More praise for *Murder in Minnesota*

"A fine example of true-crime writing
for all devotees of that form."
Lenore Glen Offord · *San Francisco Chronicle*

"As authentic history as wars, depressions,
and Presidential elections."
Sergeant Cuff · *Saturday Review*

"A virtual *Who's Who* of Minnesota murderers."
Susan Hamre · *Minnesota Monthly*

"A classic of regional popular history."
D. J. Tice · *St. Paul Pioneer Press*

MURDER IN MINNESOTA

A Collection of True Cases

Walter N. Trenerry

Minnesota Historical Society Press
ST. PAUL

♾ The paper used in this publication meets the minimum requirements of the American National Standard for Information Science—Permanence for Printed Library Materials, ANSI Z39.48-1984.

International Standard Book Number 0-87351-180-8
Manufactured in the United States of America

10 9 8 7

Library of Congress Cataloging in Publication Data

Trenerry, Walter N., 1917–
Murder in Minnesota.
Reprint. Originally published: St. Paul : Minnesota Historical Society, 1962.
1. Murder—Minnesota—Case studies. 2. Crime and criminals—Minnesota—Biography. I. Title.
HV6533.M6T7 1985 364.1'523'09776 84-20652

All photographs and sketches in the illustrations section are from the Minnesota Historical Society Collections unless otherwise noted.

Cover design: Percolator

Preface

THIS BOOK surveys the art of murder as practiced in the North Star State between 1858, when Minnesota was admitted to the Union, and 1917. The volume arbitrarily ends in 1917, not because Minnesotans stopped killing each other in that year, but because murders do not take place in a vacuum and reviving those which occurred after 1917 might bring needless embarrassment to numerous living persons who have already suffered the notoriety that surrounds a murder case.

Minnesota is surprisingly rich in homicidal lore, and I freely admit that other equally interesting collections could be made without duplicating the examples I have chosen. These cases which include several well-known ones as well as others that are obscure — appealed to me because each seemed to have some slight touch, some little flair, that took it out of the humdrum. In making this selection, I attempted to put together a readable book that would introduce a number of lively people who have not found their way into classic history texts. For Minnesota has had its great criminals as well as its important social builders. Many of the latter have received Clio's attention. Most of the former have not. I hope partially to redress the balance and give the historical underdog his day. Some of these murderers had great ability; they outshone in ingenuity their contemporaries in public life, albeit they might have put their abilities to better uses.

In these pages, too, some of Minnesota's leading men appear in unusual roles. Isaac Atwater, a member of the state's first supreme court, hears a habeas corpus petition based on allegations of fraudulent arrest; his colleague on the supreme bench, Charles E. Flandrau, defends a drunken rioter and pleads his case before Horace Austin, a district judge, who is better known as Minnesota's governor from 1870 to 1874. Jay Cooke, nineteenth-century builder of financial empires, brings political influence to bear in the case of a plasterer, and Ignatius L. Donnelly, as fiery a politician and versatile a pioneer as any state produced, signs a petition requesting the pardon of a woman. William Mitchell, one of Minnesota's great jurists, presides over a case involving a drunken party that began in a house of joy, while his famous son, William D. Mitchell, who later became United States attorney general, acts for a woman indicted for murder. William W. Erwin, who is well known as a Populist orator but who was also considered one of the greatest American criminal lawyers of his day, defends three accused murderers.

To read through these cases chronologically is to see a large segment of Minnesota history. To view history in terms of murder is perhaps extracanonical, but this angle of sight, like many others, illuminates changes in attitudes, laws, and fashions which are the substance of man's record. During the period from 1857 to 1917, motives for murder did not change, but Minnesota did. In 1857 the area was a largely unsettled wilderness on the verge of becoming a state. It had its lynchings and vigilantes, its two-gun men and speculators. Sixty years later it had substantially developed into the modern commonwealth we know today — urbanized and orderly, with the headaches caused by automobile traffic. Indians were no longer a menace; the wild frontier had been conquered, and the rich prairies and forests of the red men supported a prosperous agricultural and industrial society.

Until 1911 the penalty for murder in the first degree was the rough, old, English method of death by hanging. During the years from 1858 to 1911 approximately twenty-six persons were hanged in Minnesota. It is necessary to say approximately because the executions were carried out in the counties of conviction. No central registry exists and some records may have been lost. A summary of the hangings known to have taken place in Minnesota may be found at the end of this book.

As Minnesota developed, attitudes toward criminals and punishment shifted dramatically. Psychologists in comparatively recent times have managed to arouse a not wholly merited sympathy for the criminal. Today it is often "Society" which is said to be responsible, rather than the individual who pulls the trigger. The development of this attitude, which flowered during the reform movements of the early 1900s, was in part responsible for Minnesota's abolishing capital punishment in 1911.

It is fairly safe to say that capital punishment was never really popular in the state. Judges pronounced the death sentence with distaste and governors commuted more sentences to life imprisonment than they issued warrants for hanging. Once abolished, capital punishment was never restored. Life imprisonment is still the maximum penalty imposed in the North Star State, and in 1960 Minnesota was one of only nine states in the nation which did not inflict capital punishment, according to the *New York Times* of March 3, 1960.

The year following the abolishment of the death penalty, the Minnesota Supreme Court articulated the state's new policy toward criminals. In the State of Minnesota *ex rel.* John F. Kelly *v.* Henry Wolfer (119 *Minnesota* 368), the court said that "one of the principal aims, if, indeed, not the predominant one, of our penal system is reform. . . . Anciently, when, under the barbarous doctrine of an eye for an eye and a tooth for a tooth, 'punishment' was deemed to be, as the word implies, largely compensatory, the natural and logical conception of a sentence for a crime was that the 'punishment' should be nicely graduated to the nature and circumstances of the offense. . . . The modern conception of 'punishment,' however . . . takes practically no account of compensation; the only survival thereof being found in the attempt at prevention by means of deterring examples and by confinement of and restrictions upon criminals considered dangerous to be at large. . . . No longer is proportionate punishment to be meted out to the criminal, measure for measure; but the unfortunate offender is to be committed to the charge of the officers of the state, as a sort of penitential ward, to be restrained so far as necessary to protect the public from recurrent manifestations of his criminal tendencies . . . but, if possible, to be reformed, cured of his criminality, and finally released, a normal man, and a rehabilitated citizen." Both concepts of punishment are reflected in the cases here presented, which mirror varying attitudes toward criminals over the years.

In spite of social change, however, the public attitude toward murder seems to have remained constant between 1858 and 1917. It continues to be the most serious crime in the statute book and it is still punished the most severely. For this reason, homicide makes interesting reading; the stakes are high for both murderer and victim.

My investigation of Minnesota murders over the years revealed no new motives for killing anyone. The old ones are perfectly satisfactory. People murdered to get rid of wives, husbands, mistresses, and lovers; to speed wealthy relatives to their eternal rest; to collect life insurance; to satisfy resentments; and for all the other reasons generated by social friction. Nor did I discover any new or unique ways of killing people. Minnesotans apparently found the oldest and simplest methods entirely adequate. In the frequency of use, firearms come first in Minnesota, then, oddly enough, axes and other blunt instruments. Poisoning is comparatively rare; in the most celebrated Minnesota cases women administered the dose, so there may be some truth in the saying that poison is a woman's weapon. Minnesota murderers who used guns seemed to have a favorite point of aim. A surprising number of their victims were shot behind the ear.

I hope you will find the following Minnesota murders interesting. I regret that I could not report the most ingenious and remarkable ones that took place in the state. They looked like accidents or natural deaths and were never discovered.

Walter N. Trenerry

ST. PAUL, MINNESOTA
July 10, 1962

Contents

Dedicated to

CLOTHO, LACHESIS, AND ATROPOS,

whose inexorable decisions are
recorded herein

MURDER IN MINNESOTA

1

Death Travels by River Boat

ON THE MINNESOTA FRONTIER of the 1850s, the settlers praised the majesty of the law but often ignored it. The story of John B. Bodell and Charles J. Rinehart is a classic tale of frontier life, moving through river boat traffic to isolated settlements, peopled with Indians, greenhorns, and sharpers, and concluding with a grim necktie party to avenge the death of a traveler whose lonely wife awaited him in the East.[1]

Like many good workmen, Bodell, a thirty-six-year-old carpenter of Leominster, Massachusetts, was thrown out of employment when the Panic of 1857 drastically upset the American economy. Finding nothing in his own part of the country, he took Horace Greeley's famous advice and went west to St. Louis, Missouri, in May, 1858. There he secured work and remained over the summer. When his wife visited him in August, he told her that "there was a man" in St. Louis "who had some land to sell in Minnesota."[2] A month later Bodell made his way up the Mississippi River to the region that had become a state only four short months before.

Charles J. Rinehart had Minnesota land to sell and, one suspects, a keen eye for a greenhorn. He had gone to Minnesota in 1855. After following the usual pattern of moving from place to place and trying occupation after occupation, he had settled down in 1857 to saloonkeeping in the thriving village of St. Peter on the lower Minnesota River. Some time between 1855 and 1858 he established a claim to 160 acres of land near Lexington in the northeastern corner of heavily timbered Le Sueur County.

Between the time of Rinehart's arrival and the Panic of 1857, speculation in Minnesota lands exceeded all bounds. Fortunes were made and lost overnight as gamblers and legitimate settlers fought to establish claims to the recently opened lands of the Minnesota River Valley. After the panic hit in August, 1857, the speculative bubble burst, and there was no market for land that formerly sold at high prices. By the fall of 1858, Rinehart may well have been worried about how to find a buyer for his claim near Lexington.

In September of that year he abruptly left his saloon in charge of his father-in-law, sent his wife and children back to their original home in Springfield, Ohio, and went to St. Paul, the Minnesota capital. Soon, as though answering some prearranged signal, he left St. Paul to travel southward along the Mississippi. In those days rivers served as highways, for few roads and no railroads existed in the new state.

Rinehart and Bodell met around October 1, 1858, probably at the Mississippi River town of Winona. Exactly how they met is not known, but both men had connections in Winona, where they must have had some mutual acquaintance. Before he left Winona, Bodell told friends there that he would soon return.

By October 4 the two strangers were cruising up the Mississippi aboard the steamer "Pembina." While on the boat, Bodell wrote his wife that he "was going to see a farm of 160 acres, that could be bought for $200, in Lexington."[3] Rinehart wrote his wife, telling her to return to Minnesota with the children.

When the men reached the village of Hastings, Bodell made inquiries about his traveling companion. One man warned him strongly against continuing the trip, even though Bodell said that he found Rinehart a "good, sociable sort." Apparently impressed by the warning, Bodell asked his informant to write Mrs. Bodell in Leominster "if anything did happen to him." The carpenter was thought to be carrying three to four hundred dollars in cash — a sizable sum in those days. He never revealed exactly how much money he had and made no effort to create an impression of wealth. Wearing a coarse, heavy overcoat, he carried a valise as his only luggage.[4]

Leaving the Mississippi, the two men continued their journey westward to Northfield and Union Lake. They reached the latter Rice County settlement on October 5. The next morning they set out in a rented buggy. Bodell told the family with whom they stayed that he would return that night or the next. About noon on October 7, 1858, the two men were seen walking the last six miles toward Rinehart's claim.

An hour and a half later, at 1:30 P.M., Rinehart stopped at a farmhouse and asked the owner if he could have something to eat. Bodell was not with him. After eating, Rinehart borrowed a spade, saying that he wanted to fix a place in the road. He left the farmhouse taking the spade with him. By 2:00 P.M. he was back at the house, where he drank some coffee, chatted easily for two hours, and left.

Rinehart spent the next five days in the small, near-by village of Lexington. Bodell did not appear and his companion made no inquiries about him. On October 13 Rinehart left Lexington; by October 16 he was in St. Paul, where he told a friend that he was on his way to Rochester to buy a saloon.

Although Bodell's absence excited no alarm at Lexington, it did cause comment at Union Lake and Winona, where he had said that he would return. Late in October Bodell's Winona friends made the long trip to Lexington to look for him. Speedily organized search parties combed the fields near Rinehart's claim. By accident, the searchers found what they sought. One of the group stepped off a log and, feeling the ground yield under his feet, dug in the soft spot and found Bodell's valise. Another lost his footing in a swampy area. He grasped a willow shoot to break his fall, but it came away in his hand. Noticing that the end had been cut and the shoot apparently set there deliberately, he tested other willows nearby. They, too, had been set out.

A little digging revealed Bodell's body. It had a bullet hole above the left eye and stabbing wounds on the back of the head; in addition, Bodell's throat had been cut from ear to ear. The shallow, willow-covered grave lay about half a mile from the place where Bodell and Rinehart had last been seen walking together, and an equal distance from the farmhouse where Rinehart had borrowed the spade.

The aroused citizenry of Lexington swung into action. Firmly convinced of the murderer's identity, they sent S. J. Wise, Le Sueur County sheriff, and a deputy down the Minnesota River in pursuit of Rinehart. The citizens also convoked an extraordinary public meeting on October 26 in which they appointed a Committee of Five "to draw up a letter of condolence to the widow and distressed family of the deceased," to prepare an account of the murder for newspaper publication, and very likely, as later events suggest, to consider summary penal measures.[5]

The committee's account of the murder is, to say the least, a curious outpouring devoid of regard for fair play or due process of law. It opened: "The following is undoubtedly, one of the most foul and atrocious murders ever committed in any community. For barbarity, it has scarce an equal in the annals of our country, and committed, as it was undoubtedly, to obtain a paltry sum of money, we can but look upon the perpetrator as a villain of the blackest die." The "perpetrator" was indicated to be Rinehart. The intemperate report was printed in the *Minnesota Free Press* of St. Peter on November 3, 1858, before any formal charges had been made.

Meanwhile, Bodell's wife in Leominster received a letter postmarked October 15 at St. Paul. Purportedly from her husband, the missive advised her that he had fallen ill and would return to Massachusetts when he recovered. Mrs. Bodell pronounced the letter an absolute fabrication, saying that it was neither in the style nor the handwriting of her husband.

Unaware of his pursuers, Rinehart left St. Paul aboard the steamboat "Denmark" on October 17. Two weeks later he was in the river village of La Crescent near the Minnesota-Iowa border, where his wife and children met him and where he planned to open another saloon. There three men visited him on October 30 — Sheriff Wise, his deputy, and Alfred B. Brackett, deputy sheriff of Ramsey County, who was then at the beginning of a career that was to make him a well-known manhunter. Beyond the borders of their own counties, and acting before a formal accusation had been made, these officers had no legal authority.

Brackett demanded that Rinehart surrender. As it happened, Michael E. Ames, a St. Paul lawyer who was known as "the Chesterfield of the Minnesota bar," was present when the pursuers confronted the pursued.[6] Advising Rinehart that the arrest was absolutely unlawful, the lawyer said that Rinehart would be justified in shooting his way out and that if he did so, he, Ames, would defend him. Brackett then drew a large pistol, aimed it at Rinehart's head, and threatened to fire if he moved. Rinehart submitted, but he denied knowing about the murder or having any connection with it. He would be glad, he said, to have an immediate trial to clear himself. Concealing the fact of his arrest from his wife, he told her that he must make a business trip to Lexington and departed with his captors.

The people of St. Paul let Rinehart pass quietly through the city, but the villagers along the Minnesota River did not. The inflammatory account of the Lexington committee had done its work. Various unofficial receptions were organized when it was known that "Rinehart the Murderer" was coming. Mobs gathered at Shakopee, Belle Plaine, and Henderson. At Le Sueur — amid cries of "Hang him! Hang him!" — Rinehart's captors transferred him to a wagon and drove him to Lexington.[7]

That village had no jail. Under such circumstances it was usual at the time to send prisoners to the nearest military post, the Ramsey County jail in St. Paul, or the state penitentiary at Stillwater to await trial, but the aroused Lexingtonians would have none of this, "so strong is their determination that in this case justice shall be meted out to the guilty," reported the *Free Press* of November 10. The people of Lexington promptly built their own jail — for one prisoner.

Rinehart's preliminary examination, set for November 4, 1858, took place in a violently hostile atmosphere. The newspapers must be blamed for a great deal of this, and they, in turn, were undoubtedly influenced by the Lexington Committee of Five. On November 3, the day before the hearing, the *Free Press* indulged in a long article about the case. The paper stated that lynching Rinehart was a daily topic of conversation at Lexington, and concluded, moralistically but suggestively, that "Lynch law is never justifiable, except *when all other remedies fail.*"

From other valley towns as far away as Mankato, the curious crowded to attend the hearing, which served as a combined preliminary examination and coroner's inquest. Rinehart had competent counsel in the person of Martin J. Severance of Henderson, and in spite of the hostile atmosphere the proceedings went forward under the regular forms of law. Unfortunately for the prisoner, who may have been intimidated by them, crowds of the same people who had threatened him on his way to Lexington attended the hearing, where they glared at him, quietly and ominously.

Rinehart testified that he had separated from Bodell at noon on October 7, 1858. A short time later, Rinehart said, he had met a party of Indians on the road, and when Bodell did not reappear, Rinehart thought that the Indians must have seized him. The saloonkeeper was not so clear about why he borrowed the spade. At one time he said he used it to fix the road; at another, to dig a drainage ditch; and in still a third version, he claimed to have used the implement in repairing a shanty on his claim.

The prosecution introduced testimony showing that no Indians had been seen near the area on October 7. It also brought out several new and interesting facts: Bodell's body had heel marks imprinted on it, as if someone had stamped it into the ground; the marks corresponded with those made by Rinehart's boots; the spade borrowed by Rinehart had a broken corner which left a characteristic mark; such marks were found at Bodell's grave.

The defense offered nothing in rebuttal.

On this evidence the coroner's jury on November 5, 1858, brought in its verdict that the death of John B. Bodell was "caused by wounds from a knife and pistol in the hands of Charles J. Rhinehart [*sic*]."[8] The prisoner was accordingly bound over for trial at the next term of the district court, which was expected to convene in March or April, 1859. Rinehart was remanded to his solitary jail.

The day after the hearing ended, a story in the *St. Paul Pioneer and Democrat* suddenly alleged that Rinehart's brother-in-law accused him of having taken a trip in the spring of 1858 with another stranger who was never seen again. This tale was soon shown to be completely false.[9] A few days later, on November 9, basing its account upon an undisclosed source, the *Pioneer and Democrat* published an article headed "IMPORTANT NEWS! — RINEHART, THE MURDERER, LYNCHED!" It painted a lively picture of the prisoner's summary trial and his sudden demise. This, too, was a complete fraud, which the newspaper retracted on November 13. On November 10 the *Free Press* published a true account of Rinehart's preliminary examination, but used it as the basis for an extraordinary editorial defense of lynching. The true public enemies, the editor said, were those so concerned with safeguards for criminals on trial that they overlooked the just claims of law-abiding citizens. "It is this laxity of our laws," he continued, "and their application, too, which has, and ever will, lead to . . . mob violence and lynch law." Were these articles, which appeared so close together, planted by the Lexington committee?

While the newspapers tried his case, Rinehart did his best to escape. A powerful man, he broke the handcuffs which he wore by day and would have been free if his jailer had not discovered the broken manacles. The jailer then told him that he must now be more securely chained; hearing this the prisoner fell into a "fit." Although Rinehart appears to have been quite sound mentally and physically, his nerves gave way on several critical occasions under the tension to which he was subjected. After this attempt to escape, he was additionally secured by leg irons fastened to the floor. Somewhat later he managed to break these, and when his jailer unlocked the handcuffs for the night, Rinehart sprang to the door and was away. Snow covered the ground, and it was easy to follow his tracks. He was found little more than a mile from the jail lying unconscious in the snow. He had fainted. The newspapers gave prominent space to his efforts to escape. In these attempts, the prisoner undoubtedly played into the hands of the Lexington group by making himself appear a dangerous criminal using every means to evade just punishment.

Imprisoned again after a taste of freedom, Rinehart awaited his fate. He did not have to wait long. On December 26, 1858, a mob gathered around the Lexington jail and demanded Rinehart. Upon the jailer's very proper refusal, the crowd went away. The jailer, however, took no steps to secure additional guards or to move his prisoner to a safer place. Next day, just after noon, an unruly assortment of some sixty men, claiming to come from adjoining Rice County and purportedly made up "principally" of Irishmen, Germans, and Indian half-breeds, surrounded the jail and demanded the key. The jailer again refused, but was overpowered after defending "himself and his prisoner with great courage." The key was taken from him and the jail door speedily opened.[10]

This time Rinehart did not faint. Pulling his hands through his handcuffs with such force as to strip the skin, he wrenched from the floor the clamp which held his leg irons, broke the leg from the jail stove to use as a weapon, and faced his attackers. Holding the stove leg in his raw and bleeding hands, Rinehart single-handedly held off the mob for an hour and a half. No one dared approach him. During this time, some of the attackers jabbed a sharpened stick at him through the jail window, but succeeded only in bruising him and inflicting a gash above his left eye. Lacking courage to close with their victim directly, some of the rioters finally managed to remove a portion of the jail roof. At this, Rinehart's nerves again failed him, and he fainted. The mob swarmed in. Rinehart was taken.

The unconscious man was flung upon a sled, a rope was fastened around his neck, and he was driven a short distance to a convenient tree. There the mob strung him up, but the amateur hangmen bungled. The noose tightened around Rinehart's chin instead of his throat, and he was lowered to the ground. At this terrible moment the unfortunate man regained consciousness. Realizing what was happening, he pitifully asserted his innocence of any crime and then asked that someone pray for him. A bystander volunteered, delivering a short prayer during which all the lynchers knelt reverently as if in appreciation of a blessing on their work. When the prayer ended, Rinehart again shouted that he had not murdered Bodell. He was nevertheless hanged at once. A few minutes later his body was thrown into a shallow grave at the foot of the gallows tree and briskly covered with dirt.

The Leominster carpenter was avenged. For a time the air was full of denunciations of the lawless act and clamors for action against the rioters, but nothing was ever done. In Lexington and the surrounding area, where the Committee of Five seems to have handled its public relations well, nine out of ten residents were reported to feel that Rinehart's punishment had been just.

Was justice in fact done? Since the case never came to trial, there is very little evidence to consider. The only purportedly complete account of the trip made by Bodell and Rinehart from Winona to Lexington appears in the newspaper release furnished by the Committee of Five. There is, nevertheless, enough information to indulge in some legal speculation.

In criminal cases the prosecution must prove the defendant guilty beyond a reasonable doubt. In the Rinehart case the question must turn on whether or not defense counsel could insinuate a reasonable doubt into the minds of a jury.

It must be admitted that the defense would have an uphill fight after the jury heard the prosecution's evidence showing that Bodell disappeared on a trip with Rinehart, the man's phenomenal lack of curiosity about his companion's disappearance, the similarity of the heel and spade marks at Bodell's grave, and Rinehart's confused explanations about why he borrowed a spade. Moreover, it looked as if everything unrolled in accordance with a careful, preconceived plan. Even as he traveled northward with Bodell, Rinehart wrote his family to rejoin him at La Crescent; and after throwing an inquirer off the track by saying that he was going to Rochester, Rinehart, his mission apparently accomplished, rejoined his wife and children at La Crescent. The circle was complete. Although it is purely circumstantial—as is the evidence in most murder cases since murderers are not usually obliging enough to act before witnesses—this evidence is sufficient to justify a verdict of guilty.

The argument for Rinehart is not, however, hopeless.

(1) What happened to Bodell's money? The murder was assumed to have been committed for money, but no one showed that Rinehart needed cash, or that he had any more funds after the murder than before. If Bodell's money were on his person when his body was found, it is quite possible that the finder appropriated it, and it is not likely that he would speak up.

(2) Bodell's throat was cut. This usually produces a torrent of blood; yet no one who saw Rinehart within an hour of the probable time of Bodell's death noticed any blood or stains on him.

(3) Were there indeed no Indians in the area? During the Sioux Uprising, which took place not far west of Lexington four years later, it was apparent that the Indians, like ghosts, may appear to some and remain invisible to others.

(4) Who wrote the letter which Mrs. Bodell said was a forgery? It was never sent to Minnesota for handwriting comparison as it would have been if the case had come to trial, and it was obviously written by someone who knew a great deal about Bodell's activities.

(5) Rinehart's conduct after Bodell's disappearance was strangely lethargic for a murderer. After staying five days in

Lexington, he drifted down the Minnesota and Mississippi rivers, taking two weeks to make a trip which could have been made in three or four days. When seized, he was calmly and openly going about his regular business.

(6) The defense's best argument, however, turns on a question of time. The only source of information — the newspaper account made up by the Lexington Committee of Five, which was certainly not friendly to Rinehart — states that the man asked for lunch at 1:30 P.M., ate it, borrowed a spade, went out, and returned by 2:00 P.M. Thirty minutes is a very short time in which to eat, walk half a mile, bury a body in one place and a valise in another, and walk half a mile back.

A jury might well have had reasonable doubts if these points had been argued, but Rinehart had no chance to present them or to offer any substantive evidence in his favor.

Like King Charles I, nothing in Rinehart's life became him like the leaving of it. The bitter scene of his capture — one injured man defying and holding off a mob determined to seize and hang him — is a somber corrective to those adulators of the past who find every virtue in the crude life of the frontier.

2

War in Wright County

THE WRIGHT COUNTY WAR of 1859, which ended a spiral of murder and violence, accomplished for Minnesota what the Whisky Rebellion of 1794 did for a young American nation. Each firmly established an infant government on a basis of law. By a chain of events the murder of Henry A. Wallace in 1858 led to the so-called Wright County War and the military occupation of that county a year later. Each link in the chain increased the degree of violence, until it culminated in an armed mob threatening the state's attorney general in the courtroom and snatching his prisoner from custody. The murder of Wallace and the lynching of Oscar F. Jackson were high points in Minnesota anarchy — an anarchy which often prevailed in the process of subduing the American wilderness — and it called for extreme measures to assert the authority of the state.[1]

When Henry Wallace of Antrim, New Hampshire, and Mr. and Mrs. Oscar Jackson of Pittsburgh, Pennsylvania, left their homes in 1857 to journey to Minnesota Territory, they joined the floodtide of humanity pouring onto the rich southern Minnesota lands recently opened to settlement. Wallace, a bachelor of about twenty-five, and the Jacksons took up adjoining farms in Rockford Township, Wright County, in the Big Woods area of east central Minnesota. At that time the county was only three years old. It was on the very edge of the frontier, which was moving slowly westward as the Sioux evacuated their traditional homelands. Wright County had as yet no telegraph lines, and mail arrived once a week by stagecoach. Times were hard, for the Panic of 1857 had drained money from the territory. Everyone was in debt; banks were closed; and business in Minnesota was at a virtual standstill. Many citizens had to rely on barter for life's necessities.

Jackson was poor. He made no secret of it, complaining to his neighbors about his poverty and asking for credit. One gets the impression that he made a nuisance of himself with his complaints and solicitations, since later events show a curious amount of ill will toward him in the community which only recently had elected him town supervisor and justice of the peace. Wallace, on the other hand, had money. This in itself was unusual in those hard times; Wallace, moreover, had unusual money. He consistently used, and was the only man in the Rockford area to have, notes issued by the Amoskeag Bank of Manchester, New Hampshire.

A man trying to farm alone inevitably needs help in some things, and in midsummer of 1858 Wallace, who was also the local tax assessor, hired Jackson to help him with the haying. The two made a common type of farm agreement under which Jackson was to receive half the hay in exchange for his labor in cutting and storing it. On August 27 the men were observed working together in Wallace's fields.

Nearly a month later a neighbor remarked that he had not seen Wallace since that day. Jackson, however, had been frequently in evidence. He had, in fact, mysteriously acquired money — all of it in the form of Amoskeag Bank notes. When asked about Wallace's disappearance, Jackson showed no curiosity, but other neighbors were concerned. On September 19 a group of them went to Wallace's cabin and found it empty and in perfect order. Two days later the neighbors made up a search party, which Jackson did not join.

After combing the fields briefly, the group found Wallace's body lying in a clump of bushes near the spot where he had been seen mowing with Jackson twenty-five days earlier. His head had been crushed by repeated blows. According to the *Monticello Times* of October 2, 1858, a promptly summoned coroner's jury "of 12 of the best citizens" found that Wallace "came to his death by blows from an axe or heavy instrument in the hands of a person or persons unknown."

Unknown but not unsuspected. The grand jury convened at

Monticello, and on October 6, 1858, indicted Jackson for Wallace's murder. In the absence of a local jail, the prisoner was sent to Fort Ripley, a military post near Brainerd, for confinement until his trial at the next district court term to be held in the spring.

While Jackson languished in the guardhouse, Hiram L. Wallace, the dead man's brother, arrived from New Hampshire to spur the prosecution and to act as a kind of avenging Nemesis. Hiram had his brother's body exhumed from its burial place on the Rockford claim and reinterred at St. Anthony, the flourishing town that later became a part of Minneapolis. Hiram also dutifully went through the dead man's possessions and found that Henry's money, rifle, gold watch, and a blanket were missing.

On March 29, 1859, Oscar Jackson came to trial in a cold and hostile atmosphere. He had already received threats against his life, and he saw little warmth in the eyes of his neighbors who crowded the courtroom. The prosecution quickly showed that Wallace died by violence, that he was last seen with Jackson, and that Jackson had suddenly come into possession of bank notes known to have been used locally only by Wallace.

Jackson's defense was handled ably by three St. Paul lawyers, one of whom was Willis A. Gorman, former territorial governor of Minnesota and soon to be colonel of its first Civil War regiment. Their argument was ingenious and, as it turned out, convincing. The defense contended that no one could establish the date of Wallace's death, and that between August 27 and September 21 any number of persons could have visited his claim and killed him. Jackson, testifying in his own behalf, explained his lack of curiosity about Wallace's disappearance by saying that he had enough to do on his own farm without taking time to pry into other people's business. As for the money, Jackson claimed that he sold his half of the hay to Wallace, who paid for it in Amoskeag Bank notes.

After deliberating for eighteen hours, and once interrupting their deliberations to ask the judge for further instructions on reasonable doubt, the jury on April 3, 1859, brought in a verdict of not guilty. While apparently unconvinced of Jackson's innocence, his peers gave him the benefit of the doubt.

The verdict was, to say the least, unpopular and the acquitted man quickly left the area. "It is known that threats have been made against Jackson's life, should he re-appear in the county," reported the *Pioneer and Democrat* of April 13, 1859, "and it is said that fifteen men followed him on the night of his acquittal for the purpose of lynching him, but he managed to elude them by escaping into the woods."

Led by the murdered man's brother, a determined group of Wright County citizens did not intend to let the matter rest with the verdict, apparently planning to get Jackson back into the county where they would take the law into their own hands. In furtherance of this scheme, George M. Bertram, Wright County sheriff, Cyrus C. Jenks, justice of the peace, and Wallace's brother set out in pursuit. On April 8 the three men were in Hennepin County, where the sheriff and the justice had no authority. There they learned that Jackson was in St. Paul. A legal mockery then took place among the travelers. Hiram Wallace filed a complaint with Justice Jenks accusing Jackson of stealing molasses, flour, and money from Henry Wallace's cabin. The justice promptly issued a warrant for Jackson's arrest and handed it to Sheriff Bertram. The sheriff, in turn, delivered the warrant to Alfred Brackett — the Ramsey County deputy sheriff who had apprehended Rinehart in 1858 — asking him to arrest Jackson.

Brackett found Jackson in St. Paul's Apollo Saloon the next day. Handcuffing his prisoner, the deputy set out with him for St. Anthony by buggy. Jackson pleaded for time to call his attorney, but at first Brackett would not allow it. On the ride Jackson insisted that his arrest was based on a false charge, the purpose of which was to get him back to Rockford where he would be murdered. Remembering the unfortunate outcome of his arrest of Rinehart not more than five months before, Brackett reconsidered. When the two men reached St. Anthony, he sent word to Jackson's counsel and persuaded the Wright County sheriff to spend the night in town before starting back to Rockford.

Jackson's lawyer moved swiftly, and before the day ended a writ of habeas corpus was served upon Sheriff Bertram. "The excitement at Monticello, and the fears that Jackson will be lynched, are the causes for the issuing of the writ," said the *Pioneer and Democrat* of April 11. A dramatic hearing began that day before the Honorable Isaac Atwater, Minnesota Supreme Court justice and the most convenient jurist of plenary authority. William Lochren, later to serve with distinction in the Civil War and as a United States district judge, appeared for the prosecution. The hearing had to be adjourned when two prosecution witnesses — Jenks and Wallace — "were discovered to have vamosed," as the *Pioneer and Democrat* of April 13 put it.

These men, doubtless advised by counsel, realized that they had made a legal error in serving a warrant made out in Hennepin County. They secured a fast team and returned to Wright County, where Wallace filed another complaint on the basis of which Jenks quickly issued a new arrest warrant. Next morning it was delivered to Sheriff Bertram in the courtroom just after Justice Atwater had ordered Jackson released. The sheriff promptly rearrested the unhappy Jackson, and Jackson's attorney just as promptly secured and served a new writ of habeas corpus.

That the purpose of the arrest was clear to all is indicated by an account in the *Pioneer and Democrat* of April 13, which reported that the courtroom crowd watched Jackson after his rearrest "to see how he looked under the immediate prospect of being hung to the first tree after he crosses the line into Wright County. . . . It is rumored that one hundred men are waiting over the line to take summary measures with Jackson if they can lay their hands on him."

In a second hearing, held on April 13, Jackson was again released on the grounds that the burglary charge was a sham. Freed, he went to St. Paul, where friends and sympathizers raised enough money to enable him to leave Minnesota.

After being acquitted on a first degree murder charge and twice escaping by an eyelash from men who had no scruples about using legal processes for illegal purposes, Jackson should have taken his money and left the state. But those "whom the gods destroy, they first make mad." On April 21 — eight days after his second release — Jackson returned to Rockford.

His enemies moved swiftly to take advantage of his folly. This time a neighbor named Aymer or Emery W. Moore went to Buffalo, the county seat, and swore to a complaint before a different but equally obliging justice of the peace. It again alleged that Jackson had stolen flour and other articles from Henry Wallace's cabin. The justice issued a warrant for Jackson's arrest and delivered it to his tireless pursuer, Sheriff Bertram, who in this chronicle carries on the evil tradition exemplified by the sheriff of Nottingham.

Meanwhile an armed mob surrounded the house of Jackson's father-in-law, George Holdship. After shouting for Jackson to come out and being told that he was not there, the crowd camped about the house, building fires near it. They then went to Jackson's own near-by cabin and literally tore it apart, throwing furniture and bedding from it, breaking down partitions, and setting more fires. The crowd continued its siege from Friday until Sunday, April 24, when Bertram and a small party appeared at Holdship's house to serve the warrant. The sheriff was admitted and Jackson, who had been hiding upstairs all this time, came down to talk with him. When Bertram read the warrant, Jackson expressed fears for his life, but the sheriff assured him that if he went quietly no harm would come to him. With stupendous credulousness, Jackson submitted. Bertram then dispersed the mob, and started down the road with his prisoner.

The sheriff had sent a man ahead to act as lookout and warn against any possible mob. The lookout's eyesight must have been calculatedly poor, for the group had gone only half a mile when an armed crowd reappeared and swarmed toward Jackson and the sheriff. In a moment Bertram and his party were overpowered — without resistance — and the Wright County mob had possession of Jackson. The sheriff and his men rode off. Bertram did not report the occurrence and made no attempt to interfere.

After taunting the helpless man all night, the lynchers strung Jackson up just as his wife arrived to plead for his life. The leaders paid no attention to Mrs. Jackson but, in the sickening way that a cat plays with a mouse, hauled Jackson down and asked him if he now had anything to say. He denied murdering Wallace and said he knew nothing about the missing watch, rifle, and blanket — the absence of which had annoyed the murdered man's brother and furnished the basis of the fraudulent arrest warrants.

This was not the answer the mob wanted. After sending Mrs. Jackson away, the men again hauled Jackson up, let him strangle once more for a moment, and brought him down. By this time his throat was so badly mangled that although he tried to speak, he could not. A sudden cry arose that a rescue party was on the way.

The alarm was false, but the mob's leaders — who by now wanted to get the job done and over with — quickly strung Jackson up again, this time breaking his neck. The crowd then scattered, leaving the body hanging from a beam that projected from a gable of the late Henry Wallace's house. Thus Oscar Jackson died about 2:00 P.M. on April 25, 1859, on the site where his supposed victim had lived.

Of this cruel performance a Monticello correspondent wrote in the *Pioneer and Democrat* of April 28, 1859: "The people arose in their majesty and might, and executed the laws of our Commonwealth." A coroner's jury of local men, called on the day Jackson died, found that he had met his death at the hands of a person or persons unknown. The jury was not likely to accuse its own members.

While these events were taking place, Minnesota had been admitted to the Union on May 11, 1858. The state's first governor, Henry H. Sibley, was resolved that such lawlessness should not go unpunished. Calling the lynching a "high-handed outrage . . . against the peace and dignity of the State," Sibley on April 29, 1859, offered a reward of five hundred dollars "for the apprehension and conviction of any or all persons concerned." The governor said that Jackson "was entitled to the protection of the laws, in common with every resident of the State, and all those who participated in the act which deprived him of life, or who aided and abetted it, Should be Severely punished." Alluding to the Rinehart case, the governor noted that "Once before . . . the life of a human being was taken . . . under Similar circumstances, and the State disgraced thereby. These deeds of violence must cease," he said sternly, "or there will be no Safety for life or property in our midst." No one ever claimed the reward, and the Jackson lynching might have drifted into obscurity had it not been for an implausible coincidence that revived the entire matter and brought it to the wildest phase of its spiral.[2]

On July 25, 1859, a short-lived fraternal order called the Sons of Malta was holding a celebration at Minnehaha Falls, a favorite scenic haunt near the infant city of Minneapolis. Among the visitors was Mrs. Jackson. While strolling the grounds, she saw Aymer Moore, who had sworn to the complaint which led to Jackson's final arrest and who had been among the lynching mob. Mrs. Jackson immediately notified John W. Crosby, St. Paul's chief of police, and by nightfall Moore was under arrest, charged with Jackson's murder.

As soon as Governor Sibley learned of Moore's arrest, he ordered the prisoner returned to Rockford to stand trial. To prevent further collusion among local officials, the governor directed Charles H. Berry, the state's attorney general, to conduct the prosecution in person. Berry opened the preliminary examination at Monticello on July 31, 1859, with an angry mob swarming about the building, shouting and threatening the agents of law enforcement. Mrs. Jackson, testifying for the prosecution, clearly and unequivocally named the leaders of the lynching party and described the circumstances under which her husband died. When the Wright County sheriff took the stand to explain how the mob overwhelmed him and took Jackson from his custody, the attorney general found the sheriff's explanation so unsatisfactory that he ordered Bertram arrested and held as an accomplice in the lynching. Berry then discovered that certain prosecution witnesses had mysteriously disappeared before they could testify, and he was forced to adjourn the hearing before it had been in session a full day.

Where the witnesses had gone became clear that evening. About 9:00 P.M. a large, apparently well-organized crowd suddenly appeared and forcibly released Moore from his place of imprisonment. After threatening the attorney general's life and those of any other persons who dared inquire further into Jackson's death, the men rode off into the night.

The attorney general sped to St. Paul and reported to Governor Sibley that a Wright County mob had sabotaged proceedings in the very forum of justice and that county officials would do nothing about it. The act was a direct challenge to the state's authority. Could the executive power of Minnesota tolerate open revolt? Could the citizens of an organized government be allowed to ignore the law and defy the officials charged with its enforcement?

Governor Sibley thought not. On August 5, 1859, he issued a proclamation declaring Wright County "to be in a state of insurrection" in which its civil officers were "utterly powerless to execute the laws." The governor proclaimed: "For the first time in the history of Minnesota, it has become the stern but melancholy duty of the Executive to employ a military force to suppress a combination against the laws in one of the counties of the State. Twice has an armed mob in Wright county outraged the public sentiment." He warned that "To assert the majesty of the law and to subdue the spirit of ruffianism which has thus manifested itself by overt acts, prompt measures will be taken."[8]

Before the day ended, Sibley ordered three state militia units to Wright County. At that time, Minnesota's armed forces were in theory composed of all the area's able-bodied men and were constantly prepared for action, but actually the militia existed chiefly on paper. Its units were little more than marching clubs made up of volunteers with fancy uniforms which they purchased themselves. Fortunately, the units Sibley ordered to active service — the Pioneer Guards, the St. Paul City Guards, and the Stillwater Guards — were somewhat better than that. (Three additional units — the St. Paul Light Cavalry Company, the Washington Light Artillery, and the Dakota Rifles — were placed on alert but were not ordered to the front.) Accompanying the soldiers to Wright County were thirty-five special policemen, among whom were Police Chief Crosby and the murdered man's father-in-law. John S. Prince, a St. Paul banker who was also a candidate for mayor of the city, commanded the expedition.

Although mobilization plans for these units are not preserved, it may be conjectured that the job of rounding up the soldiers, sobering them up, finding their uniforms and equipment, and shepherding them to the point of rendezvous, proved more complex than planning and conducting the expedition. The three units marched away on August 6 in the pride, pomp, and circumstance of glorious war. They were ordered to execute a three-pronged offensive, proceeding by different routes to Wright County. Attorney General Berry reached Monticello on August 6 with the Pioneer Guards; the other military units attained their objective the following day.

On the surface they found everything calm, but the citizens' reactions to their arrival were varied. "Some for us," wrote Berry to Sibley on August 6, "but many more with alarm and hostility." W. J. Wheeler, the governor's secretary, who had accompanied the troops, reported to Sibley the same day that "people here sympathise with the Lynchers," who were nowhere to be found. They had fled to the woods, and local men showed the densest ignorance of where they had gone. Sheriff Bertram and I. R. Lawrence, Wright County attorney, refused outright to co-operate with Berry. Lawrence informed the attorney general that "there was an agreement by the people to do the harvesting" of the men sought by the troops "and to aid them in any manner necessary to keep them out of the way." He told Berry that the missing men "had taken shelter on the north side of the Mississippi," but he would not say where. Before night, Berry reported to Sibley, "it was apparent that all expectation of assistance from the Sheriff or the people of the County of Wright must be abandoned." [4]

Lawrence then indicated that the rioters would "voluntarily give themselves up to the authorities of the County" if Berry and the troops would not "interfere." The attorney general and Commander Prince agreed, but still the county officials did nothing. At this point Sibley himself started for Monticello to take personal charge. At that, the county officials, hoping to satisfy the governor, abruptly discovered three members of the rioters, arrested them, charged them with Jackson's murder, bound them over until the next grand jury should meet, and then released them on five-hundred-dollar bonds. One of the men so arrested and charged was Moore.

There was really nothing more for the militiamen to do. They had carried out their objective as far as they could. The arrest of Moore and the others gave formal satisfaction to the governor. When the military occupation of Wright County had continued for three days, jokes began to circulate about the war against phantoms — jokes which the opposition party might put to good use politically. Governor Sibley, never one to tolerate humor at the expense of his dignity, recalled the troops on August 10. But he warned the local officials that if they failed to execute the laws, he would again "interfere in such mode as I may deem expedient." The St. Paul units reached home on August 11 and staged a grand banquet, complete with songs, toasts, and boasts. The Stillwater Guards got back on August 12. The legislature set the official duration of the war as August 6–14, 1859. [5]

Wright County, duly pacified and seemingly chastened, convened its grand jury on October 2. After considering the charges against Moore and the other two men accused of taking part in

Jackson's hanging, the grand jury not surprisingly failed to indict any of them. They were discharged, and no one was ever punished for Jackson's death.

Time passed. In 1861–65 all the militia units involved in the Wright County War performed valorous service on the bloodier fields of the Civil War. In 1877, long after the Jackson affair had been forgotten, a gold watch was found near the place where his cabin had stood; in 1880 someone also found a rifle there. Old settlers identified both articles as having belonged to Henry A. Wallace.

A jury said that Jackson was not guilty of murder. Was he unjustly hanged? Working with Wallace in a sparsely populated area, it is obvious that Jackson had the opportunity to kill him. But so did any of his neighbors. One contemporary newspaper reported that just before his lynching Jackson said "Wallace had endeavored to coax his wife to run away, and ain't that enough to make a man do something."[6] If true, this statement might explain some things about the case that remain dark, but it seems inconceivable that the prosecution would have failed to bring this out in presenting its case. Moreover, throughout the desperate affair, Mrs. Jackson exhibited only courageous devotion to her husband and his memory. Circumstantial evidence suggests that poverty could have given Jackson a powerful motive. His story that Wallace paid him in cash for his promised half of the hay is unconvincing. In a period of tight money, it would have been more logical for Wallace to barter part of his crop for labor. Moreover, if Wallace needed hay, why would he offer half of it to Jackson in exchange for his work?

Whether Jackson was guilty or innocent, the atrocious circumstances of his death testify that Minnesota, too, had its share of lawlessness. The *Pioneer and Democrat* remarked on May 5, 1859: "Till the infamy of that horrible crime is wiped out in a prompt and full measured retribution, Wright County will be painted black upon the map of Minnesota — a patch of loathsome leprosy upon the fair surface of the land." Even an admitted murderer is entitled to due process of law and to meet his death without torture. It is no honor to early Minnesota that its pioneers on occasion took the law into their own hands and that some of its sworn officials mockingly used legal process to accomplish unlawful purposes.

The Wright County War, semiludicrous as it was, served notice that anarchy and rebellion would not be tolerated in Minnesota. In forcing steps to pacify the frontier, the deaths of Wallace and Jackson brought positive results valuable to the civil government. They also were to have indirect and unforeseen consequences. Public officials, shrinking under the publicity given the lynching and the calling of troops, tried to vindicate the state's tarnished reputation for law and order by omitting the quality of mercy in dealing with criminals in 1859 and 1860. The Wright County War may have claimed an indirect victim in the events described in the chapter which follows.

3

Not to Foster, But to Slay

DURING THE YEAR 1859 Minnesota was subjected to a series of crises as bewildering to the citizen of that day as the issues of a century later were to his descendants. Everything was going wrong and no one seemed to be doing anything about it. The slavery issue was splitting the country. Before the excitement caused by the Lincoln-Douglas debates in 1858 could subside, events in 1859 were to lead to John Brown's rebellion and his hanging. Ignatius Donnelly, the state's leading orator and Republican candidate for lieutenant governor, kept the political fires blazing by stumping Minnesota for the Republicans and forecasting a day of doom if the Democrats, who were the slavery party, should carry the state and nation in 1860.[1]

An irritating local issue also plagued Minnesotans. Bonds worth five million dollars, issued in 1858 to finance the building of badly needed railroads, had become nearly worthless in less than a year, and no track had been laid. Get-rich-quick hopes based on future railroad lines evaporated, leaving the full faith and credit of an infant state pledged to redeem bonds for which the commonwealth would not get a single mile of railroad. Elsewhere in Minnesota frontier lawlessness was getting the upper hand, as Oscar Jackson's lynching set off riots challenging state authority, and Governor Sibley called out the militia to control the situation.

All these events were quickly overshadowed by the Bilansky imbroglio, which burst upon the scene in March, 1859, and quickly seized first place in the public's interest. Its fascination was irresistible, for when lovely woman stoops to folly she is not likely to do it halfheartedly. Throwing her cap over the moon, she follows where passion leads her and all the world enjoys watching.

Somewhat before two o'clock on the afternoon of March 12, 1859, a small group met in the Stanislaus Bilansky home on Stillwater Avenue in St. Paul. It was a sad occasion. During the preceding day Stanislaus had died of acute indigestion after a nine-day illness, and he now lay in his coffin poised for that last ride which all mankind must finally take. Gathered for the funeral were his friends, his widow, Ann; a young carpenter named John Walker, who was said to be Ann's nephew; and Rosa Scharf, a girl who had been hired to attend Stanislaus in his illness.[2]

Suddenly, without warning, a strange group appeared in this house of death. Led by Ramsey County Coroner John V. Wren, the party consisted of three doctors, the coroner's jury, and witnesses. Right then and there, the coroner abruptly announced, he would hold an inquest into the death of Stanislaus Bilansky. Faced with the law's majesty the stricken widow had no choice but to let authority proceed, which it did with considerable thoroughness.

First the doctors examined the corpse but stopped short of carving up Stanislaus' remains in the parlor. Then the coroner called for testimony. From this it was learned that Bilansky had fallen ill on March 2, that he seemed unable to keep his food down, vomiting after every meal, and that in the later stages of his illness no doctor had been called because Mrs. Bilansky seemed opposed to it. A certain Captain Pettys, who had visited Bilansky every day, reported, "I asked him to have a physician, but his wife was ugly about it, and did not like to have me call."[3] This had made Pettys suspicious, and he was probably the one who summoned the coroner.

Pettys' misgivings appeared unfounded, however, when it developed that during his lifetime Stanislaus was a heavy drinker and a man of violent temper predisposed to digestive upsets. Dr. Alfred Berthier, the deceased's personal physician for nine years, said that he examined Stanislaus during his illness, diagnosed it as nothing more than a particularly aggravated case of indigestion, and did not prescribe medicines because he preferred to wait until the man's stomach became stronger.

The coroner's jury concluded that Bilansky "came to his death naturally," adding that "there was apparently great want of care in proper attention being given to him in his sickness" because his wife had not again called a doctor.[4] The widow was allowed to proceed with the funeral. In a short time the little mourning party drove to the cemetery where the remains of Stanislaus Bilansky were laid in the earth.

Ann Bilansky went back to town with Rosa Scharf, the hired girl. Just after Stanislaus' death Ann had commented to Rosa in a puzzled way that her husband must have taken poison, and now the matter seemed still on her mind. If Mr. Bilansky "was poisoned, he poisoned himself," she told Rosa during the drive.[5] She may well have wondered what provoked the coroner's unexpected visit.

Ann, Rosa, and Walker returned to the Bilansky home. As many a servant girl has done — to gain information which she may use later to her profit or out of sheer curiosity — Rosa Scharf kept an eye on her employer. She observed that Ann was not too unhappy about her husband's death and limited her display of grief to conventional social formulas. Rosa also noticed that after Stanislaus' funeral Walker settled down in the Bilansky house without any apparent intention of leaving. Late in the evening the girl was able to make her most interesting observation — she saw "Mrs. Bilansky undress right before Walker."[6] At this point Rosa's eyewitness reports necessarily cease, but the imagination is not left altogether powerless.

The following dawn probably came as it does on other days — too soon for lovers, too late for the impatient. There is no record of what Ann Bilansky and John Walker did on that Sunday for they were not seen in public, but they may very well have taken advantage of their time. At nine o'clock that evening, March 13, their idyll came to an abrupt end when they were both suddenly arrested and imprisoned in the city hall on suspicion of murder.

Who were these mortals so involved in each other's fortunes? Stanislaus Bilansky, recently deceased, had been a middle-aged Pole who went to St. Paul in the 1840s when the future capital consisted of little more than a log chapel and a few shanties clustered on muddy flats near the Mississippi River. By the standards of 1859 he was an old settler. He had kept a saloon for a time, but in the year of his death he was no longer in business, living on the capital he had accumulated. Bilansky appears to have been an unlovable sort of person — obstinate, moody, cantankerous, suspicious, tyrannical, and jealous. In spite of this catalogue of undesirable traits, he managed to marry several times; rumor credited him with four trips to the altar. Ann's predecessor set the apparent endurance record for wives by staying with him for nine years, but Stanislaus' "constant abuse and ill-treatment" finally exhausted her and she took the youngest of their four children with her to other quarters. The other children remained with their father.[7]

John Walker was a fair, curlyheaded, blue-eyed, young carpenter from North Carolina. He was living in St. Paul in 1858 and was acquainted with Bilansky. In May, 1858, Walker fell ill and wrote to a woman in Fayetteville, North Carolina, whom he called his aunt, asking her to go to St. Paul as his nurse. She went. Whatever Walker's illness, it responded famously to her remedies, and the two lived on close and affectionate terms.

Walker's aunt was Mary Ann Evards Wright, a tall, blonde, gray-eyed, vivacious, and talkative widow of thirty-four. She was attractive and dressed well. Although St. Paul was a substantial small city by 1858, one can imagine that this striking southern woman would attract attention on the streets of Minnesota's new capital.

Through the good offices of Walker, Ann Wright met Stanislaus Bilansky, who in 1858 was without a wife and apparently unhappy in his single blessedness. Acquaintance ripened into desire and in September, 1858, Ann undertook the role of Mrs. Bilansky which three women before her had apparently tried and found too intolerable to play. Shortly after the wedding young John Walker quietly moved into the Bilansky residence.

In Ann, Stanislaus appears to have met his match. Here was a woman who would not be cuffed and who firmly went her own way in defying him. He did not like Walker's presence in his house, and he liked it even less when obliging friends hinted that Walker was not really his wife's nephew. He wanted the young carpenter to move. Ann did not want Walker to leave. He stayed. Over Stanislaus' protest Ann and Walker took a trip to the near-by village of St. Anthony (now Minneapolis); not a long journey, but one made in spite of her husband's disapproval. Unknown to Bilansky but made known to him later, as soon after Ann and Stanislaus' nuptials as November, 1858, Ann had been seen tiptoeing into Walker's bedroom at night and stealing away between three and four o'clock in the morning. When told, Stanislaus simply grumbled to his old cronies at the saloon — the immemorial release valve of henpecked husbands — and did nothing.

It is impossible to understand why this woman married Stanislaus Bilansky; it puzzled her contemporaries as much as it does those who come after her. Mrs. Bilansky seems to have made no effort to conceal how she felt about her husband. "She said they lived unhappily; she hated him, and could not treat him well." Ann was also quoted as saying that "she did not want to sleep with him."[8] Her feelings for Walker were a matter of common gossip, although the details did not become public until after Stanislaus' death. By February, 1859, the Bilansky marriage had reached a deadlock resolved only by Stanislaus' illness and death in March; on March 13 Mrs. Bilansky and John Walker found themselves confined under suspicion of murdering Ann's husband.

What caused the sudden reversal of fortune, a peripeteia as abrupt and complete as that of any Greek tragedy, was someone's attack of conscience. At the preceding day's inquest Mrs. Lucinda Kilpatrick, a friend and neighbor of the Bilanskys, had testified concerning Ann's care of Stanislaus during his illness. Her testimony had been edited, however, and she completely omitted — at Ann's request — any reference to a shopping trip made by the two ladies on February 28, just before Stanislaus came down with his puzzling ailment. One of Ann Bilansky's purchases on that shopping trip was a packet of arsenic.

After the inquest Mrs. Kilpatrick told her husband what she had withheld from the coroner, and added that Mrs. Bilansky hid behind a curtain all the time Lucinda was testifying to be sure of hearing what was said. Mr. Kilpatrick was shocked and on Sunday morning immediately got in touch with Police Chief Crosby. The chief ordered Stanislaus Bilansky's body exhumed for further examination. While Ann and Walker dallied on March 13, grim work was afoot which would affect them both.

A routine autopsy on Monday, March 14, disclosed neither poison nor any natural cause of death. The coroner then ordered chemical tests for arsenic. He also summoned his jury for another inquest to be held the next day.[9] The second inquest brought out additional pertinent facts. Mrs. Kilpatrick described the shopping tour she and Ann had made on February 28. Along their route Ann mentioned to Lucinda that Stanislaus wanted some arsenic. Would Lucinda buy it for her? Ann asked. Lucinda replied with some asperity that if she wanted arsenic she would buy it herself. The two women then went into W. H. Wolff's drugstore at Third and Wabasha, where Mrs. Bilansky asked for arsenic to poison rats. Wolff said that he had something better than arsenic, but Mrs. Bilansky made an excuse for not buying the substitute. Later she bought the desired poison at Day and Jenks' drugstore.

Testifying further, Mrs. Kilpatrick now disclosed additional conversations she had with Ann. On February 28, at the same time that she said Stanislaus wanted some arsenic, Ann also said she "would not mind giving him a pill if the Dr. was attending him." She did not say what the pill would contain. On March 12, just before the first inquest, Ann asked Lucinda to swear that she, Lucinda, was the only one who had bought arsenic on February 28. After asking Ann why she was afraid, Mrs. Kilpatrick testified, "I said unless they find arsenic in his stomach they could do nothing with her." The first inquest did not, in fact, find any arsenic; nevertheless, just after Mrs. Kilpatrick finished giving her evidence Mrs. Bilansky had remarked anxiously, "if arsenic was found in the stomach they would have to prove who gave it."

As a neighbor Mrs. Kilpatrick knew that Stanislaus was ailing, and she occasionally called during his illness. She saw no physician nor did she see Mrs. Bilansky give her husband medicine or anything else during his vomiting spells. She remembered that Stanislaus complained chiefly about a sensation of heat in the stomach. If he asked for something to drink, his wife or the children gave it to him. So far as Lucinda could see the disease did not look serious and, in fact, neither Ann nor Stanislaus appeared to think it so.

Lucinda Kilpatrick was followed by Rosa Scharf, the girl hired by Mrs. Bilansky soon after her husband fell ill. When Rosa arrived on March 2, she testified, Stanislaus was only mildly under the weather, but two days later he began to have vomiting spells and took to his bed. He blamed his indigestion on an overdose of pills and expected the upset to pass soon. When it did not, two doctors were called. Both examined him, found nothing serious, and recommended a light diet. Stanislaus also dosed himself to no effect with a favorite patent medicine.

Whatever Stanislaus' illness was, Rosa remembered that it produced immediate nausea after eating. He had a constant burning sensation in his stomach which became worse as soon as he ate. Both Rosa and his wife cooked for him: soup, which he alone ate and which he could not keep down; toast, which proved indigestible; and once some arrowroot which John Walker brought. Bilansky's illness did not seem to respond to dietary treatment. As it became more acute, Walker wanted to call the doctors again, but this time Mrs. Bilansky was opposed and no physicians came.

While Rosa noticed that Mrs. Bilansky treated her husband in a "rough manner," the two nevertheless seemed on good terms. If the sick man needed food, drink, or attention, his wife was always hovering over him, ready to provide it. Ann alone nursed him; Ann alone fed him, said Rosa. In spite of this loving care the man died. His doctors could not explain it at the time, Rosa said, and Mrs. Bilansky could only say that he "must have taken poison." [10] Possibly Bilansky was despondent because he thought, rightly or wrongly, as two people testified, that Ann was about to desert him for Walker, but this would have nothing to do with his illness unless he indeed had moodily poisoned himself. He had not drunk whisky during the last six weeks of his life; for once his favorite liquid could not be blamed for his indisposition.

Technical medical evidence might furnish an answer. Dr. Thomas R. Potts, who happened to be Governor Sibley's brother-in-law, could only tell the coroner's jury that he found the deceased's stomach and bowels inflamed, but he could not tell the reason. Dr. J. D. Goodrich had more sensational information. The late Mr. Bilansky's symptoms, the doctor said, were a burning sensation in the stomach, inability to keep food or liquid down, and a brownish tongue of cracked appearance. These, Dr. Goodrich told his tense listeners, were consistent with arsenic poisoning.

When the autopsy proved inconclusive, Dr. Goodrich, Dr. William H. Morton, and Wolff, the druggist, conducted standard tests for arsenic which consisted chiefly in heating the suspected substance (a segment of Bilansky's stomach or intestines) and passing its vapor over metal columns or through glass tubes. If arsenic were present, it would be deposited on a surface where its crystalline structure could be examined and identified.

St. Paul's homespun scientists were somewhat less than positive in stating their results, which made the *Pioneer and Democrat* of March 17, 1859, crackle angrily that the evidence was "about as unsatisfactory as it was possible to make it." There was reason for the newspaper's sarcasm. A jury of laymen trying to fix the cause of death heard supposed experts make the following remarks. Wolff, after reporting that the physicians examined Bilansky's internal organs, said, "In one of our experiments there was a crystal discovered, which, under the microscope, resembled arsenic." Dr. Morton testified: "I made the examination spoken of by Mr. Wolff. It had the appearance of arsenical congestion. I saw one of three tubes after the experiments. The grayish ring testified to by Mr. Wolff, I believe was arsenic. . . . The metallic ring I think is never found except where arsenic is present." Dr. Goodrich stated: "With the exception of the rings I have not seen but one crystal, that I could pronounce with any particularity, to be arsenic. . . . As far as I have been able to examine, the tests give the results of tests for arsenic."

Although this evidence lacked the positive authority which scientific men have persuaded the world to expect from them, the cumulative effect of all the testimony apparently convinced the jury that "the deceased came to his death by the effects of arsenic administered by the hands of Mrs. Bilansky." John Walker was not implicated and was released on March 15. Ann was held on a charge of first degree murder, which carried the unpleasant penalty of death by hanging.

Three days later, represented by counselors John B. Brisbin and A. L. Williams, Ann Bilansky appeared for her preliminary examination. Isaac V. D. Heard, who was to serve as reporter for the military commission trying the Sioux rebels in 1862, conducted the state's presentation. On evidence substantially the same as at the inquest — except that now the doctors were somewhat more positive about the presence of arsenic — she was ordered held for trial at the next district court term.[11]

Her trial opened on May 23, 1859. The case had created a sensation in St. Paul, which rarely had the treat of finding out how a pretty woman managed to carry on a liaison with a young lover under her elderly husband's very roof. Heard, who again conducted the prosecution, easily proved that Mrs. Bilansky bought arsenic two days before her husband fell ill. In fact, Lucinda Kilpatrick testified that Ann felt uneasy about buying the poison, saying at the time that if her husband "should drop away suddenly" people would have suspicions of her. When Mrs. Kilpatrick underwent extensive cross-examination by Ann's counsel, the public had an unexpected diversion in learning that Lucinda, too, might have fallen under Walker's spell and aspired to be Ann Bilansky's rival. After realizing where repeated questions about her relations with Walker were leading her, Mrs. Kilpatrick abruptly refused to answer any more. Over Counselor Brisbin's objection that he had just found valuable information probably showing the witness' bias toward his client, Judge Edward C. Palmer ruled that Mrs. Kilpatrick was not required to answer further cross-examination on these lines.[12]

Ann seems to have watched the proceedings as though they were a spectacle arranged for her amusement. She was "quite composed and self-possessed," the *Pioneer and Democrat* of May 25, 1859, reported. "She does not show a deep concern in the proceedings, but an interestedness, more of gratification of feelings of enmity, while attacking the character of the witness, Mrs. Kilpatrick; frequently smiling behind her handkerchief, as if intent on bringing scandalous information to light."

Rosa Scharf, the only person other than Ann who had watched Stanislaus during his illness, was again the chief prosecution witness. This time she had new revelations to make. She said, for example, that Ann warned her not to use any utensil which Stanislaus touched, and that Ann had been very careful to wash all her husband's dishes herself and to segregate them from the other china. This seemed peculiar to Rosa, who was hired to keep house. Rosa testified that one day Mrs. Bilansky pointed to an elderly man walking by the house and told Rosa to "set her cap for him" because he had money. When Rosa said she was not interested, Ann replied, "if you could not love him, you could give him something to sleep himself to death; and said there were a great many things it could be done with, and mentioned arsenic, opium, laudanum, paregoric, etc., but that one must know how much to give them so they would not wake up." What may have impressed Rosa the most was that when Stanislaus seemed to be dying, she offered to run across the street to ask if Mr. and Mrs. Kilpatrick could help, only to be told tartly by Ann that "there was no use of hurrying."

Scientific evidence at the trial was positive. Dr. Morton had spent three days in Chicago with the best technicians, equipment, and reagents. No longer bumbling and uncertain, he smartly reeled off the results of the tests made: reduction tubes, positive; ammonic sulfate of copper, positive; ammonic nitrate of silver, positive; Reinsch's test, positive; sulfurated hydrogen, negative; and Marsh's test, positive. Conclusion: the stomach and intestines of Stanislaus Bilansky contained arsenic in a lethal amount. Dr. Morton said that he also secured some of Bilansky's patent medicine, had it analyzed, and found no harmful ingredients.

The testimony of Mrs. Kilpatrick, Rosa Scharf, and Dr. Morton contained the substance of the state's case. Counselor Brisbin, defending, concentrated on rats. He proved that the Pied Piper himself could not have rid the Bilansky household of the plague of rats that had descended upon it. Furthermore, Stanislaus himself gave away the cat, which had at least held the rodent menace at bay, and without the cat it was necessary to use arsenic, which Ann admittedly bought.

Other defense witnesses testified at length about the peculiar character of the late Stanislaus. He had been a heavy drinker; he drank until he was violently sick; he was a hypochondriac who had a premonition that he would die in March. While no one testified to it, the defense tried cleverly to insinuate that Bilansky might have committed suicide. It would be, however, a most unusual suicide who chose to spread his death agony over nine painful days.

Curlyheaded, young John Walker, who had agitated the bosoms of at least two women involved in the trial, was the defense witness about whom the public had the greatest curiosity. He bore up well. In spite of searching and sarcastic inquiries into his personal life, he loyally maintained that Ann Bilansky was really his aunt, that he had no improper relations with her, and that she never entered his room after he was in bed. So far as her nephew could see, Ann behaved as a proper wife, was attentive to her husband, and, when she might have been expected to go to pieces, "he discovered no emotion or agitation on the part of defendant, when the Coroner called; that she looked perfectly composed and grieved." His testimony substantially completed the defense. Ann Bilansky did not take the stand.

In his final argument Counselor Brisbin concentrated skillfully on the prosecution's weak points: no one proved that Bilansky died of poisoning or that Ann administered any poison to him. The prosecution relied upon circumstantial evidence, which as Thoreau pointed out is often quite strong, as, for example, when a trout is found in the milk. The case reached the jury at 12:30 P.M. on June 3, 1859, and by 5:30 that day the jury announced its verdict: guilty. Ann showed "emotionless indifference." [13] It is almost impossible to believe that she was not the victim of some grand delusion or schizophrenia which made her feel that she stood above these events and that they had no relevance for her.

The newspapers did not hesitate to draw moral lessons from the verdict. On June 5 the *Pioneer and Democrat* remarked in a long editorial that the case was "the repetition of a tragedy, which has been enacted all the world over, wherever a woman, bad enough to be a harlot and bold enough to be a murderer, has wished to get rid of a husband whom she disliked, for a paramour whom she preferred." The case puzzled the editor, however, because it appeared to lack a motive. Bilansky had little property, and Ann's marriage to him had not interrupted her dalliance with Walker.[14]

Mrs. Bilansky's attorney moved for a new trial, but the motion was denied on June 22. Eight days later, however, troubled by questions Ann's counsel had raised, Judge Palmer certified the case to the Minnesota Supreme Court for review. It was argued before the state's first supreme court justices — Lafayette Emmett, Isaac Atwater, and Charles E. Flandrau — on July 8.

Counselor Brisbin exercised considerable ingenuity in his appellate argument. Among other things he tried to claim that as a woman Mrs. Bilansky should be entitled to benefit of clergy, a curious practice, long abolished, that once allowed those who could read or write to escape with light sentences for serious crimes. Brisbin also argued that under medieval law a wife who killed her husband was guilty of a crime called petty treason. Since the Minnesota legislature had abolished this crime, counsel argued, it must also have abolished the death penalty for the crime. The whole argument was obviously aimed at avoiding the death penalty—hanging—which Minnesota then imposed upon murderers. The supreme court, however, on July 25 declined to interfere, affirmed Mrs. Bilansky's conviction, and ordered her remanded to the district court for sentencing.[15]

Walker was visiting Ann in the Ramsey County jail when news of this decision reached her. She had made herself a favorite with the jailers and, contrary to regulations, they had not confined her to a cell but allowed her to wander through the central hall until late in the evening. After Walker departed, she was still in the hall when the jailer on duty left for a moment to get his keys. In a split second Minnesota's most famous contemporary prisoner ran downstairs, crawled through a small open window, and was at large.

Trying to ignore denunciations of criminal carelessness, bribery, and general maladministration, Ramsey County Sheriff J. Y. Caldwell organized a great manhunt and offered a five-hundred-dollar reward for Ann's capture. Veteran detective Brackett, whose actions were so critical in the Rinehart and Jackson cases, disguised himself and tried to entice Walker into revealing Mrs. Bilansky's hiding place by offering to lend him a skiff for their escape. Walker did not accept the bait. Other deputies combed St. Paul looking for the woman described by the sheriff as "tall in stature, long featured, sharp visage, teeth a little projected — the two front teeth in the upper jaw lapped — is very talkative, uses good language, voice rather masculine, grey eyes, light hair, Roman nose. Had on when she left a dark dress; wears a delicate watch chain with silver watch." [16]

Suspicion centered about the Lake Como section of St. Paul. After covering that area for nearly a week, two deputies on August 1 found Mrs. Bilansky dressed in men's clothing, walking toward St. Anthony with Walker. Although she "manifested considerable emotion on being arrested," neither she nor Walker resisted. That night both were back in the Ramsey County jail, where Walker remained for a month and a half, to be released when the grand jury again failed to indict him.[17]

Ann had first hidden in the brush near the lake; a farm boy brought her food. As soon as she succeeded in getting a message to Walker, he found her a better refuge in a friend's barn. The two had hoped to escape by pushing west, feeling that the shortest way out of the state was not necessarily the safest.

It appears that Mrs. Bilansky realized what had happened to her only after her unsuccessful jail break. Her indifference faded as she came to understand that now no *deus ex machina* would swoop from the clouds to free her. She came to know depression and, one suspects, fear.

It was not until December 2, 1859, that she finally came before the district court for sentencing. In a clear voice she addressed the judge, saying, "If I die in this case, I die an innocent woman. I don't think I have had a fair and just trial. You can proceed." Before passing sentence, Judge Palmer told her that she stood convicted of having taken a human life without cause or justification, and that society must exact its penalty. She must not expect pardon, and he advised her that nothing could avert her doom.[18]

A formal sentence of death in the old form is solemn and dreadful. Even the once indifferent Ann Bilansky sobbed as she listened. "It is the judgment of the law," Judge Palmer pronounced, "that you, Anne [*sic*] Bilansky, be hence removed to the common Jail of this County, and therein kept in solitary confinement for the period of one month, and that thereafter at such times as the Governor of this State shall by his warrant appoint, you be taken to such place within the County as the Sheriff shall select, and there be hung by the neck until you are dead. And may God, in His infinite compassion, have mercy upon your soul." At the conclusion, the prisoner burst into uncontrollable tears.[19]

Judge Palmer then certified the record of the case and sent it to Governor Sibley, who, under the law, must order the execution and fix the date.

Now the case entered a new phase. To order a woman hanged in 1859 was a political question of the first magnitude. No woman had ever been executed in Minnesota. At that time women still occupied the pedestal upon which men had placed them, and a certain popular sentiment argued against punishing them. As soon as Ann Bilansky's sentence was announced, Governor Sibley faced all kinds of protests demanding commutation of her sentence, whether she was guilty or not.

Minnesota's leading citizens imposed substantial pressure on the governor. For example, on July 25, 1859, the day the Minnesota Supreme Court affirmed Mrs. Bilansky's conviction, Justice Flandrau wrote to Sibley: "It is my firm conviction that a strict adherence to the penal code will have a salutary influence in checking crime in the State, but it rather shocks my private sense of humanity to commence by inflicting the extreme penalty on a woman. I believe she was guilty, but nevertheless hope that if you can consistently with your view of Justice and duty, you will commute the sentence which will be pronounced, to imprisonment." To say the least, this was an unusual private letter for a member of any court to write. Democrat Sibley stalled until his term expired on December 31, 1859, and left the problem in the lap of his successor, Alexander Ramsey, a Republican.[20]

Reformers and busybodies worked to commute Mrs. Bilansky's sentence, carrying their attack to the legislature where they hoped to abolish capital punishment. On December 13, 1859, the Minnesota House of Representatives instructed its judiciary committee to "inquire into the propriety of abolishing capital punishment within this State." Only thirteen days later the committee made its report. Its members were "unanimously of the opinion" that capital punishment "ought not to be abolished." The House accepted the report and took no further action, but this was not the end of the matter. When a new governor and a new legislature took over on January 1, 1860, the Bilansky forces appealed simultaneously to the governor for clemency and to the legislature to amend the law requiring the death penalty.[21]

While Governor Ramsey pondered, Rosa Scharf was found dead on January 5, 1860. Without her testimony the state might have had trouble proving its case against Ann. A coroner's inquest showed that Rosa bought laudanum and took it herself. On the evening before her death she visited the Kilpatricks to ask what the authorities "were going to do with Mrs. Bilansky." Although the jury decided that Rosa "came to her death from an overdose of laudanum," she may well have taken it deliberately. What led her to do so was never explained. Could she have advised Ann to use arsenic? Did she rather than Ann make the statement about marrying an old man and hurrying him off to sleep? Had she testified falsely in order to save herself? Had she committed suicide from remorse? Was she another woman jealous of Ann's relations with Walker? These lines of inquiry were not pressed. If they had been, the governor might have been led to reconsider the case.[22]

During this time Ann enjoyed a degree of social success which she could not have imagined. She was in a sense *de rigueur*. It became the fashion to visit her at the Ramsey County jail, and several members of the legislature were among her callers. She spent her time brooding on what she felt to be injustices in her case, could recall the most minute details of all the proceedings, and retold them again and again, at length, to her listeners. In telling her version, she was guilty of such obvious fabrications that for a time whenever anyone in St. Paul told a particularly tall tale he would draw the comment: "You have been to see Mrs. Bilansky."[23]

Governor Ramsey would not hurry his decision, which was a difficult political question in a critical year when the Republican party hoped to carry the nation. He made it three weeks after Rosa Scharf's death. On January 26 the governor issued his warrant directing the sheriff of Ramsey County to carry out the sentence of the law upon Ann Bilansky between the hours of 10:00 A.M. and 2:00 P.M. on Friday, March 23, 1860.[24] Ann Bilansky then knew what it is given to few mortals to know — not that she would die, but when she would die.

As time grew shorter the Bilansky forces worked with greater frenzy. Knowing that they could expect nothing from the governor, they concentrated upon the legislature, where they succeeded remarkably well. The 1860 legislature took up the cause at once and acted with speed. A bill "to commute the sentence of Mrs. Anna [*sic*] Bilansky to imprisonment for life in the State['']s prison" was introduced on February 1. Although the opposition hooted that it should be retitled "an act to encourage prostitution and murder," the bill passed both houses and went to the governor for signature on March 5.[25]

Ramsey promptly vetoed it, which took great political courage. Sibley himself could not have hoped to set a neater trap for his old friend and opponent. In a long message on March 8, Ramsey pointed out that the bill unconstitutionally invaded the governor's pardoning power. Moreover, remembering the Rinehart and Jackson lynchings, he stressed the unsavory reputation which Minnesota was acquiring for lawlessness. "On the one hand," Ramsey wrote, "is the awful responsibility of permitting the sacrifice of a human life . . . and on the other the no less awful apprehension of endangering the safety of society, promoting a contempt for law and encouraging the mob spirit by ill-advised interference with the regular cause of Justice." The world should see Minnesota adhering to regular procedures of law. In the specific matter of Mrs. Bilansky's crime the governor saw no special occasion for mild treatment. "She procured poison and administered it," Ramsey wrote, "not in such quantities as at once to destroy life, but little by little, that no suspicion might arise. She sat by the bedside of her husband, not to foster, but to slay. She watched without emotion the tortures she had caused, and, by and by, administered no healing medicine, no cooling draught, but ever, under a guise of love and tender care, renewed the cup of death."[26]

The veto finished all practical attempts to save Ann Bilansky from the gallows. She was reported to be "very much depressed" by it and "constantly weeping." Her friends, however, did not give up their lawful and unlawful efforts to set her free. More petitions to commute her sentence were circulated in St. Paul, and people were caught trying to smuggle clothes to her, chloroform to overcome guards, and even nitric acid to eat through locks.[27]

As her death approached, Mrs. Bilansky became interested in the clergymen whose calls she had previously scorned in the certainty that somehow she would be set free. After some hesitation, she embraced the Catholic faith and was received into that church by Bishop Thomas L. Grace on March 22, the day before her execution. On that same day she gave her last interview to the press. The reporter found her "very pale and thin, with dark circles" under her eyes, but "perfectly composed" and still protesting her innocence. She told him that she never gave her husband poison "in large or small doses," asserting "I have suffered enough this day for all the wrongs I have ever done in my life."[28]

The custom in those days was to carry out the execution in the jail courtyard during the daylight hours. Aaron W. Tullis, who was now the sheriff of Ramsey County, had his gallows ready on the morning on March 23, 1860. A plain, black coffin lay at its foot. A detachment of Pioneer Guards was on duty to keep the crowd beyond a fenced enclosure.

On that morning Ann Bilansky was awakened about five o'clock. After prayers she spent the next several hours saying farewell to other prisoners and a few friends who were admitted to the jail.

Walker, for whom she was supposed to have committed the murder, was not among them. He was no longer in St. Paul. At 10:00 A.M. the sheriff appeared with the black robe she must wear, and fifteen minutes later a small procession, made up of the prisoner, a few officials, two physicians, a priest, and several Sisters of Charity paced slowly through the jail corridors. Upon reaching the gallows outside, the entire party mounted the stairs. Mrs. Bilansky knelt on the drop. The others knelt on the platform while the priest read prayers for five minutes.

The prisoner was then asked if she had anything to say. Addressing herself to all who could hear, she said: "I die without having had any mercy shown me, or justice. I die for the good of my soul, and not for murder. May you all profit by my death. Your courts of justice are not courts of justice — but I will yet get justice in Heaven. I am a guilty woman, I know, but not of this murder, which was committed by another. I forgive every body who did me wrong. I die a sacrifice to the law. I hope you all may be judged better than I have been, and by a more righteous judge. I die prepared to meet my God." [29]

When she finished, a deputy sheriff came forward and slipped the noose over her head. She seemed startled, then indignant, asking, "How can you stain your hands by putting that rope around my neck — the instrument of my death?" The deputy "assured her that duty compelled him" to do so and then swiftly dropped the black cap over her head. To this she only murmured, "Be sure that my face is well covered."

Repeating her prayers rapidly, Ann Bilansky stepped onto the drop. Her last words were "Lord Jesus Christ receive my soul." Sheriff Tullis released the drop. The woman fell about four feet; her body made a slight convulsive movement and then was still. The priest and sisters remained kneeling on the platform for twenty minutes, reading prayers continuously. The corpse was then cut down, and Ann Bilansky was pronounced dead. Her body was laid in the black coffin at the foot of the gallows. A crowd estimated at fifteen hundred to two thousand persons jammed the streets and roof tops near the gallows. The spectators, many of them women, broke through the cordon set up by the Pioneer Guards and fought for pieces of the rope to keep as souvenirs or as a remedy for disease.

4

The Christmas Murders

THE SO-CALLED "New Ulm Christmas murders" of 1866 had their origin in a series of blood baths caused by unsatisfactory relations between whites and Indians. In a way, they were among the last Minnesota reverberations of the Sioux Uprising of 1862, a short-lived but bloody frontier war that has been called one of the worst Indian uprisings in American history.

Provoked by what they regarded as violations of treaties signed in the 1850s, and spurred on by hotheads among them, the Sioux rose on August 18, 1862, attacking settlers and settlements up and down the Minnesota River Valley. Although the uprising soon lost its momentum and was checked within six weeks, the war cost at least five hundred white lives and probably more. At its conclusion their captors treated the Indians as war criminals rather than as honorable belligerents. A military commission tried 392 of them for violating the laws of war, and on December 26, 1862, thirty-eight Sioux were hanged at Mankato. Not satisfied with this public humiliation, troops in 1863 and 1864 pursued the Sioux into the Dakotas, where several more bloody battles were fought.[1]

The effects of the Sioux War lingered long in southern Minnesota, retarding settlement in the rich valley that was in the 1860s still on the edge of the westward-moving frontier. Its citizens remained jumpy, for large numbers of able-bodied men were absent serving with the Union forces in the Civil War. Indian and white relations, never very good, deteriorated still further. The Indian, once regarded merely with contempt, now became an object of suspicion and hatred. For their part, the Sioux, driven from their traditional Minnesota homelands, occasionally managed to slip through the cordon of military posts to attack isolated settlers.

On May 2, 1865, less than a month after the Army of Northern Virginia surrendered at Appomattox, Minnesotans were shocked to learn of a sudden Indian raid which almost wiped out the Andrew J. Jewett family of Garden City, a village in Blue Earth County some ten miles south of Mankato. The attackers shot Mrs. Jewett and her husband, tomahawked Jewett's elderly parents and his hired man, and tried to kill his two-year-old boy, who miraculously survived. The question in every white man's mind was: Were the Jewett murders a prelude to another state-wide Indian insurrection? [2]

Jewett's neighbors quickly formed a search party and captured a half-breed named John L. Campbell. When he was brought to Mankato for examination, Campbell was wearing two pairs of women's stockings and trousers identified as Jewett's. The half-breed had deserted from the Civil War cavalry battalion commanded by former St. Paul detective Alfred Brackett and had been roaming about Minnesota with an Indian band.

When he was interrogated, Campbell, boasting in the Indian fashion, told his captors that his was only one of nine Sioux bands then lurking near Mankato. The Indians, he said, were planning to attack the city and burn it. A panic immediately developed in the Minnesota Valley, for memories of 1862 were still vivid. Mankato called upon other near-by towns for help in its defense, and throughout the valley farmers began to leave their fields and take their families into the towns.

Campbell was speedily brought before an irregular court organized by the citizens of Mankato on May 3. Twelve "impartial, substantial businessmen" constituted a jury; Sheldon F. Barney was appointed judge and John A. Willard, judge advocate. For four hours a succession of witnesses gave their testimony which Campbell, still wearing Jewett's trousers, heard impassively. No one testified for him and no one represented him. Since one of the witnesses was allowed to describe Campbell as a "known desperado," it would seem that the so-called court overlooked a few formal rules of evidence. At the end of his mock trial, the half-breed was found guilty of Jewett's murder and was sentenced to death. A few men who kept their heads advised holding the prisoner until the next district court term, but they were overruled.[3]

Taking their victim to a large tree at the corner of Hickory and Fifth streets, the Mankato men immediately tied a rope around his neck and hauled him up over a convenient branch. Since they had forgotten to pinion his arms, Campbell was able to hold himself up and keep from choking. He was brought down quickly. After letting their victim speak briefly to a priest, the mob then tied Campbell's arms, set him on a wagon, restrung the rope, and pulled the wagon away. The fall did not break his neck and he slowly choked to death. His body was sent to his mother at Traverse des Sioux.

It was fortunate for Mankato that Campbell had only been boasting about the number of lurking Sioux bands. The Indian reaction to Campbell's lynching was loud and bitter. His mother denounced the act so violently and tried so hard to stir the Sioux into vengeful action that she was placed under military arrest and held in detention. The whites also reacted violently. Blue Earth County revived the Draconian practices that had followed the Sioux Uprising when on May 17, 1865, it offered a two-hundred-dollar bounty for the scalp of each Indian killed in the county.[4] Nothing was ever done to punish John Campbell's murderers.

These events lay behind those which led to the Christmas murders at New Ulm a year later. In 1866 the town of New Ulm, a German settlement in Brown County, sponsored a Christmas festival in the courthouse. Four years earlier during the uprising, New Ulm had withstood two attacks that helped break the Sioux offensive and turn the tide of war in the whites' favor. In the battles the town had largely been destroyed, but it was quickly rebuilt. Now prosperous, the Germans were celebrating Christmas Day. Since the saloons were open, one may reasonably suppose that toasts and libations in the holiday mood were frequent.

Into this buoyant, alcoholic atmosphere drove two men from Mankato in a hired sleigh. Both were trappers who had just returned from the woods near Leavenworth in Brown County. One of the men was Alexander Campbell, a bachelor of nearly twenty-eight who was not related to the unfortunate John; the other,

George Liscom, twenty-five, had left his bride of six months in Mankato while he accompanied Campbell to New Ulm. Before entering into the festivities, the trappers sold some of their furs to a local trader. Campbell, although a Yankee, was dressed in Indian fashion wearing a dark blue hood, moccasins, and a sheath knife in his belt. His normally light complexion was tanned and he wore a short beard. Liscom, who was also a Yankee, was dressed similarly in clothes suited to the woods.[5]

When they finished their business, the trappers entered the National Saloon, where they played a friendly card game. Liscom lost and although a teetotaler ordered drinks good humoredly. After the liquor arrived, a dispute developed over the bill. Liscom was told that he owed seventy-five cents because several Germans had apparently taken advantage of his order to obtain free drinks. The trapper maintained that he owed only fifteen cents and refused to pay the rest. Another companion paid the difference and said, "Give me the drinks for us Yankees."[6] Since the vast majority of men present were Germans, this statement was unwise; the Germans had little love for Yankees even though they cheerfully swilled drinks for which the Yankees paid.

Some time after four o'clock in the course of this bibulous Christmas afternoon, a New Ulm Civil War veteran named John Spenner joined the trappers — who, incidentally, were also veterans. Campbell and Liscom promptly stood Spenner a drink, which was followed by others. As the afternoon progressed, Spenner coaxed these men in Indian dress into representing Indians. While Spenner pounded on a kettle, Campbell and Liscom performed a Sioux war dance whooping convincingly, imitated Sioux braves scalping their enemies, and otherwise acted as the Sioux might when on the warpath. As the saloon audience remembered it, the performance was spectacular.[7]

Suddenly, in the twinkling of an eye, the jolly atmosphere vanished. Spenner turned abruptly on Liscom, the smaller of the trappers, forced him outside, and began to maul him. The Germans crowded around Campbell and tried to keep him from helping his friend, but he forced his way forward. As in all fracases, what happened is not entirely clear, although it seems that Spenner managed to hit Liscom over the head with an ax before Campbell burst through the crowd. Campbell closed with Spenner. As they fought,

Campbell slashed out with his hunting knife. By one of those freak turns of fate, a slash which was meant to intimidate Spenner severed the principal artery in the man's leg.

Friends immediately thronged to Spenner and secured medical attention for him. Liscom, badly injured, bleeding, and prostrate, received none. Campbell gave what help he could, hoping that Liscom would regain enough strength to stagger away. It was obvious that the Germans were leagued together to pitch into the Yankees, and the two trappers had no wish to linger where they were so decidedly outnumbered.

At this point the Brown County sheriff arrived and took Campbell and Liscom into custody. Both surrendered with pleasure, feeling that here was someone who could get them out of the saloon and protect them. The trappers were handcuffed and taken to jail, where they undoubtedly reflected that this Christmas was turning out to be anything but merry.

They were allowed to reflect only a short time. Late that night John Spenner died of his knife wound. The news spread rapidly through the drunken German crowd and a mob gathered quickly outside the jail, shouting, "Bring out the half-breeds! Out with the Indians!" [8] Someone called out that Campbell was the brother of John Campbell, who had been lynched at Mankato the year before. These accusations, which were untrue, suggest that Spenner and his Teutonic associates may have deliberately induced the trappers to impersonate Sioux braves. The Germans perhaps hoped later to claim that, after all, only a couple of Sioux were roughed up — and who cared about Indians?

After working itself into a frenzy, the mob rushed the jail. A detachment overwhelmed the sheriff and his deputies, although later examination showed that it was not necessary to force the doors. Someone had apparently opened them. Swarming into the jail, the men seized Campbell and Liscom. Both were still handcuffed. A rope was placed about Liscom's neck and he was dragged by it from the building. As he emerged someone struck him with a club. He fell to the ground but was quickly hoisted and hanged on the rung of a ladder. Campbell's turn was next.

Among the drunken mob was a soldier named John Gut, a member of Company H, Tenth Minnesota Regiment, and A.W.O.L. on this lively Christmas night. He made the rioters' cause his own.

Forcing his way to the forefront, he cried, "These two half-breeds killed my best friend, John Spinner [*sic*], and I will kill them; let me alone or I will stab you!" The crowd let him through. Seizing a knife, Gut stabbed Campbell again and again while the prisoner was in the jail and as he was being dragged out. With others, Gut bludgeoned, kicked, and beat the helpless Campbell until he was strung up from the jail window gratings. Gut's frenzy did not end when the man died. As the trapper's body swung grotesquely at the rope's end, Gut repeatedly stabbed Campbell's corpse.[9]

Not many minutes later the soldier was seen washing blood from his hands. When asked what he had been doing, he replied that he had been killing two Indians or half-breeds because they had been killing a Dutchman. The mob dispersed. The two bodies vanished during the night.

Even in that day of meager communications news quickly traveled to Mankato (some twenty miles to the east) that the Dutchmen of New Ulm had lynched two of its citizens. Feelings reached the boiling point. Mankato's mildest plans for New Ulm seemed to be "Wipe out the place! Burn it down." A detachment of Mankato men armed with muskets and artillery was rumored to have begun marching upon New Ulm to arrest the rioters. If the group existed, it did not reach its destination, but the rumor accurately reflects local sentiment.[10]

A few determined men did go to New Ulm on December 27, demanding the bodies of Liscom and Campbell and insisting that legal proceedings to determine who was responsible should begin at once. They were met with little but blank stares. No one knew anything and no one seemed disposed to act. When asked where the bodies were, one New Ulm resident said, "they got down and walked off in the night." Next day the Mankatoans conducted a thorough search. They successfully traced the bodies "from the jail to the river by the trail of blood." Having no means of dragging the frozen Minnesota River, they were forced to return to Mankato for reinforcements. Back in New Ulm again on December 31, a larger group of Mankato residents found the trappers' bodies "within eighteen inches of the hole [in the ice] through which they had been shoved like dead dogs." Wesley Campbell saw his brother's head frozen into the ice.[11]

When the corpses were recovered, it was seen that the mob had not been content with killing the men but had exhausted its rage in mutilating their bodies. Campbell's corpse had fifteen major wounds and the marks of innumerable other blows. His right leg had been chopped off at the knee, and his right hand had been severed at the wrist. Liscom had eighteen major wounds as well as the marks of a general battering. His head was crushed, and someone had cut off his right forefinger. On January 6, 1867, Campbell and Liscom were buried at Mankato. Nearly six hundred people attended their funeral, and the procession to the cemetery was said to be the largest yet seen in that city.

Realizing from the atmosphere that they should not count on New Ulm to undertake punitive measures, the Mankato group had been careful to remove the trappers' bodies on the Nicollet County bank of the Minnesota River rather than on the Brown County side where New Ulm is located. This procedure would have given a Nicollet County coroner jurisdiction to inquire into how the men met their deaths. But Nicollet County did not have a qualified coroner, and the bodies were taken to Mankato, where the Blue Earth County coroner convened an inquest. Its sessions lasted from December 31, 1866, to January 11, 1867. After hearing exhaustive testimony, the jury concluded that the two trappers died from "being struck with a hatchet, pounded on their heads with clubs and sticks of cord-wood, kicked by feet, stabbed in the breast with knives and hung by the neck with ropes until dead." John Gut was ordered held; others were charged but managed to secure bail, which they promptly defaulted.[12]

On January 18, 1867, Gut, who until then had been held at Mankato, was taken to New Ulm after Brown County at last issued a warrant for his arrest. The Mankato sheriff took the precaution of delivering his prisoner at the jail door. Then he waited to see the man actually incarcerated. An editorial in the *Mankato Weekly Union* of January 18 commented: "It now seems probable that the citizens of New Ulm will yield to the popular voice and give at least passive acquiescence to the administration of the law."

The New Ulm authorities held a preliminary examination on January 21, 1867, into the charges against Gut and certain other members of the mob. As a result, orders were issued holding Gut and twelve others for the next Brown County grand jury session.

It was common gossip, however, that the action was taken only to meet formal legal requirements and that no indictment could be expected in the solidly German community of New Ulm.[13]

Acts of violence like those which took place in New Ulm on Christmas Day could not remain local matters. The indifference of its law enforcement officials gravely concerned Governor William R. Marshall, since similar events had resulted in the Wright County War of 1859. As his emissary and representative of law and order, the governor sent to New Ulm Attorney General William Colvill, the Civil War hero who had commanded the First Minnesota Regiment at Gettysburg. After investigating, Colvill reported that a fair trial was impossible in the town. The governor sent Colvill's report to the legislature which was then in session, with a request for legislation "which will bring order out of chaos, and social quiet and safety out of anarchy." The legislature responded. The statutes already attached Cottonwood, Murray, Pipestone, and Redwood counties to Brown County for judicial purposes, since all but Brown were relatively unsettled and had no court organization. But as the law stood, criminal cases had to be tried in the county where the offense was committed, and jurors had to be drawn from that county. An act of the legislature approved on March 9, 1867, authorized the judge to hold court in any county in the district whenever he considered it "to be in furtherance of justice or for the public convenience" and provided that jurors might be drawn from all counties.[14]

Under the new law, the New Ulm rioters' cases were transferred to the grand jury convening at Redwood Falls on June 18, 1867. That body, however, failed to return an indictment, much to the astonishment of Judge Horace Austin. According to the *Weekly Union* of July 5, 1867, the judge "administered a severe rebuke" to the jury. He charged that "the jurors had shamefully stultified themselves by failing to present the parties for trial. . . . He talked to them for about half an hour, during which time many of the jurors held down their heads with shame." Austin said he would continue to subpoena new jurymen "until the accused are tried, and if guilty, properly punished." Then he adjourned the court until September, 1867. When a new grand jury convened on September 17 and 18, it promptly indicted John Gut and twelve others on charges of first degree murder.[15] These indictments, incidentally, appear to have been the earliest district court matters acted upon in two-year-old Redwood County.

Later in the year Gut's case was again transferred, this time to Nicollet County, where his counsel thought he would have a fairer trial. After several continuances, the trial opened at St. Peter on January 23, 1868. Two noted Minnesotans, both Indian war heroes and old acquaintances, appeared on this occasion. One was the presiding judge, Horace Austin, who had helped defend New Ulm in 1862 and had later served against the Sioux as captain of a Mounted Ranger company. The other was Charles E. Flandrau, Gut's counsel, a former Minnesota Supreme Court justice and the commander of New Ulm's defense in 1862. Conducting the prosecution was Francis R. E. Cornell, who had replaced Colvill as attorney general of Minnesota. His presence indicated the importance of the trial to the state administration. It was the first time in Minnesota's brief history that a local grand jury had indicted citizens of its area involved in a lynching, and the state authorities apparently felt that a conviction would be highly desirable.

The state had no trouble proving that John Gut stabbed Alexander Campbell. The defense as much as conceded this, hoping that justifications and constitutional arguments would carry the day. By way of justification the defense asserted that Gut was drunk when he took part in the riot, and then claimed that he was of unsound mind and not legally responsible for his acts. These matters were for the jury.[16]

The constitutional argument alleged that the 1867 law allowing the place of trial to be changed violated the requirement that the accused has a right to trial in the district where the crime was committed, "which county or district shall have been previously ascertained by law." [17] As Gut's counsel, Flandrau also argued that the 1867 statute amounted to an ex post facto law—that is, it made an act a crime which was not a crime when done. These matters were for Judge Austin to decide.

Flandrau tried to introduce the most ingenious part of his prepared case by offering to prove the following: (1) that the United States and the Sioux were at war, (2) that unrevoked general orders issued by Minnesota's adjutant general offered bounties for the scalps of Sioux warriors, (3) that Campbell looked like a Sioux, wore Indian clothing, and danced Sioux war dances, (4) that Gut was misled by Campbell's appearance and acts into thinking him a Sioux, and (5) that Gut was a soldier who only carried out what he considered his duty to kill his country's enemies. Attorney General Cornell objected that all these points were irrelevant. Ruling against his former commanding officer, Judge Austin sustained the objection. If he had not, he would in effect have revived the medieval law of outlawry, which placed outlawed persons so far outside the law that anyone could kill them with impunity.

Flandrau's unique offer completed the defense efforts. As the trial ended, Judge Austin again decided against his former commander by overruling his constitutional arguments. Austin instructed the jury to consider only whether Gut had been too drunk or too far out of his mind to know the consequences of his acts. On January 31, 1868, the jury returned a verdict of guilty "with a recommendation of the clemency of the Court." [18] Austin ignored this and on the following day sentenced Gut to be hanged.

Flandrau promptly appealed his client's case to the Minnesota Supreme Court. After hearing the same arguments that Flandrau had presented to Judge Austin, the high court reached the same conclusion. The statute permitting Gut's trial to take place outside Brown County did not infringe upon any constitutional rights, the court said, because jurors were drawn from the whole area, including Brown County, and the law did not change the district. The court considered Flandrau's arguments about Indian enemies untenable. War is not waged by stabbing handcuffed enemy prisoners, even if Gut could possibly have considered Campbell and Liscom to resemble enemies. As for general orders and governmental proclamations issued by overzealous executives, Chief Justice Thomas Wilson wrote: "The evidence that war existed between the Sioux Indians and the United States, and that the deceased was supposed to be a Sioux Indian, was therefore immaterial.

"It is not pretended that there was a law of our state authorizing the killing of a male of that tribe, and the proclamation or order of any officer of the state could not make that right which is wrong, or legal which is illegal. If such a proclamation or order was made, and if on account thereof any ignorant person was misled into the commission of crime, it is for the governor to determine whether that would be a proper case for the exercise of executive clemency."[19]

After the Minnesota court's decision, Flandrau again appealed, this time to the United States Supreme Court. Considering only the constitutional arguments, the high court affirmed the two lower courts in a brief opinion stating that changing the place of trial did not amount to altering the "previously ascertained" district, and that merely giving the judge a choice of counties without imposing additional punishment was not ex post facto legislation.[20] The case was finally resolved. All that now remained was for the governor to fix a definite date for John Gut's hanging.

By this time, however, it was February, 1870, and the fortunes of politics had brought about changes in circumstances. The Judge Austin who tried Gut's case in 1868 was the Governor Austin of 1870. Moreover, in 1868, not long after Gut's jury had recommended clemency, the legislature had amended the law on punishment for murder to provide that the death penalty would not be imposed unless the jury recommended it. Mindful of the law's change, and doubtless recalling the anti-Indian hysteria of earlier years and the natural tendency of soldiers to get into trouble, Governor Austin commuted to life imprisonment the death sentence imposed by Judge Austin in 1868. On December 29, 1873, Gut's sentence was further reduced to ten years, beginning in December, 1866. In commuting Gut's sentence the governor noted that the other twelve men who had been indicted were never punished "owing to their fleeing the country."[21]

Although criminal proceedings in the 1866 Christmas murders centered on one of the least attractive human beings ever to skulk across the landscape, Gut's acts were not without result. Final judgment in the case he provoked reminded men of ancient legal principles which settlers on the frontier sometimes conveniently overlooked: that threats to the body politic from without do not justify highhanded acts within, and that executive orders and proclamations are not law unless previously authorized by law. The anti-Sioux hysteria which probably lay behind the New Ulm lynchings gradually vanished as Civil War veterans returned to their interrupted pursuits, settled the frontier in a businesslike way, and relaxed into comfortable prosperity. With accumulations of property came increased respect for the law that protected it.

5

Rally, Philadelphians!

IN THE SUMMER OF 1869 Duluth was undergoing its first real boom. Railroad connections with St. Paul were a certainty for 1870, and the area at the western end of Lake Superior was beginning to show the growth which had earlier led such Eastern speculators as Jay Cooke to invest in its land. A typical mongrel port city was in the making. Shapeless frame buildings lined streets of mud; dingy hotels overcharged visitors; those who lifted their eyes unto the hills beheld naked slopes ruthlessly stripped of trees; a few patched-up sailing vessels shifted at their moorings; and in the saloons, which were the real social centers, crowds of drunken men talked, sang, fought, made business deals, and boasted incessantly about the town's future.

Duluth's sudden emergence attracted a variety of new citizens — among them Anson Northup, one of Minnesota's earliest settlers. When he reached the adolescent town that summer, its boom was in full swing. Northup intended to contract with railroad builders to haul materials for the new line. During his varied career, he had been a hotelkeeper in other parts of the state, and in 1839 had driven the first herd of cattle into the St. Croix Valley. He also put the first steamboat in operation on the Red River of the North in 1859. During the Civil War, Northup served as a teamster, and he received a special reward from the legislature for his part in the Sioux campaign of 1863–64. He had taken his family with him to Duluth, where his two sons worked for him as teamsters. Charles, the eldest, was the first white child born in the

St. Croix Valley; George had enlisted in Company E of the First Minnesota Regiment at the age of sixteen and served honorably throughout the Civil War. In 1869 Charles was twenty-six years of age, and George was two years younger.[1]

The hard-working Northups were not the only new residents which the railroad attracted to the booming city. Railroads are designed by people with acute minds, but they are built by people with strong backs. In 1869 the contractors for the projected Lake Superior and Mississippi Railroad had found it convenient to import into Duluth certain strong-backed Hibernians from Philadelphia whose uncouth manners had earned for them the name of "Philadelphia Roughs." When they reached Duluth, the men liked neither the place nor the job, refused to work, and spent their time — so long as they had any money — going from saloon to saloon.

A Philadelphian of different background who had also found his way to Duluth was Thomas H. Stokley, a "beardless boy" of twenty. He was the son of William S. Stokley, a prominent Philadelphian who had been a collector of internal revenue and in 1869 was an alderman of the city of brotherly love. Although he was a watchmaker, the boy for some unexplained reason was working in Duluth as a lather and plasterer. He was unquestionably the only such artisan of his day to carry on his trade in a black frock coat.[2]

Saturday, August 14, 1869, was a local election day. In 1869 laws against buying drinks for voters or tippling on election days were unknown, and frontier saloonkeepers enjoyed their usual lively business. A number of idle Hibernians indulged in their customary potations and soon caused the troubles which drunken idlers often provoke.

Two Irishmen whose credit was exhausted asked for drinks at a saloon on First Street where they had already run up a considerable tab. When the bartender refused to serve them, they tried to rush him but were thrown into the street. There, brooding over their wrongs, one of the men threw a stick through the saloon window. The owner, Nicholas Decker, had been away voting. When he returned, the bartender showed him the broken window and pointed out the guilty man, who stood not far away among a small crowd of friends. Decker strode over to him and asked if he had broken the window. The man responded by taking a mighty swing at his questioner. Charles Northup, who had approached the group, caught the man's arm and prevented the blow. The drunken Irishman tried again; Northup parried and struck him in the face. At this one of the other Roughs cried, "kill the son of a bitch!" The group began to close in on Northup who, seeing himself heavily outnumbered, started to run down Superior Street while the inflamed sons of Erin chased him, shouting.[3]

Hearing the noise and probably carried away by mob spirit, Tom Stokley, who apparently knew the Roughs but was not one of them, left his work and joined in the pursuit wearing his black frock coat. Just as Northup seemed to be outrunning his pursuers, a Hibernian bellowed what must have been the gang's war cry—"Rally, Philadelphians!"—hoping that other Roughs would join in heading Northup off.[4]

By this time the chase was nearing the Northup home, and George, who had been driving a team not far away, realized that his brother was in trouble. Leaving the team, he ran to help Charles, who had actually outdistanced the group. Although the Philadelphians had almost decided to retire, when George appeared as a reinforcement, they renewed the chase. This time they closed in on George, who stooped to pick up a rock. At that moment, a man gave him a quick, underhand blow. In another instant, he cried, "Charley, I am stabbed."[5]

Pursuers and pursued had now reached the Northup house, where Anson himself came out, ax in hand, and dispersed the mob. Charles went inside, but George followed the retreating gang. When he returned twenty minutes later, he appeared ill. His family at once called Dr. Thomas Potts, one of the physicians who testified at Ann Bilansky's trial. Finding his patient with a one-and-a-half-inch knife wound in his belly, a barely perceptible pulse, a cold and clammy skin, and his abdomen swollen from internal bleeding, Dr. Potts dosed him with whisky and morphine. Later in the evening a second doctor was called. George Northup died at eleven o'clock, whispering that he thought Edward McGovern, one of his principal assailants, had stabbed him.

The St. Louis County sheriff had meanwhile rounded up nine suspects including McGovern and Tom Stokley. Since Duluth did not yet possess enough of civilization's amenities to have a jail, the men were confined in a "dark hole at Decker's Brewery." They must have spent uneasy hours, for throughout the night a large crowd stood outside the brewery shouting, "hang them! lynch them!" On the next day, which was Sunday, a group of citizens held a formal meeting in the new Masonic Hall, trying to organize a vigilance committee which would hang the prisoners at once. It took strenuous persuasion, including that of Anson Northup on the very day of his son's funeral, to dissuade them.[6]

On August 16, 1869, two days after George Northup was killed, the accused men had their preliminary hearing. Four of them were released. The other five were charged with first degree murder, and ordered held in the Ramsey County jail at St. Paul until the grand jury for St. Louis County should meet. McGovern and Stokley were among the group held. Tom's attorney, Albert N. Seip, complained by affidavit that securing a fair hearing for Stokley had been rather hard. "One person," Seip said, had come to him in court while he "was cross examining a witness for the prosecution, and whispered in a threatening tone" that if he "did not cease cross examining such witness, said person would see that measures were at once taken to stop him."[7]

The prisoners left Duluth about one o'clock that night, taking the steamer "Keyes" to Superior, Wisconsin, and the regular stagecoach to St. Paul the next day. Knowing the frontier temper, the four men who had been freed chose to travel in irons to St. Paul with the others. Upon reaching the capital, three who were veterans promptly re-enlisted in the army. Some two months later, on October 24, the other four, including McGovern, were released on bail of two thousand dollars each.

The Ramsey County district court, however, would not allow bail to Stokley, who had to stay in jail until the grand jury finally met in Duluth nearly a year after George Northup's death. On August 9, 1870, the grand jury indicted Stokley, McGovern, and the three others for first degree murder, charging that they killed George Northup by "stabbing him . . . in the left side of the abdomen, with a knife."[8]

The court decided to try Stokley's case first. His counsel asked on August 11 to have the trial held outside Duluth, arguing that feelings had run so high at the time of Northup's murder that "an impartial jury could not be impaneled." The attorney also pointed out that Anson Northup, not content with hiring two extra jail guards at his own expense, had also retained four additional lawyers to help Edward F. Parker, the county attorney, conduct the prosecution. Two of these were unquestioned leaders of the Minnesota bar — Gorman, former territorial governor, and Charles Flandrau, former supreme court justice. James J. Egan of Duluth and James N. Castle of Stillwater were also retained by Northup.[9]

Judge James M. McKelvy refused to allow the place of trial to be moved after the prosecution showed that the population of Duluth had changed markedly since 1869. County Attorney Parker said that among its some 3,500 residents — as opposed to its not more than 1,000 sojourners and speculators a year before — "at least three-fourths" had never heard of either the crime or the defendants.[10] The trial accordingly opened in Duluth on August 17, 1870. With four lawyers active in the prosecution, and three — Seip, Isaac Heard, and Henry J. Horn — appearing for the defense, every technicality was presented, argued, and fought over. With this battery of counsel, it took some time to pick a jury and several venires were exhausted. Even then one of the jurymen, unknown to counsel, turned out to be the Reverend Henry Elliott, the Methodist minister who had preached George Northup's funeral sermon.

The prosecution had no easy time proving its case, for it is usually difficult to find witnesses to a mob scene who are positive about who was there and what was done. Although Stokley was reported to have confessed to Anson Northup that he stabbed George with his pocketknife, excusing himself by saying that he was under the influence of liquor and, moreover, acted in self-defense, Anson did not testify at the trial, and the prosecution did not establish that Stokley actually made such a statement.[11] The record in the Stokley case shows that the fracas which cost George Northup his life took place so quickly and in such confusion that no one person comprehended it all. The following facts, nevertheless, were established to the jury's satisfaction.

On the day of the murder Tom Stokley was wearing a long, black, frock coat. Someone saw him carrying a knife. Although Charles Northup said, "I saw no one strike George," another witness testified that some man struck George "an underhanded blow"; the witness went on to say, "don't know positive who the man was; my judgment is that it is Mr. Stokely [*sic*]; at the same time Northrup [*sic*] struck him with the stone; at the same time they were as near together as well could be; George Northrup then hollered that he was stabbed." Still another witness reported that a man standing about eight feet from George stepped forward and seemed to pick up a stone. Then, the witness said, "George Northrup put his hand to his side and cried out; 'I am stabbed; the son of a bitch has stabbed me!' . . . I could not say who struck the blow; the man was about five feet six; dressed in a long black tailed coat." The witness was not personally acquainted with Stokley, but the description applied accurately.[12]

The defense contented itself with introducing evidence of young Stokley's good character, presenting nothing to contradict the prosecution or to justify or excuse the act. On August 19, after hearing the court charge that all who took part in the affray were guilty as principals, the jury retired and on August 20 brought in a verdict of guilty — not of first degree murder, but of murder in the second degree. The jurymen had apparently given way a little because of Stokley's youth. On August 25 the defense moved for a new trial and stay of sentence which was denied on September 1, 1870. Young Tom Stokley then came before the court and heard himself sentenced to imprisonment for the remainder of his natural life.

An appeal to the Minnesota Supreme Court proved fruitless, although it permitted Stokley to remain for another year in the county jail instead of the state penitentiary. During August, 1871, however, Stokley took up residence along the shores of Lake St. Croix in what the *Stillwater Messenger* of August 25 jokingly called the "Hotel de Jackman" for Henry A. Jackman, the popular new warden of the state prison.

The four Philadelphia Roughs indicted with him — McGovern, Thomas J. Courtney, E. J. Paulin, and Benjamin F. Zaracher — were cleared of the charges against them. A Duluth jury acquitted McGovern in August, 1870. The trials of the other three were transferred to St. Paul, where in September the jury after twenty hours of debate disagreed in Courtney's case and acquitted Zaracher. The St. Louis County attorney, satisfied with Stokley's conviction, decided not to retry Zaracher, and declined even to prosecute Paulin. In so doing, he may have been moved by the state of the county treasury, for the *Duluth Minnesotian* of October 8, 1870, noted that the "expenses of their trials will bear very heavy on the new and yet comparatively feeble county of St. Louis."

If he had been of obscure family, Tom Stokley's saga might have ended when the Stillwater prison doors closed behind him, but he was not. By 1871 his father was the Republican candidate for mayor of Philadelphia. It was soon apparent that very great influence indeed was at work to secure Tom's release. Governor Austin received numerous petitions from sympathetic Minnesota citizens—five members of the grand jury, six members of the trial jury, Parker and Gorman who had conducted the prosecution, three former governors and one future governor, four former members of the Minnesota Supreme Court, and Ignatius Donnelly, who would not be kept out of any controversy—as well as from the Stokley family in Philadelphia. Although these did not seem to convince him, he must have been moved by a letter from Mr. and Mrs. Anson Northup which said: "The dead cannot be brought to life, the majesty of the law has been maintained, and we hope and believe a repentant heart has obtained mercy and pardon above. We earnestly write . . . that the lonely son may be returned to his Parents and Society and that a life of usefulness and honor may be placed in his power."[13]

Pressure from another direction was also at work. On September 1, 1871, Jay Cooke, Philadelphia railroad tycoon and financier who had large holdings in Duluth, wrote to Austin. He hoped that the governor could see his way clear to pardon young Stokley, because his father's "heart is almost broken by this great misfortune." Cooke also sent letters of introduction for Charles O'Neill, veteran Pennsylvania Republican Congressman, who journeyed to Minnesota to work for Stokley's release. In addition Cooke apparently arranged to have Tom's father approach Alexander Ramsey, who was then a senator from Minnesota and longtime chief of the state's Republican party. Governor Austin, of course, was also a Republican.

In 1871 the Republicans were genuinely concerned that the Democrats, by carrying local elections, might regain enough power to influence national affairs. If this happened, the Republicans feared that the treatment of the South would be softened and the gains of the bloody four-year Civil War dissipated. Thus local elections, like that in which Stokley's father was engaged, assumed monumental importance. The lines of party pressure tightened about Austin.

The Union Republican City Executive Committee of Philadelphia wrote Austin that "Naturally Mr. Stokley's mind is very much distressed on this subject and it being an important epoch in our local politics we would like him to have an assurance that at the appropriate time he will be relieved of this affliction." The chairman of the Pennsylvania Union Republican State Central Committee, writing to Austin on September 4, 1871, was more blunt: "To carry the State of Pennsylvania in this campaign," he declared, "we must carry the City of Philadelphia, and to carry Pennsylvania in the great contest of 1872, we must control the police force of the City [*for patronage*]. Much at this moment depends upon the activity of Mr. Stokley in the campaign, who since the sentence of his son is almost paralyzed with grief, and we ask you as the Committee representing the great Republican party of the State of Pennsylvania to grant the pardon of the condemned, and by so doing infuse new life and vigor in our candidate for Mayor of Philadelphia, and recover the City to republican rule and control." John W. Geary, governor of Pennsylvania, seconded this plea in a letter written the following day, as did Edward M. Paxson, the Philadelphia judge who was soon to be a member of Pennsylvania's supreme court, and other Republican notables of the Keystone State.

Under these pressures and perhaps anticipating reciprocal favors some day, it is no wonder that Governor Austin decided to grant the pardon. His decision was made known to Tom Stokley's father by Ramsey before election day and before the pardon was actually issued. Mr. Stokley was elected mayor of Philadelphia in November, and no one can say how much the knowledge that his son would be pardoned infused vigor and confidence into his campaign.

On December 22, 1871, possessing a full and entire pardon, Thomas Stokley left the Minnesota State Prison and sped to Philadelphia. There in less than ten years he became a deputy sheriff.

6

Bobolink's Last War Whoop

IN MILITARY CAMPAIGNS of 1862, 1863, and 1864, Minnesota volunteers and federal troops had cleared the Sioux from southern Minnesota and pushed them westward. The Chippewa remained in the north. As ancient enemies who had driven the Sioux from the Mille Lacs region in the mid-eighteenth century, the Chippewa refused to join the Sioux rebellion in 1862 and stood with folded hands while the whites exterminated a common foe. Although Chippewa-white relations in the state were generally peaceful, the tribe later proved itself capable of causing substantial trouble for some northern Minnesota settlers.

By 1871 when John Cook took up a claim at Oak Lake in Becker County the Chippewa were largely confined to reservations. Oak Lake, now vanished, was a village near the western Minnesota White Earth Reservation, where Cook once worked for the government. Earlier he had been a fur trader among the Indians there and at Leech Lake to the northeast. Now he wanted to farm.

The Oak Lake settlement near which he chose to live came into being in 1871 when the westward-building Northern Pacific Railroad reached that point and established a station. Like many another frontier hamlet it had its brief hour of life and disappeared, but unlike many the actual date of its death sentence is known. On May 27, 1872, the railroad moved its Oak Lake station to near-by Audubon.[1]

John Cook was a native of New Hampshire; his wife, Deantha, was born in Maine. During the Civil War Cook served as assistant engineer on the "Little Ada," attached to Admiral David D. Porter's command. As did veterans of that and other wars, Cook kept his uniform after leaving the service and was often seen about Oak Lake wearing his navy coat, on which Mrs. Cook had substituted black buttons for the brass ones. In 1872 the Cook family consisted of John, about forty years of age; Deantha, about thirty-two; Freddie, just over eight; Mary, seven; and young John, about twenty-one months. They had lived on their Becker County claim little more than a year.[2]

Although Cook was now a farmer, he continued trading in furs. On April 26, 1872, a friendly Indian known as Frank brought him a hundred muskrat skins, which he stored upstairs in his house. Freddie, John's young son, was so impressed with "Mr. Frank's" visit that he ran over to tell his aunt, Mrs. Nellie Small, about it. The Smalls lived on an adjoining claim about three-quarters of a mile from the Cooks. Several other Indians were seen in the vicinity that day. Two stopped at Cooks'. Three called at the house of a neighbor, solemnly lighted pipes at the fire, and left without saying a word. In Oak Lake one member of a Chippewa band moving through the area bought two gallons of whisky. Other Indians camped in the neighborhood that night. Among them was one known as Kahkahbesha, whose name is spelled various ways and is usually translated Bobolink.

On the following morning, April 27, 1872, the Indians who camped near Oak Lake departed early and abruptly, leaving partly cooked food which they seemed in too great a hurry to eat. On that same morning Mrs. Small, who was Mrs. Cook's sister, sent her young son to the Cook home for milk. The lad returned empty-handed and told his mother that the house "was all burned down." Mrs. Small ran to the Cook place where she saw a mass of smoking timbers, spots of blood on the cellar walls, and fragmented remains of the Cook family in the cellar. She quickly sent for other neighbors who combed the wreckage and confirmed her worst fears.[3]

A coroner's inquest was called while the ruined house was still smoldering. Members of the jury put the fire out, searched the rubble, and found some charred bones, a few children's teeth, some gold fillings, and a set of false teeth. The local physician, Dr. David Pyle, found traces of blood on fragments of clothing.

Nothing indicated how the tragedy took place or who might be guilty, but these people living at the edge of white settlement immediately thought of Indians. The sheriff telegraphed Governor Austin at once, reporting the crime and asking him to send a detective, while the citizens of Oak Lake sent a petition asking the governor to confine all Indians to their reservations. Otherwise, the petitioners said, the people "must arise in the majesty of the first law of human nature (self-preservation) and exterminate the race of Indians." [4]

Early in May Governor Austin issued the requested proclamation warning all Indians to stay within their reservations. Recognizing that he needed better information and fearing that the incident might provoke further bloodshed, he also sent Dr. David Day, a St. Paul physician, as his special emissary "to ascertain if there were any real danger from an Indian outbreak." When he came back from the Chippewa country, Dr. Day reported that the Pillager band — reputedly the bravest and fiercest of the Chippewa — "meditated mischief" so far as he could see, but he could not judge the form or direction it would take. "A continual vendetta is going on between the Indians, and whites of the border," he commented, "and if indulged in much longer the Law of the savage will have superceeded [*sic*] that of Civilization." [5]

Meanwhile, the conduct of a particular Indian was drawing attention. Two days after the Cook home burned, Bobolink, who had been observed near there on April 26, sold a hundred muskrat skins to a white trader. To fellow tribesmen he sold a woman's cloak and a gold watch chain and pencil, charging fifteen dollars for the cloak and three dollars for the other items. Some days later he appeared in Oak Lake wearing a navy coat on which the brass buttons had been replaced by black ones. He had with him a gold watch, which he pawned for a dollar, and a navy revolver of the type Cook had owned, which he tried unsuccessfully to sell.

News of Bobolink's conduct must somehow have reached Governor Austin, since he very shortly sent into the north two well-known men. To apprehend Bobolink, the governor dispatched James Whitehead, a St. Anthony lumber dealer who had lived among the Indians and had known Bobolink as a boy. To investigate the Oak Lake crime, Governor Austin sent Alfred Brackett, the St. Paul detective who had taken part in many important early Minnesota criminal cases.[6]

Whitehead's assignment was anything but simple. It required walking into a large reservation, finding a particular man, arresting him, securing him, and taking him away, all before the hostile eyes of his friends and relatives. Bobolink's band and his social standing made Whitehead's task even more difficult, for the Indian was a member of the Otter Tail band of Pillager, who lived near Leech Lake. Tradition says that they acquired their peculiar name — in Ojibway, Muk-im-dua-win-in-e-wug, meaning "men who take by force" — in 1781 when they defied the British and seized the goods of a British trader passing through their country. Their reputation for boldness endured. Moreover, Bobolink was a nephew of the respected Chief Flat Mouth. To complicate things further Bobolink had sold the watch chain and pencil to a brother of Red Turtle, another Pillager chief. Knowing that Whitehead might have hard going, Governor Austin telegraphed Captain I. C. Walters, militia commander at Brainerd, to hold his troops ready to protect Bobolink, Whitehead, and Brackett if necessary.[7]

At Sandy Lake on May 20, 1872, the Pillager were holding a ceremonial of the Grand Medicine Lodge, a complex socioreligious society of considerable importance to the Chippewa. By late afternoon the group of several hundred men and women was in a mixed state of religious exaltation and drunkenness. Into this lion's den walked three white men to arrest the principal chief's nephew: Whitehead, the special agent, and D. O. Preston and George W. Holland, Brainerd attorneys.[8]

Ignoring the surly looks which met him everywhere, Whitehead calmly walked through the crowd seeking Bobolink, whom he finally found playing the moccasin game with friends. After speaking a few words to his quarry in Ojibway, Whitehead waited until the Indian finished his game and returned to his lodge. The agent followed him there, told him why he was wanted, and arrested him. When Bobolink realized what was happening, he tried to snatch a knife from under the blanket he was wearing, but Whitehead was too quick and pinioned his arms. The special agent had taken precautions, asking the two Brainerd lawyers to follow him and station themselves outside any lodge he might enter. They did so and were able to help secure the prisoner.

The three men had their captive but in this Indian stronghold it was a question who was imprisoning whom. To leave the place, the white men had to take Bobolink past the Grand Medicine Lodge itself, where the Indian's wife and family saw him and rushed out to ask what was the matter. Chief Red Turtle also appeared with a group of braves and began to follow Whitehead. For a moment it was touch and go.

Whitehead later recalled: "The chief said it seemed strange the whites could come here and take away a man without consulting him. [I] told him we took prisoners first and then told them about it. [I] told him he was always supposed to be a good Indian and not to meddle with this matter; if they would rescue him I would return in 10 days with 1000 troops. He said to tell the Governor he had not meddled with me." At the same time Red Turtle, who had no wish to provoke reprisals, instructed Bobolink "that if he had done anything wrong to tell the truth what ever he knew about it."

The white men took their prisoner from the Indian camp. When they reached the river about a mile away, Whitehead, who must have had extraordinary *sang-froid,* left Bobolink in the custody of the other two men and revisited the Chippewa lodges to search for missing items from the Cook residence and to talk with other Indians. His visit brought results. Whitehead later revealed that he "had seen a heavy, winter woman[']s cloak on an Indian before this" and went looking for him. "When I found him he was partially drunk and said he had hid the cloak. I next found the chief and told him what I wanted. . . . Got the chief and the Indian I had seen with the cloak together and asked the chief to get it for me. He asked me what I would pay. I said set a price. He said $15.00. I said very well bring it along. In about ½ hour, the Indian . . . returned with the cloak and I paid him the money." After a while Red Turtle's brother handed Whitehead a gold chain and pencil, telling him he had paid Bobolink three dollars for them. Whitehead paid him the three dollars.

With his prisoner and his evidence, the agent was now ready to leave. As the afternoon progressed the Indians had become drunker and some of the squaws were taunting the men, calling them cowards and urging them to rescue Bobolink. By great good luck the white manhunters were able to take their captive away before the Chippewa tribesmen became sufficiently inflamed and decided to try a rescue.

On the journey from camp to the nearest railroad station at Aitkin, Bobolink nearly escaped when, given permission to wash in the river, he dived in and began swimming away rapidly. But the white men chased him in their canoe, caught up with him, and finally subdued him by hitting him over the head with a paddle. After he was safely on the train, Bobolink was confronted with Mrs. Cook's red cloak and was asked if he recognized it. Looking uneasy, the Indian said, "I think I do." [9]

In spite of the incriminating circumstances and after being questioned twice, Bobolink denied having had any personal contact with the Cook family. He was nonetheless taken to Oak Lake by Whitehead and Brackett for preliminary examination on May 24. At that time he admitted knowing about the murder but continued to deny having taken part in it. Three Rainy Lake men committed the crime, he said. He had been innocently sleeping under a tree when three Indians awakened him, told him they had murdered the Cook family and plundered the house, and gave him some of their spoils to secure his silence. The examining justice was not convinced. He ordered Bobolink taken to St. Paul for confinement in the Ramsey County jail until the grand jury met.[10]

While in jail, Bobolink was visited by Allen Jordan, a half-breed whom he knew. Their conversation resulted in a startling confession. Bobolink admitted to Jordan that he had taken part in attacking the Cook home but said he had done so only under duress. Indians from the Leech Lake Pillager band, among whom were Kahbemahbe (One Who Seems to Sit in Different Places), the ringleader, and Okemah (King) had coerced him.[11]

According to the story Jordan heard, Kahbemahbe learned on April 26, 1872, that an Indian had left a large quantity of furs with John Cook. Kahbemahbe then found Okemah and the two of them dragged Bobolink with them to Cook's farm. Reaching the house about 8:00 P.M., they stood outside the door. Kahbemahbe pushed Bobolink forward, telling him to shoot when the door opened. Bobolink shot John Cook in the chest. He fell dead instantly.

Continuing his story, Bobolink said that Mrs. Cook rushed to her husband's side. Kahbemahbe stepped forward and struck her with his hatchet. Although she kept crying, "Oh, don't! Don't kill me!" she was struck again, this time a deadly blow. Telling the others to wait, Kahbemahbe ran upstairs where he found two children in bed. He promptly killed them. The three Indians then divided the spoils, including a package of furs Kahbemahbe had thrown downstairs. After setting fire to the house, the three separated, Bobolink hurrying eastward while the others turned west.

On the strength of this confession, Brackett and two others set out on June 20 to arrest Bobolink's supposed confederates. Kahbemahbe and Okemah were found together on the White Earth Reservation, quietly and peaceably gambling. When arrested they made no resistance, Okemah saying only, "What? What?" in the Ojibway language. Neither seemed to know anything about the raid or to have property connected with the Cooks. Both waived preliminary examinations and were sent to St. Paul on June 30 to await further proceedings. Kahbemahbe was described as "a large, stout, well-dressed" man of about twenty-eight who wore "a profusion of ear and finger rings." Okemah was a boy of not more than eighteen.

In that same month of June, 1872, a Chippewa chief named Anoke went to St. Paul with Jean Baptiste Bottineau, a half-breed, to interview the most famous contemporary Chippewa prisoner then languishing in jail. It appeared that the Indians dreaded white reprisals for the Cook affair, welcomed the governor's order keeping them on their reservations where they felt safer, and were just as anxious as the whites to see the Cook matter investigated. When Anoke and Bottineau questioned him about the murder, Bobolink kept to the story he told at his preliminary examination. This time he named the three Indians who supposedly awakened him and told him what they had just done. Further interrogation showed irreconcilable contradictions in Bobolink's story, and law enforcement officers decided to take no action against these Indians, who were much luckier than others in the same situation.[12]

As matters stood Bobolink had told two versions of one story in which he admitted guilty knowledge but claimed not to have taken part in the murder, and one version of another story in which he confessed to shooting John Cook. He suddenly became the author of still another confession in which he appeared as the lonely killer. This report appeared in the *Duluth Minnesotian* of June 29, 1872, and doubtless contained some editorial embellishment. "I made up my mind to commit this crime because I was poor and needed clothing," Bobolink is quoting as saying. Upon reaching the Cook home, the Indian continued, he opened the door and shot Cook as he sat reading. Mrs. Cook ran to her husband. Bobolink shot her. After killing the husband and wife, the Indian said that he entered the house, found the three children, and killed them with a club. "They did not cry or moan," he commented. After choosing the goods he wanted, he set fire to the house and went away. "I do not consider the above a brave act," the newspaper quoted him as saying, "and have never felt brave until to-day since I have told the truth. I know I will be hanged and I intend to give the war-whoop on that occasion."

As if to confound the investigation further, Bobolink shortly repudiated this second confession and said he really told the truth at his preliminary investigation. On August 8 Bobolink indulged in a third confession, this time in the presence of Franklin Cook, the slain man's brother, Whitehead, who captured him, and Jean Bottineau, who had interviewed him before and now served as interpreter. He had a hand in the murder, Bobolink said, but his hand was forced. On the day before the Cook family met its doom, he was hunting near Oak Lake. In the evening, he went on, he met another Indian named Mascaabeoson who bragged about the goods he had amassed by killing white people and proposed killing the Cook family for plunder. Bobolink held back, he said, until Mascaabeoson taunted him repeatedly with being a coward. Then he decided to go along.[13]

At the Cook residence Bobolink was still reluctant, he insisted, and he and his companion stood under a tree talking until it was nearly midnight. Finally Bobolink stood guard outside while Mascaabeoson shot John Cook through the window as he sat at a table reading. Mascaabeoson entered the house, killed Mrs. Cook with a hatchet, ran upstairs, threw a packet of furs down, and killed the children. Bobolink heard only one short cry. The two Indians then divided the plunder. As they were leaving the neighborhood, Bobolink said, Mascaabeoson returned to the Cook house on some pretext and set it afire.

Having confessed to murder in three different ways and having twice confessed to knowing about a felony but not disclosing it, the unhappy and unquestionably confused Bobolink stayed in the Ramsey County jail until he was formally indicted for first degree murder by the Becker County grand jury on November 12, 1872. The jury refused, however, to indict Kahbemahbe and Okemah, whom Bobolink had tried to implicate in his first confession. Neither would it indict one Bowahness, another Chippewa of no good reputation who was suspected of complicity in the Cook murders as well as that of another white settler. On the advice of counsel, Messrs. R. Reynolds of Detroit Lakes and D. O. Preston of Brainerd — one of the men who helped capture him — Bobolink pleaded not guilty. Since Oak Lake had no jail, he was taken to the Wilson House at Detroit Lakes for confinement until his trial.[14]

During all this, Bobolink's tribe had not forgotten him, but the year 1872 was a singularly unpropitious time for the Chippewa to try using what little influence they had. On April 28, 1872, the day after the Cook tragedy was discovered, a white girl named Helen McArthur disappeared under circumstances suggesting that Indians abducted her. The hysteria caused by this event again threw white Minnesota into a mood of Indian extermination, and it is a real wonder that Bobolink was not lynched.[15]

Chief Flat Mouth was nevertheless courageous enough to try to help his nephew. He first took care to assure the whites that if Indians had a part in the Cook tragedy they acted on their own individual responsibility without encouragement from any band or tribe. Flat Mouth said "that they had some sense left in them. He knew his obligations to their Great Father that his people would never spill the white man[']s blood. If it was done by some foolish young man he did not think the whole tribe should suffer for it."[16]

After making this statement Flat Mouth seems to have become more devious. Dr. Day, Governor Austin's emissary in the Indian country, was surprised to receive a telegram saying that on June 10 the Pillager chiefs would deliver to him three men involved in the Cook murders. They asked Day to meet them at Brainerd, the regional metropolis. Founded in 1870 when the Northern Pacific indicated that its line would cross the Mississippi there, it was a railroad division point and a bustling little settlement by 1872.

To Brainerd, suspecting treachery but curious, went Dr. Day, only to find that the Indians did not appear. On June 6 Flat Mouth had wired Governor Austin, "We cannot go down to Brainerd," and asked the governor and Henry B. Whipple, Episcopal bishop and long-time friend of the Indians, to bring Bobolink with them to a meeting at Leech Lake. There, said Flat Mouth, they could discuss the Cook affair as well as ways and means of finding the guilty parties. Governor Austin countered by asking Flat Mouth to come to St. Paul with two other principal chiefs and the three suspected men. Flat Mouth declined the invitation and stayed home. The three suspects were never named.[17]

Although there is no evidence of it, Flat Mouth may have had some idea of luring Austin and Whipple into Indian country, rescuing Bobolink, and holding the white men as security against a general white attack on the Indians. If that was his plan, it did not work. The Indians made no further moves in Bobolink's behalf and left him to the white man's justice.

Rumors of Indian troubles persisted, however, as long as Bobolink remained a prisoner. Some influence was at work magnifying the risk so that other parts of Minnesota—as well as other states—would get the impression that a serious Indian outbreak threatened. Curiously, all Indian problems seemed to be brewing only along the Northern Pacific right-of-way. Local newspapers obviously interested in the prosperity which a railroad line would bring their frontier communities accused rival railroad lines, land speculators, and even the governor himself, of drawing wild pictures of Indian conditions in northern Minnesota in order to divert workmen and investors to the southern part of the state where they had large stakes.[18]

The Indian outbreak did not materialize. On January 15, 1873, Bobolink's trial opened without fanfare in Byron's Hall at Detroit Lakes. This large room over a billiard parlor was the only suitable place to hold court in the tiny village which had no courthouse. Francis Cornell, attorney general of Minnesota, conducted the prosecution in person before Judge McKelvy, who had presided over Tom Stokley's trial in 1870.

In a murder case the prosecution must not only prove that a human being came to his death, but how he did so. This is not so simple when physical remains are scanty. When the state introduced all that could be found of the Cook family, the evidence consisted of a few charred bones, a fragment of a female skull, a few children's teeth, some gold fillings, and a set of false teeth. A stone crock held all that searchers could find of the bodies of John and Deantha Cook and their three children. For the remainder of its tangible evidence, the prosecution brought into court John Cook's watch chain, and Deantha's watch, cloak, belt, and pencil, which Whitehead had bought at the reservation.[19]

Dr. Pyle was able to state positively that the charred bone fragments were those of human beings and that the small teeth were those of children. He could also identify the skull fragment as that of a human female. Pointing to traces of subcutaneous hemorrhage in the skull, he explained that someone must have struck this woman on the head with enough force to kill her. Apart from testimony that blood stained the cellar walls, this was the only evidence that death might have resulted from violence.

Dr. Philo S. Calkins, a Minneapolis dentist, identified the false teeth as a set he had made for John Cook. This is probably the first instance in Minnesota criminal jurisprudence where a dentist made the critical identification of a murder victim. Other witnesses then restated the evidence which had originally led to Bobolink's arrest. A storekeeper recalled seeing the defendant in Cook's navy coat and described how the Indian tried to sell Cook's property. A trader told of buying a hundred muskrat skins from Bobolink within a day or two of the Cook family's holocaust. The two Indians who bought Mrs. Cook's belongings testified through an interpreter. Whitehead related the circumstances of Bobolink's arrest and his later confession to him and Franklin Cook. When Dr. Pyle, who identified the Cook family's remains, disclosed that he had seen Bobolink and several other Indians in the Oak Lake area on April 26, 1872, the prosecution rested.

Bobolink's defense was feebly presented. His counsel did not even try such obvious tactics as hinting at another guilty party, or showing that Bobolink had no weapons on the day in question — the prosecution did not show that he had — or minimizing the confession by showing the circumstances under which Bobolink made it and the Indian psychology which lay behind it. The Indians had two strong temptations when speaking with whites: boasting, to show their valor; and lying, because they did not trust the whites and would say anything to keep from bringing down the white man's wrath on them. Bobolink's counsel made nothing of this.

No one demanded the presence of any men Bobolink had accused. The first three mentioned at his preliminary examination, for instance, were never investigated, and no one argued very hard that while Bobolink's possession of Cook's goods looked guilty, it could nevertheless be consistent with innocence. Brackett, Whitehead, the court, and the jury accepted at their face value the statements of the Indians who said they bought from Bobolink trinkets belonging to the Cook family.

The defendant did not take the stand. The defense effort really consisted only of arguing that the prosecution had no positive evidence linking Bobolink with the crime, and of introducing two so-called medical men, who must charitably be called quacks, to raise doubts about the identification of the Cook family's remains. The first defense witness described himself as a practicing physician of the Eclectic School, which flourished in Adams, New York, and had no connection with any recognized American medical school. The second revealed that, while he had not gone so far as to spend a day studying in any institution of medical learning, he had nevertheless read with great care several illustrated volumes on anatomy. Both these savants solemnly testified that they knew no difference between a male and a female skull and that the prosecution's expert must be mistaken in identifying the skull fragment as that of a woman. With this fragile effort the defense rested.

On January 18, 1873, an hour and a half after retiring, the jury returned with its verdict. It found Bobolink "guilty of murder in the first degree" and recommended death. This appears to be one of the few cases where the death penalty was actually recommended by jurors acting under the 1868 law, which left it to the jury to decide whether a convicted murderer should hang. Three days later Judge McKelvy pronounced the formal sentence of death by hanging, and the prisoner was taken to St. Paul for confinement until the governor should fix the day. Counsel for the Indian made a faint motion for a new trial but withdrew it before the court heard it argued.

Back in St. Paul Bobolink startled the authorities by making yet another confession. He had been a forced bystander, he now said, while a White Earth Indian named Bowahness, who had planned the crime, killed Mr. and Mrs. Cook, and another White Earth man named Musquaobethung finished the bloody work of killing the children. Bowahness had been arrested before, but had been dismissed for lack of evidence by the same grand jury which indicted Bobolink. Musquaobethung is surely the same name as Mascaabeoson whom Bobolink implicated in his confession to Whitehead and Franklin Cook.[20]

Feeling that even though the story was doubtful they ought to take action, the authorities found Musquaobethung and arrested him. Bowahness was known to be at the White Earth Reservation and placing him under arrest called for more elaborate preparations. Having in mind the preceding year's Indian difficulties, Governor Austin ordered the forty-man Brainerd militia company to go with Whitehead, who was to arrest Bowahness. The militia took its assignment reluctantly, dawdled, approached the reservation gingerly, and, after meeting a half-breed who said Bowahness had "skedaddled," sighed in relief as one man and returned to Oak Lake without investigating the half-breed's story. Whitehead, however, continued into the Indian country, where he found that the half-breed had told the truth. Bowahness, who was described as "an artful old Indian reprobate," half Sioux and half Chippewa, was on his way to Pembina in Dakota Territory.[21]

Meanwhile, what to do with Bobolink presented a tremendous political problem—more difficult to decide and having more momentous possible consequences than Ann Bilansky's case. Should Bobolink be hanged? If he were hanged when other men accused of the crime had not been cleared or even investigated, the governor took the chance of serious trouble from the warlike Pillager and perhaps other Minnesota Indians. It was only ten years after the great uprising of 1862. If, on the other hand, Governor Austin commuted Bobolink's sentence, the Indians might overstep their bounds in reliance on the white man's leniency. Whatever the governor might do appeared to be wrong.

Fate resolved this dilemma so neatly that one cannot but suspect that someone lent a helping hand, although the passage of time has made it improbable that the truth will ever be known. On May

20, 1873, Bobolink died of "the quick consumption" in the Ramsey County jail. Never was consumption so quick or so convenient. The sheriff of Ramsey County immediately buried the Indian's body in a secret place, and some future archaeologist may stumble over the remains of the unfortunate Bobolink who never got his chance to give the war whoop at his hanging.[22]

Some time later Bowahness, who had been found, and Musquaobethung were released for lack of evidence. Bobolink's last confession had been as untrustworthy as the others. The case was closed.

Was Bobolink guilty? He had too many associations with the Cook family and its possessions to sustain a claim of perfect innocence, although he may have been, and probably was, only one of a group. His contradictions — for example, misstating the number of Cook children in his first confession — made everything doubtful. Yet in a casual statement Bobolink corroborated an equally casual statement made by Mrs. Small — that John Cook had stored furs upstairs in his house. As early as July 7, 1872, the *Detroit* (Lakes) *Weekly Record* said, "It is not believed by the people of this county that one Indian alone was concerned in the Cook tragedy." The number *three* was peculiarly persistent throughout the investigation. On the night before the Cook murders *three* Indians made a call in the neighborhood; Bobolink twice asserted that he was one of *three* men who did the deed, and at other times said that *three* men from Rainy Lake committed the crime; and Chief Flat Mouth spoke of delivering *three* men of his band concerned in the murder. One cannot help feeling that the Indians probably knew who killed the Cooks, and knew that three men did it.

Upon the evidence presented at Bobolink's trial, however, a jury might easily have reasonable doubt that the Cook family was *murdered*, since the outward evidence of death by violence was of the flimsiest — spots of blood on walls and extravasated blood in a female skull, without anything to show who inflicted violence. It is somewhat unlikely for five people to die in an accidental fire, but it has happened.

A lawyer of today, unaffected by white Minnesotans' 1873 attitudes toward Indians, cannot help feeling unhappy about the way Bobolink's own counsel sped him toward the gallows. Such a lackluster defense, it is hoped, was seldom presented in a Minnesota criminal case. The presiding district judge should probably have appointed new or additional counsel when he saw the very unsatisfactory case for Bobolink, and could have adjourned the trial until counsel could produce more evidence. A vigorous defense or an intelligent appeal might have set Bobolink free, however politically undesirable that might have seemed.

The Cook family tragedy passed into history and is now almost forgotten. In July, 1872, citizens of Oak Lake filled in the cellar of the former Cook home and interred the family remains on the site.[23] It is marked by a small bronze plaque set there in 1923 by the Grand Army of the Republic and reading: "This plot marks the site of the home of John Cook, pioneer settler who, with his wife Diantha [*sic*] J. and children Freddie W., Mary E. and John W. were murdered by Indians on April 26, 1872." It will be noted that the marker says Indians and not an Indian. In this it is probably correct.

7 The Lady Vanishes

HARDLY A MAN IS NOW ALIVE who has heard of Minnesota's Blueberry War. It lies unsung among history's pages, awaiting the Homer who will immortalize this hayseed *Iliad*. Farcical though it was, it had its beginnings in mystery, tragedy, and death; and, like the Trojan War, it began with the abduction of a Helen.

On April 28, 1872, two days after the John Cook family was killed at Oak Lake, twenty-two-year-old Helen McArthur set out from her home to walk two and a half miles through the woods to the village of Crow Wing, a bustling pioneer settlement that no longer exists. Her sister accompanied her part of the way, but then turned back. On her way home the sister met two Indians of unsavory reputation and noticed that they were walking a short distance behind Helen. These men were Gegoonce, also known as Albert Smith, and his brother, Tebekokechickwabe, whose name provokes curiosity because an Indian refused to translate it, saying its meaning was "unmentionable to ears polite."[1]

Helen McArthur was not seen again. Her family, thinking that she was visiting in the village, did not at once take alarm. Later, search parties combed the area, but Helen was not found. One party claimed to have tracked the girl to the river. Its members maintained that they recognized Helen's tracks because "she was considerably lame, one limb being shorter than the other." From this, her parents reluctantly concluded that Helen had drowned. There the matter rested for nearly three months.[2]

In mid-July Tebekokechickwabe and his squaw had a falling out.

Reacting as women will, the squaw decided that she would have her revenge by disclosing certain extraordinary matters hitherto confined to her domestic circle. Her husband and his brother, she said, had followed Helen McArthur into the woods, seized her, ravished her, killed her, cut her body into small pieces, and trampled the pieces into the mud. The squaw claimed to have heard Tebekokechickwabe tell the story to someone else. Acting on the squaw's information, John Gurrell, Crow Wing County sheriff, early in July arrested the two men on the White Earth Reservation, charged them with murder, and took them to Brainerd for trial.[3]

Gegoonce had earlier been mixed up with the law in two nasty cases. One involved the attempted rape of a white woman over sixty years old; the other, the murder of a soldier at Fort Ripley for which the Indian was arrested only to be released for lack of evidence. In addition to these peccadilloes, he had spent the entire summer of 1871 in jail following conviction of theft. Tebekokechickwabe had no criminal record but seems not to have been liked, perhaps because of his brother's lurid career.

Once in jail the Indians were separated. Each was told that the other had been hanged by the citizens. Gegoonce gave way without additional pressure. He admitted that he knew about the crime, but insisted that he had not taken part in it, and accused his brother's squaw of having stabbed Miss McArthur and burned her body. His brother and sister-in-law, Gegoonce said, were persons of bad character.[4]

The other defendant, Tebekokechickwabe, would at first admit nothing and made no effort to blame anyone else. His captors felt that his memory needed jogging, so they put a rope around his neck and strung him up for a short period. When lowered, he recalled that he and his squaw had met Helen in the woods. For some reason Miss McArthur and his squaw got into an argument, during which Miss McArthur struck the squaw across the face with a shawl. Angered, Tebekokechickwabe had then smashed the white girl's head with the butt of his rifle, breaking its stock; his squaw finished the work by stabbing the girl. Both of them then cut up Helen's body, burned it, and buried the bones.

After hearing these stories, the authorities dragged the Indians from jail and ordered them to point out the place where they had buried the bones. In a short time the two Chippewa led them to what appeared to be a cooking area. Upon digging, the investigators found a number of charred bones, which they accepted as corroboration of the confessions. They then took the Indians back to jail and turned the bones over to Dr. Samuel W. Thayer, a Brainerd medical man. The squaw had also been arrested and both men's stories implicated her as a principal. But when a physical examination revealed that she was pregnant, she was released, and no charges were ever filed against her.

The preliminary examination of the two Indians was held at Brainerd on July 16 in a packed courtroom. Both prisoners pleaded not guilty. When Tebekokechickwabe's attorney asked for more time to procure witnesses who would, he said, establish the Indians' innocence, the hearing was adjourned until July 25. "There was very evident disappointment on the part of the crowd of spectators at the adjournment," reported the *Brainerd Tribune* of July 20, 1872, "as the case is one fraught with horrible details, without a doubt, and one in which the deepest and finest feelings of sympathy . . . are enlisted in the fate of this estimable young lady." The same issue of the paper noted that the citizens of Brainerd had raised the sum of two hundred dollars as a reward for finding and producing Helen's body. "This is right, liberal, and just as it should be," the editor added.

It is doubtful that the Chippewa braves were seriously meant to have a trial, even though they had been furnished counsel from the beginning. As early as July 13, 1872, the *Brainerd Tribune* commented that the McArthur disappearance "coming upon the heels of the Cook family tragedy, is calculated to excite the most orderly and law abiding community to take the law of self preservation into their own hands." On July 22 a good many Brainerd citizens stayed up all night "to see the hanging" and were disappointed when nothing happened.[5]

A good deal of piquancy left the situation when a rumor spread that someone had seen Helen McArthur alive. It proved false, and on July 23, 1872, an obviously prepared plan went into effect. At 9:30 P.M. a mob of some three or four hundred men, women, and children swarmed around the jail. They quickly broke down the door, overwhelmed the sheriff, seized the prisoners, and dragged them to the foot of a tall pine tree, which stood near a saloon at the corner of Front and Fourth streets grimly but appropriately named

"The Last Turn." At the foot of the gallows tree Gegoonce still insisted that he was innocent. He had admitted nothing, and his brother had not accused him of having taken part in the crime. While he was still protesting, someone shouted, "Haul him up," and the unfortunate Indian was hanged at once.[6]

As Gegoonce struggled and kicked in his death agony, Tebekokechickwabe pleaded for his own life. Pointing to the writhing man, he shouted, "That's the man that killed the girl. Let me go and I will show you where her head is hid away!" But the crowd had come for a spectacle of death and was not to be put off. In a moment Tebekokechickwabe was also dancing on air. His arms were not tied tightly, however, and he was soon able to get them free. As he was climbing the rope to the limb from which it was suspended, someone suddenly shouted, "Indians!" About twenty shots rang out and Tebekokechickwabe, whose body was later found to have eight bullets in it, fell dead, his corpse jerking to a halt at the rope's end. The mob dispersed, leaving the two bodies hanging, twisting slowly in the evening breeze.[7]

The next day the bodies were cut down and buried in an undisclosed place. A coroner's jury found that the two men had met their deaths at the hands of persons unknown. Here the dreadful affair might have ended had not the Comic Muse accompanied her sister Tragedy. The unfortunate Helen McArthur was now to become a nineteenth-century Helen of Troy, firing a Minnesota Agammemnon to make a thousand slips and rouse the endless guffaws of newspaperdom.

The Chippewa living nearby were naturally curious about the uproar which involved two of their men, and some went into Brainerd to inquire about it. The sheriff became nervous and ordered them to return to their reservations. He also apparently told tall tales to certain reporters, who sent inflammatory dispatches to their newspapers. The *St. Paul Daily Pioneer* of July 25, for example, said that "news of the summary vengeance meted out to the red fiends who participated in the outrage upon Miss McArthur . . . spread like wild fire among the Indians . . . and it was not long before signs of threatened trouble began to manifest themselves, finally culminating in a most warlike demonstration on the part of the Indians, a body of whom, between 100 and 200 strong have appeared in front of town, bedaubed with paint and bedecked with feathers, and swearing vengeance upon those who participated in the hanging."

Convinced by his own rhetoric, the sheriff on July 24, 1872, sent a telegram to Governor Austin which read: "Please send troops *immediately*; town full of Indians and have been ordered to leave . . . but do not. Three white families left to day. The Indians hung last night by a mob, by breaking jail and taking them out." [8]

Austin, fearing that the lynching might inflame the uncertain situation created by the Cook murders, accepted Sheriff Gurrell's telegram at its face value. On July 25 the governor authorized Mark D. Flower, the state's adjutant general, to call out whatever troops might be needed to keep order. He also wrote to Sheriff Gurrell and the Crow Wing County attorney reminding them of their duties. "I have heard with much regret," he said, "of the lynching of two Indians at Brainerd. Such acts of lawlessness are always to be regretted, and their occurrence now is especially unfortunate. . . . Indeed our criminal code thus administered is no better than that of the savages, and whenever hereafter they suspect any of our people of infringing upon their rights they might as well demand that the white offenders be delivered up to be dealt with according to their barbarous fashion.

"I here pass no judgment on the guilt or innocence of the executed Indians," Austin continued. "If guilty of all they were charged with, they deserve a thousand deaths, but *that very question* they had a right to have determined in the legally authorized manner, and I neither admit nor receive any excuse for a violation of this right in a State, where the Courts and other legal authorities stand ready to do their full duty.

"I desire that you as the law-officers of the county, whose duty it is to make arrests for violations of the law, and initiate the proper proceedings for the trial and conviction of offenders, should make complaint or cause the same to be made, against the active participants in the mob, and have them arrested and examined for the offense before a civil magistrate." Austin then informed the county officials that he was sending state troops, which would be "at your service to aid you in the execution of this order." [9]

While the adjutant general was getting his troops in motion, Governor Austin asked General Winfield S. Hancock, Civil War hero and commander of the army's Department of Dakota, to send a detachment of federal troops from Fort Ripley to points along the Northern Pacific Railroad line. "Not that there is really any probability that there will be any fighting," Austin said, "but to reassure the people of their safety and prevent an undue excitement and a stampede, which would prove almost as disastrous as actual hostilities."[10] Hancock complied promptly.

About midnight on July 25 Companies A, B, and D of the First Regiment National Guard were quickly wrenched from their sleep and ordered to meet at the St. Paul Opera House to entrain for Brainerd. By the time the train left, it was crowded with reporters anxious to qualify as war correspondents.[11] As the state's Brainerd expeditionary forces pursued their slow way northward drawn by wood-burning locomotives, Governor Austin had time to cross-check his information and to learn that he might have been blessed with a more reliable informant than Sheriff Gurrell. Other sources reported Brainerd quiet, even torpid.

At a point forty miles southeast of Brainerd, just after the troops had been issued twenty-five rounds of live ammunition per man, the governor telegraphed recalling all but twenty-five of the soldiers. Inasmuch as the message did not reach the little army in time for it to catch the afternoon train back to St. Paul, the troops surged forward to Brainerd, which was indeed full of Indians — selling blueberries.

After getting off the train, the stout-hearted soldiers broke ranks and settled down to the serious business of eating fresh blueberries and buying additional supplies to take home. Heading his story "The Army of Occupation," a *Daily Pioneer* reporter wrote on July 26, "The military expedition arrived here at 7:30 P.M., and found upon their arrival that His Excellency had been most ingloriously sold." The correspondent disclosed that Brainerd was absolutely quiet, even the Indians seemed to approve of the lynchings, and that the sheriff had excitedly called for troops without consulting or telling anyone. The capital city newspaper spoofed the whole escapade in a headline which gave to the war its name:

THE BLUEBERRY WAR
Strange Dispatches from Brainerd.
The Bushes full of Indians
And no Indians There.

THE PEOPLE LEAVING AND
The People are not Leaving
OUR BOYS AT BRAINERD.
THEY FIND ALL THINGS QUIET.
The Dreadful War all Over

The next day, in an article entitled "Horrors of the Situation," the reporter told how the aroused savages had blocked all retreat with their baskets of blueberries for sale, while the troops' avid purchases had sent prices up a penny a basket.

The militiamen also received cheerful salutes from the local press. "On Saturday evening last," said the *Detroit* (Lakes) *Weekly Record* of August 3, "The State Militia, having eaten and purchased all the blueberries in the Brainerd market, returned to St. Paul. Indeed, it is said that the Indians suspended the berry business during the stay of the soldiers at Brainerd, as they were so charmed with the new uniforms and bright buttons of the militiamen, as to do nothing but gaze at them. And these curious tinsel-gazers were the 'fiercely painted Gull Lakers' which our State troops had come up to 'clean out.' Our landlords here at Detroit have been unable to get any berries since, and as in the days of the rebellion, we attribute the scarcity to 'the war, you know.'"

And so, having feasted on blueberries and strutted in their new uniforms, Companies A, B, and D, First Regiment, marched home on July 29, much as the heroes of the Wright County War had in 1859.

During the hilarity over the Blueberry War a reputable Brainerd physician's statement went almost unnoticed. The charred bones found at the place to which the two Indians had led their captors, said Dr. Thayer, were those of deer and not human beings. When the laughter over the Brainerd expeditionary force had gradually died away, and the governor who had sent it into the field had recovered from the volleys of homespun wit aimed at him, some people recalled the doctor's words and realized that the comic interlude had not displaced the real tragedy. The two Indians were dead, and Helen McArthur's disappearance was still unexplained. For a time it stayed unexplained.

Five years later a party of prairie-chicken hunters stumbled across a human skeleton at a point two miles north and one mile west of the McArthur home. With the bones were remnants of a shawl and a hair ribbon. Friends, relatives, and the family physician identified the remains as those of the missing Helen, one of whose legs had been shorter than the other. Her grief-stricken mother stored the bones and pitiful shreds of clothing in a cedar chest for a long while before consenting to their burial in the McArthur farmyard.[12]

Were the Indians guilty of Helen McArthur's death? The only evidence lies in the respective stories of Gegoonce, Tebekokechickwabe, and the squaw. The girl's head was found with her bones. If Tebekokechickwabe's death cry about leading the white men to the girl's head meant that it was in some separate place, later events showed this to be false. The Indian was probably doing anything and saying anything which would extend his life. The squaw whose revelations set everything in motion was irritated with her husband. He and his brother, both of whom found themselves in jail accused of a crime carrying the death sentence, could not in turn have been very pleased with her, and this must be taken into account in their stories implicating her. Helen McArthur's sister did not mention seeing the squaw with the two men. Where every witness was biased, and the stakes were life and death, the truth could hardly be expected to come to light. All three persons undoubtedly knew that Miss McArthur had suffered violence and was dead. No one else could be certain that she was dead until her remains were found in 1877. Guilty knowledge, however, is far from complicity in murder.

The most likely criminals are Tebekokechickwabe and his squaw. Both Gegoonce and his brother accused the squaw of stabbing the girl. Tebekokechickwabe's story, specifically mentioning Helen's shawl — which she was known to be wearing and which was found with her bones — suggests an eyewitness. While Gegoonce accused his brother from the first, it is curious that Tebekokechickwabe did not accuse Gegoonce until after he was dead. In spite of the evidence seeming to exonerate Gegoonce, however, it is indisputable that he was seen walking after Helen McArthur in the company of his brother.

Does an examination of motives help in assessing guilt? There is nothing to show that the two men and the squaw were even acquainted with Helen McArthur. Sexual violence is the only motive suggested in the Indians' stories, but the squaw's unsupported accusation, made in a fit of pique, is the only basis for the charge. Neither brother accused the other of it.

The balance of probabilities is slightly in favor of believing that the squaw took part in the crime and slightly in favor of accepting Tebekokechickwabe's extorted confession that for some reason the squaw and Helen got into an argument which led to Helen's death. There the matter must end. Whatever their degree of guilt, the Indians deserved better treatment than they got, and their lynchings add another chapter to the inglorious record of early Minnesota's brutalities.

Long after the Blueberry War had become only a bookworm's joke, Crow Wing County planned a new road across what had once been the McArthur farm. In 1959 grading threatened to disturb Helen's grave, and her bones, which had already been buried twice, were exhumed and reburied at old Crow Wing, where this victim of a forgotten tragedy now sleeps her last, undisturbed sleep.[13]

ALFRED B. BRACKETT, St. Paul detective, figured in many early Minnesota murder cases.

ST. PAUL, Minnesota's capital, looked like this from a window of the county jail about 1859, when Ann Bilansky awaited the gallows.

HENRY H. SIBLEY, the state's first governor, called out the militia to re-establish law and order during the Wright County War that occurred in 1859.

CHARLES H. BERRY, Minnesota attorney general, tried to prosecute the lynchers of Oscar Jackson in Wright County.

ALEXANDER RAMSEY, who succeeded Sibley as governor in 1859, had to set the date of Ann Bilansky's hanging. Despite pressures, he refused to commute her death sentence and vetoed an act of the legislature which would have changed her punishment to life imprisonment.

HORACE AUSTIN (left) was judge of the sixth district when he ordered John Gut hanged in 1868. Two years later, having been elected governor of Minnesota, he commuted Gut's sentence to life imprisonment.

CHARLES E. FLANDRAU, former justice of the state's first supreme court, acted as counsel for John Gut. Flandrau had been Judge Austin's military commander during the Sioux Uprising of 1862.

THE RAMSEY COUNTY COURTHOUSE in St. Paul was erected in 1850 from a design by Dr. David Day, who acted as the governor's emissary in investigating the Cook murders. The county jail, at the rear, was built in 1857 and housed Ann Bilansky, Thomas H. Stokley, and Bobolink, among other prisoners.

THE MINNESOTA STATE PRISON at Stillwater, where Thomas H. Stokley and the Younger brothers were confined, had opened in 1853. (A. T. Andreas, *Illustrated Historical Atlas*, 1874.)

DULUTH, as it looked in 1870, when Thomas H. Stokley came to trial for the murder of George Northup. The settlement, with its wooden buildings clinging to the rocky shore of Lake Superior, had just obtained a city charter and entered a new period of prosperity. Work to improve its important harbor was beginning in earnest.

DR. PHILO S. CALKINS, of Minneapolis, in 1872 identified John Cook's false teeth. He may have been the first dentist to make a critical identification in a Minnesota murder case.

MR. AND MRS. JOHN COOK and their three children were murdered, then burned, inside the home on their Becker County claim in 1872. (A. H. Wilcox, *Pioneer History of Becker County*, 1907.)

BRAINERD'S FRONT STREET about 1873 when Bobolink gave his last war whoop and the Blueberry War was fought. (Crow Wing County Historical Society.)

JOSEPH L. HEYWOOD, the courageous Northfield bank cashier, died at the hands of the James-Younger gang in 1876. Ira E. Sumner took this photograph of Heywood as well as that of the dead bandit opposite.

COLE, JAMES, AND BOB YOUNGER, the captured and convicted outlaws, were photographed in 1889 two weeks before Bob died in the Minnesota State Prison. Jim and Cole were later paroled from that institution. (*The Story of Cole Younger*, 1903.)

THE FIRST NATIONAL BANK and the Scriver Building on Northfield's Bridge Square looked like this in 1876. (Joseph H. Hanson, *The Northfield Tragedy*, 1876.)

GEORGE WELLS, alias Charley Pitts, was photographed after his death in the Northfield bank raid.

WILLIAM MITCHELL, one of the state's most distinguished jurists, presided at the trial of Charles Richman at Winona in 1879, after the defendant had spent a lively night with French Lou.

THE OZARK FLATS in Minneapolis were the residence of all the principals in the murder of Kitty Ging on December 3, 1894. (*The Ging Murder*, 1894.)

KATHERINE GING, a Minneapolis dressmaker, was shot near Lake Calhoun while on a mysterious buggy ride in 1894. (All illustrations on this page are from *The Ging Murder*.)

CLAUS A. BLIXT was the janitor at the Ozark Flats. It was he who pulled the trigger of the gun that shot Kitty Ging on a cold winter's night.

HARRY HAYWARD, a dandy and a gambler, engineered Kitty Ging's murder. He was hanged for it in 1895 on a gallows painted red at his request. Always well-dressed, he wore impeccable evening attire for the occasion.

"SPRING Fashions for Minnesota" (left) is the title of the cartoon printed by the *Minneapolis Journal* on April 20, 1911, the day the Minnesota legislature abolished capital punishment in the state. "It seems no longer to be an effective weapon against the fiend," commented the cartoon at right from the *St. Paul Daily Pioneer Press*, April 29, 1905, referring to the Keller murders.

A DOUBLE GALLOWS was prepared for the hanging of Timothy and Peter Barrett. It was sketched with the traps open for the *Minneapolis Journal*, March 22, 1889.

LOUISE ARBOGAST (left) and her mother, Mina, the daughter and wife respectively of St. Paul butcher Louis Arbogast, were both indicted for his murder in 1909. (*St. Paul Daily News*, May 18, October 25, 1909.)

IDA ARBOGAST took the witness stand in her mother's trial but often had difficulty in remembering the circumstances of her father's death. (*Daily News*, October 21, 1909.)

THIS COURTROOM SCENE during the Arbogast trial was sketched for the *Daily News* of October 26, 1909. Then as now photographers were prohibited.

8
Highwaymen Came Riding

"The man who chooses the career of outlawry is either a natural fool or an innocent madman." COLE YOUNGER

BY 1876 PIONEER MINNESOTA was becoming agricultural Minnesota. Where once the air had resounded with Indian war whoops, the grasshopper now swarmed and constituted the state's chief problem. Respectability was catching up with the settlers and life seemed a little tame. This was the prevailing national mood. To feed America's underlying appetite for excitement, newspapers, dime novels, and cheap nonfiction of the day dramatized scandal and violence. Tales of bank robberies and stagecoach hold ups in Iowa, Texas, and Missouri, often carried out by the James boys or the Younger brothers, found a wide reading public. Complete with biographies, lurid woodcuts, and statistics on the cash and bullion taken, these volumes momentarily projected into a crudely romantic world readers who found themselves bound more and more to routine ways from which war and excitement had passed.[1]

The city of Northfield on the banks of the Cannon River was in 1876 a representative, respectable, small, southern Minnesota community, although it proved to contain a surprising number of ordinarily quiet citizens who could instantly whip out firearms. The little Rice County town had two colleges and a First National Bank, which boasted an up-to-the-minute new vault complete with a Yale chronometer lock.

The bank's teller, Joseph Lee Heywood, was thirty-nine, married, and the father of one daughter. He had been born in New Hampshire, had served in the 127th Illinois Regiment during the Civil War, and had become a Northfield resident in 1867. He was city treasurer as well as the treasurer of Carleton College. In the summer of 1876 he was serving as acting cashier of the First National Bank and was planning to take his family to the Centennial Exposition in Philadelphia later in the year.

At that time, far to the south, a nimble group of young Missourians had just completed ten years of exciting and highly profitable travel through the states of Arkansas, Iowa, Kansas, Missouri, and Texas. The band was composed of two sets of brothers who had united to form a single striking force: the James boys — Jesse Woodson James, twenty-nine, and Alexander Franklin James, thirty-three — and the Youngers — Thomas Coleman, thirty-two, James, twenty-eight, and Robert, about twenty-two.[2]

All but Robert had learned their trade with the guerrilla William C. Quantrill, Confederate butcher of women and children. When the Civil War ended, Kansas and Missouri citizens, who understandably disliked seeing their families tortured and their property destroyed, began systematically to wipe out the veterans of Quantrill's unit. At this, the James brothers about 1866 organized their own band — in self-defense they claimed — and proceeded to carry out a series of unlawful paramilitary maneuvers worthy of a general. In ten years of this kind of self-defense the James and Younger boys were said to have robbed ten banks, held up four trains, pillaged two stagecoaches, snatched the Kansas City Fair gate receipts, and, more or less incidentally, committed fifteen murders.

In the summer of 1876 they were peering northward. Before making any move, however, they brought their little detachment to its full strength of eight by adding William Stiles, who went under the name Bill Chadwell; George Wells, who used the monicker Charley Pitts; and Clelland Miller, who liked his own name well enough to continue using it. Although all eight men had taken to the road early in life and had spent most of their adult years there, apparently none had ever passed a day in jail or been arrested.

While the James and Younger boys organized, life in Northfield followed its peaceful way. On September 4, President James W. Strong of Carleton College dropped in at the First National Bank for a chat with Acting Cashier Heywood. Their conversation turned to the famous Confederate bank raid of October 19, 1864, in which armed Southerners entered Vermont from Canada and forced the cashiers of three banks at St. Albans to surrender a total of $208,000. "Do you think under like circumstances you would open the safe?" Strong asked. "I do not think I should!" replied Heywood.[3]

Even as the men carried on their desultory conversation, southern Minnesota was entertaining unusual tourists, who had arrived at the end of August and who, moving in groups of two, four, five, and even six, restlessly roamed the towns and showed a decided curiosity about banks. Minneapolis played host to these men from August 23 to 26. Upon their arrival the manager of the Nicollet House was so alarmed by their appearance that he had the house detective guard their room. After a second weary night, the watchman could only report that the six iron men had played cards from dusk to dawn without showing any fatigue.

While in Minneapolis three of the tall strangers paid a visit to one of the city's better-known houses of joy operated by Mollie Ellsworth. Mollie immediately recognized one of them as Jesse James and asked in surprise what he was doing in Minneapolis. "Oh, nothing," he drawled. "I am going out into the country for a few days and will be back soon, then you and I will go to the centennial."[4]

On the day the men left Minneapolis, Red Wing had four affluent visitors and St. Peter had two. In each town, the strangers told vague stories about their business and bought new horses and saddles. On August 29 two of the men arrived in St. Paul and spent the evening in a gambling hall. When they removed their coats to make themselves comfortable, they also took off such other impedimenta as knives, revolvers, and cartridge belts. During the evening they lost two hundred dollars.

Next day the two unsuccessful gamblers bought a black horse and a bay. St. Paul stablemen described the strangers as looking like brothers with "keen eyes, quick movements, good talkers, smart in dealing; liberal with their money, and paying prices asked without question; well dressed with linen dusters, and altogether making an appearance that was so remarkable and unusual that they at once attracted attention."[5]

Five strangers were observed in Mankato on September 2. They made purchases at some stores and obtained change for a large bill at the First National Bank. A Mankato resident hastened to tell the sheriff that one of them was Jesse James, but most of his fellow townsmen laughed at him. Next day St. Peter had two visitors who spent the night and departed. Three days later the villagers of Cleveland, a few miles east of St. Peter, noticed four tall men, two of whom had been there ten days before, about the time Madelia had hosted two visitors.

The strangers, who appeared at such widely separated places as Madelia and Minneapolis, then seemed to hover in a small area looking for a concentrating point. On September 7, 1876, five of them conversed briefly with a resident of Dundas, a few miles south of Northfield. About 11:00 A.M. five men, of whom a witness said "nobler looking fellows he never saw," rode into Northfield on fine horses equipped with new saddles and bridles.[6]

After tying their horses at the rear of the depot, they idled away an hour in town before entering J. G. Jeft's restaurant for lunch. In a way their meal was as memorable as Lizzie Borden's famous breakfast of cold mutton soup. Each man ordered ham and eggs, with four eggs per man. While eating they discussed politics in loud voices, several of them offering to bet any taker a thousand dollars that Minnesota would go Democratic in the November election. After finishing lunch, they left, walking with bold, reckless swaggers and looking as if they could be hard to handle.

At about two o'clock in the afternoon the five men rode up Northfield's main street, heading for the First National Bank. As they reached it, all dismounted. Three of them tied their horses to hitching posts and entered the bank. The other two held their horses' reins and stood talking quietly. Bystanders later remembered their handsome physical appearances and their excellent horses. From the opposite direction two other horsemen, previously unnoticed, also approached the bank.

Suddenly the air crackled with gunfire.

An onlooker, realizing what was going on, shouted, "Them men are going for the town, they mean to rob the bank!" At this the mounted men began to ride up and down the street, shooting pistols into the air and through store windows, and shouting to those on the street, "Get out you sons of bitches!" and to anyone trying to come out a door, "Get in there you son of a bitch!" [7]

Inside the First National Bank were Heywood, Alonzo E. Bunker, the assistant cashier, and Frank J. Wilcox, a clerk. They had been sitting at their desks when the three men burst in and jumped on or over the counter. One of the strangers roared, "Throw up your hands . . . and if you halloo we will blow your god damned brains out." The bank employees held up their hands. The men then asked who was the cashier. Heywood said, "He is not in." Bunker and Wilcox agreed. The leader of the bandits wrathfully turned to Heywood and snarled, "You are the cashier; now open the safe." Heywood replied firmly, "It is a time lock and cannot be opened now." [8]

Impatiently, one robber tried to enter the vault. Heywood attempted to push the man inside and close the door on him, but was dragged away and hit on the head with a revolver. Another raider scooped up some twelve dollars in loose scrip, stuffing it into a two-bushel flour sack. A moment later the men again ordered Heywood to open the safe. Once more he refused even though a knife was drawn across his neck, scratching his skin as the knife-wielder threatened to "cut his damned throat from ear to ear." To this Heywood replied that the man must cut it then, for at that time the safe could not be opened. Struggling toward the door, the stubborn acting cashier cried out "Murder!" One of the bandits fired at him but missed.[9]

At this moment Bunker drew the raiders' attention by running toward the back door. In an instant he was badly wounded by a bullet in his shoulder, but he managed to escape and spread the alarm.[10] When heavy gunfire was heard outside, the raiders hurriedly prepared to leave. Just before running out of the building, one turned and, holding the muzzle of his revolver about a foot away, shot Heywood in the right temple.

Outside the robbers soon learned that Northfield's citizens did not behave like sheep, as had been contemptuously expected, but like outraged lions. The escaping bandits ran into a Northfield man whom they grabbed and threatened to "blow his head off if he squealed," but twisting from their grasp, the citizen raced up the street shouting, "Murder, robbers!" [11] When the mounted gang members tried to control the street by shooting into the air, Northfield men quickly found guns and fired back. Every man seemed to have a weapon handy, and in after years it was said that even a clergyman had whipped out side arms and used them to advantage. The focal point of the fight was the Scriver Block, where a good many windows were shot out.

Although many residents showed unusual spirit, two especially stand out. They were Henry M. Wheeler, a medical student, and Anselm R. Manning, the owner of a hardware store. Using an old carbine, and firing from the second story of the Dampier House across from the bank, Wheeler shot one highwayman through the heart and saw him pitch over his horse's head to lie sprawled in the street. Manning, obeying the infantry field service regulations which enjoin closing with the enemy and destroying him, singled out another bandit and brought him down with one shot. A member of the gang quickly went up to the fallen man, spoke to him, took his pistols and ammunition, and rode off, while another chose to fight it out with Manning. Dismounting, the attacker used his horse as a shield, but fled in haste when Manning brought down the animal. Manning pursued the fleeing outlaw but was able only to wound him in the leg.

In the midst of the affray one of the raiders told Nicholas Gustavson, a Swedish immigrant who lived near Northfield, to get off the street. He did not obey and was shot in the head. The man could speak little or no English and did not understand the order.

The robbers quickly realized that only a speedy retreat would save them from annihilation at the hands of citizens who, instead of running for cover, acted like a growing swarm of angry hornets. Picking up their wounded comrade, the surviving highwaymen dashed out of town, through Dundas towards Millersburg and the area then called the Big Woods. The attack and retreat had taken about five minutes.

With the invaders thoroughly repulsed, the Northfield men surveyed the damage. Two bandits lay dead in the streets; a horse lay near them. Nicholas Gustavson was gravely wounded. Assistant Cashier Bunker had a bullet in his shoulder. The bank was safe, but not its brave acting cashier. As the robbers withdrew, people crowded into the bank, aghast to see Heywood "lying prone upon his face, with his brain and blood oozing slowly from a hole in his right temple." He lived for twenty minutes but died without regaining consciousness. Spectators reported that "A huge spot of deep red clotted blood and blood stain upon the matting behind the counter told where the murdered bank official had fallen. Upon his desk there lay a blotter besmeared with blood and small particles of brains. His desk was also similarly smeared with the brave man's brains."[12]

Thanks to Heywood's extraordinary courage the raid had been anything but a financial success. Fifteen dollars in silver lay in open view on the counter. In an unlocked drawer below the silver tray reposed two thousand dollars in currency. The safe, which had been unlocked the whole time, held fifteen thousand dollars. Heywood had closed the doors but had not locked them. Without his courageous dilatory tactics, the holdup men could have seized everything merely by opening the safe doors.

No one could identify the fallen bandits. One was six feet three inches tall. His pockets contained only ten cents and a Waltham watch, and, oddly, he wore mismated boots. The other was about five feet six inches in height. His pockets yielded a newspaper clipping about the new time lock on the Northfield bank vault, a pocket map of Minnesota, $5.75 in currency, a compass, a valuable gold watch, and some jewelry.

Witnesses recalled the gang's leader as a slim, muscular, smooth-shaven man about five feet six inches tall, with clean-cut features and a fair complexion. He wore a short linen duster, a cape, and white cotton gloves. Three of the men were described as having a "sharp, shrewd aspect, and would be taken rather as gamblers of the flashy sort than desperate highwaymen." All were roughly handsome and good horsemen. They were still unidentified, however, when the coroner's jury assembled to find that Heywood met his death "by the shots of a revolver in the hands of a person whose name is not known."[13]

Naturally there was tremendous speculation about the robbers' identities. It was generally believed that the men must have been a gang active in Missouri and Kansas. Two months earlier to the day, on July 7, 1876, the James band had relieved the Missouri Pacific Railroad of from fourteen to eighteen thousand dollars at Otterville, Missouri.[14] No one thought that Jesse James had come to Northfield, but it was agreed that in their audacious midday attack the Northfield raiders had been inspired by the James gang's bold methods.

A great chase began at once as police forces and throngs of "the best woodsmen" converged upon south central Minnesota in hot pursuit of the outlaws. Mayor John T. Ames of Northfield had wired the St. Paul and Minneapolis police forces for help, and twenty minutes after his telegram arrived detectives were on their way to Northfield by train. On September 8 the pursuers set up headquarters at Faribault. The robbers were seen in Rice County at Millersburg and Shieldsville, where they exchanged shots with their hunters. They were reported in Le Sueur County where they seemingly found a farmer to take them along the road to Cordova. Then they suddenly vanished into the woods at Waterville, thirty-three miles southwest of Northfield. There after a gun fight the leader had cried, "Too hot for us! Must make for the woods!"[15]

While the chase continued, attempts were made to identify the dead bandits. In the process, Mayor James T. Maxfield of St. Paul made one of the most peculiar suggestions since the invention of photography. He wrote to Mayor Ames "suggesting the propriety of severing the heads of those two robbers . . . from their bodies, and either embalming them or putting them in spirits so as to preserve the features of their countenance as perfectly as possible, so that, in case the authorities of Missouri and Iowa desire to examine them they can do so and be enabled to determine whether or not they belong to the famous Younger Brothers as some think." Ira E. Sumner, a Northfield photographer, acted more to the point by propping the bodies up and snapping their pictures. Within a month he had sold over fifty thousand of these photos at two dollars a dozen.[16]

On September 11, four days after the raid, the investigation had progressed far enough to identify the raiders tentatively as the James-Younger gang. The dead men were believed to be Bill Chadwell and Charley Pitts. It was thought that both Frank and Jesse James had been in the bank and that Frank had shot Heywood. (This may be correct; there has never been satisfactory evidence either to confirm or deny it.) And four days after the raid, Nicholas Gustavson, the second victim, died of his head wound.

Although a huge cordon, estimated at more than a thousand

men, surrounded the counties where the raiders were believed to be hiding, the outlaws continued to elude the search parties. Hundreds of amateur manhunters joined in the pursuit when the state of Minnesota offered a thousand-dollar reward for each man captured, and the First National Bank of Northfield offered five hundred dollars for each robber, dead or alive.[17]

On September 14, one week after the raid, to the astonishment and disgust of Minnesotans, the gang divided into two parties of two men and four men, burst through the cordon, outran all posses, and again vanished. A leading newspaper commented the following day: "The robbers and their pursuers appear to be continually finding and losing each other. We trust they will come together after a while to stick." [18]

While the hunt went on, St. Paul bankers were the first to think of the raid's principal victim. On September 19 eight banks of the capital city began to make up a purse for Heywood's widow and child. Within a month it totaled $12,602, a substantial sum for 1876. Of this, five thousand dollars came from the grateful management of the First National Bank of Northfield. Contributions also poured in from banks and individuals all over the United States; William W. Astor, New York millionaire, for example, gave five hundred dollars.[19]

Heywood attained that summit of contemporary cultural achievement, a bleak accolade from New England's frail and ladylike talent which was even then dying of exhaustion from rattling on didactic themes. To the expectant readers of the nation George Parsons Lathrop, of Cambridge, Massachusetts, friend and associate of poets, contributed to the *New York Tribune* his "On A Faithful Bank Cashier." Two stanzas will show the aging New England muse in harness:

Unto how few the fadeless bays
  Belong! How few the iron crown
Of virtue wear! And few the lays
  That beat a hero's honor down
Untarnished to the latest days!

. . .

If he betrayed not, death was sure;
  Before him stood the murderous thief:
He did not flinch . . . Of one life fewer

The angels turned the blood-sealed leaf
That night, and said: "The page is pure." [20]

On September 21, 1876, two weeks after the raid and a day after Lathrop's threnody appeared, the citizens of Minnesota were overjoyed to hear that a posse operating near Madelia — some eighty miles southwest of Northfield — had captured three of the outlaws and killed a fourth. It appeared that two men escaped. A farm boy, later identified as A. O. Sorlen, recognized one of the gang and led a group of manhunters to the hide-out. A lively gun fight resulted and the robbers, outfought and outnumbered, saw the wisdom of surrender.[21]

Two of the three survivors admitted to being Cole and Bob Younger. The third was thought to be either James Younger or Calvin (Cal) Carter, a famous Texas desperado whose ranch was believed to serve as the Younger gang's winter quarters. They were pretty thoroughly battered. Cole had seven wounds including a serious one near his right eye; James's lower jaw was so badly shattered that he was not expected to live; and Bob had a bullet in his lung and a smashed elbow. They had very little on their persons. James could produce a hundred and fifty dollars in cash; Cole had five dollars and a compass; Bob had five dollars; and the dead man — whom the survivors refused to identify — had five dollars, a pocketknife, a compass, and a map of Minnesota.

Although his comrades would not identify him, the dead bandit was soon declared by the St. Louis chief of police to be Charley Pitts, who had supposedly been killed at Northfield. It turned out that Clell Miller was the gang member actually killed there. The Younger boys also refused to comment on the two men who escaped, merely saying that their companions Woods and Howard had separated from them and gone elsewhere. Jesse James's middle name was Woodson, and his alias, Howard, has passed into folklore in the ballad which immortalizes him:

And the dirty little coward
Who shot Mister Howard
Has laid Jesse James
In his grave.

When they were brought into Madelia, the Younger brothers were in great fear that they might be lynched — a fate which had overtaken some of their comrades in earlier raids. It soon became obvious, however, that their only danger lay in being smothered by idolatry. Crowds came to visit them, seeing them as fearless characters in a grand drama, bestriding this narrow world like colossi. Their room was kept filled with flowers, food, and cigars. Undoubtedly great natural actors, Cole and Bob quickly took up the roles which their hayseed audiences expected them to play.

Bob, six feet tall and irresistible to the ladies, delivered the first set speech, using a low voice and carefully chosen words without slang or profanity. He "deeply regretted" Heywood's death, he said, which resulted from passion and not planning, although in assessing Heywood's acts he was "inclined to think Heywood was more frightened than brave." When asked why the outlaws had chosen the Northfield bank, Bob replied candidly that they thought it would have more money than the others. The St. Peter bank was not worth robbing, and in Mankato the money would be divided among three banks. Speaking of his own part in the raid, he muttered with lowered head that "he had tried a desperate game and lost." Countless rehearsals could not have improved it.[22]

If Bob had polish, Cole had imagination and a more varied delivery. Little brother Bob, Cole said, had not quite explained the reason for the raid. The Younger brothers would never have molested the peaceful citizens of Minnesota "if they had not encountered gamblers at St. Paul, who won their money, and they made the raid to get even with the state." They did not intend to kill anyone "as that was not their policy."[23]

When a little girl brought him a bouquet, Cole at once became the kindly, tender friend, taking the bouquet and sighing, "I love flowers, because those I love loves flowers." This wistfulness infected his other utterances. "Circumstances," he expounded in his comfortable Madelia room, "sometimes make men what they are. If it had not been for the war, I might have been something, but as it is, I am what I am." On another occasion he was overheard — as he had planned — discoursing with himself, saying: "I don't believe it — I don't believe it. . . . Byron says 'Death is the end of all suffering — the beginning of the great day of nothingness,' but I don't believe it."[24]

Realizing what great souls they had in their midst, the ladies of

Madelia called in large numbers to exhort these gentle boys to remember their Christian upbringing and have faith in prayer. To these pious females Cole admitted that he "had been brought up under Christian influences, his parents being Christians, but he had never professed religious belief," while Bob said that he had "once been a believer and member of the church, but had fallen." When someone spoke of their mother and sisters, the men "responded in the most affected manner, tears streaming down their cheeks." In a later conversation, perhaps ambiguous, "Both said they had braved every danger, but that such scenes as this was too much for them." [25]

After two days of this idolizing, the Younger brothers were forced to leave the attractions of Madelia and proceed to Faribault. There the outlaws found no need to change their roles; the women of Faribault tripped over each other trying to outdo the gentle ladies of Madelia. The three highwaymen proved such a curiosity to both sexes that within three days of their arrival at Faribault between four and five thousand people visited the jail to get a look at them.

Cole delighted his visitors by continuing the eloquence and posturing he had begun at Madelia. He refused to speak a second time to a group — which he rightly suspected was drawing him on — saying, "No, don't call them back. They are so illiterate that they cannot appreciate the sublime life I have led." As before, he accused a malign fate of having driven him to the highways. "He dates his commencement of his remarkable career of crime to the war," an interviewer reported, "which saw his father, a district judge in Missouri, shot down in cold blood for his money by [George A.] Hoyt's militia. He pleads that it was vengeance he vowed then, and after a career with Quantrill's guerrillas he found himself so hunted and charged with hundreds of crimes as to drive him into outlawry." The parade of visitors to see the prisoners caused a good deal of criticism, and the practice was stopped.[26]

At the preliminary hearing, conducted in the Faribault jail on September 26, the sheriff thought it wise to put the Youngers in irons. When questioned about the Northfield raid, Cole claimed that the gang meant to carry all by audacity, not by killing and wounding. To this someone remarked that the robbers had certainly tried hard to kill Manning. Cole insisted that the boys had only tried to frighten the man because "they were all dead shots and could have picked him off at any time if they had desired to do so." Unfortunately for the accuracy of his story, Cole forgot to tell Bob. When Manning himself came to the Faribault jail, a reporter noted, "Bob recognized Manning, and made the remark that he was rather surprised that he did not drop him, as he is positive he took deadly aim upon him. But Manning did some effective dodging which saved his life." Bob was reputedly the best shot in his gang.[27]

With three of the raiders in jail and available for questioning, the police were able to establish to their satisfaction that Wheeler had shot Bill Chadwell and that Manning had accounted for Clell Miller as well as wounding Bob Younger. Charley Pitts had indeed fallen during the last gunplay at Madelia. It was never clear who had been in the bank, but the tentative solution — uncorroborated to this day — was that Charley Pitts shot Bunker and Frank James murdered Heywood. No one seemed to know for certain who had given Nicholas Gustavson his fatal wound, but the Swede's death was generally laid at Cole Younger's door.

Oddities, crackpots, and jokers always seem to follow a sensational crime, and the Northfield raid produced its share. The first to take advantage of the case was the Northfield photographer who found such a ready market for his gruesome pictures. Not far behind for macabreness was the action of the authorities who shipped Charley Pitts's body to St. Paul packed in ice. For two days this "unpleasant and disgusting spectacle," as a newspaper called it, occupied a table in the rear wing of the state Capitol, where a crowd of more than two thousand people jostled each other to get a view. Tradition has it that a St. Paul doctor then took possession of the corpse, ultimately dissected it, and that Charley Pitts's articulated skeleton now dances in a St. Paul physician's cabinet.[28]

The newspapers of the state, too, had a field day. One sample of the humor they produced will suffice. On September 29, 1876, the *Pioneer Press* quipped, "Those captive robbers will never die Younger." Another newspaper-inspired feature of the affair developed on September 25 when Wheeler and Manning, each of whom had killed one of the desperadoes, received threatening letters. They sounded like schoolboy productions, but the *Pioneer*

Press of September 26 solemnly reproduced them as news. "I see by THE PIONEER PRESS," the letters read, "that you are the man who killed our comrade. YOU ARE A DOOMED MAN FROM THIS HOUR. A dagger or bullet will find your heart. We do not care a damn for detectives. It is not convenient now, but you cannot escape. They are hunting us in the bushes now, but we are taking our meals in Minneapolis." The letters were signed "Cole Younger & Co."

Two days later the editor of the same paper received a letter threatening his life. It was written from La Crosse, Wisconsin, by a purported sympathizer of the gang. Since the robbers had managed to escape capture for two weeks when more than a thousand men were looking for them, there was abundant speculation—prodded by manufactured rumors—that local confederates had hidden them or co-operated with them. It was also hinted that these well-wishers might try to avenge or free the bandits. These letters, however, were unquestionably promotional stunts to increase circulation. It is more than coincidence that the missives threatening Wheeler and Manning specifically mentioned the *Pioneer Press* and that the editor of that journal was the only newspaperman in the United States to receive such a threat.

Trying to keep the case alive during the somewhat tiresome period between capture and legal proceedings, the newspapers also devoted much space to the soft treatment given the raiders at Faribault, the identity of the third Younger brother, and to acrimonious debates on whether the raiders would hang. Bob Younger, beloved of the ladies, was particularly provoking to masculine editors, and the following irritable comment is representative: "Bob Younger had his bouquets in Madelia, and he has his cigars, oranges, and nuts in Faribault. We haven't a doubt that Bob could marry the handsomest woman who confers these palatable luxuries upon him, if he did not himself despise the whole simple and gushing set. Bob's sentiment, it should be remembered, doesn't get above a bawdy house."[29]

While his brothers entertained the yokelry, Jim Younger, whose serious jaw wound kept him quiet, played another kind of game, teasing his captors about his identity. Even before the Northfield raid Cole and Bob had received substantial publicity, and there was no question that the Faribault jail held these two men. But the other members of the family—there were fourteen brothers and sisters in all — were for the most part only shadowy figures in the public mind. Jim was relatively unknown. When the three men surrendered at Madelia, Jim was identified as Cal Carter. Jim did not deny it, and the police — while reasonably certain that he was one of the Younger brothers — nevertheless had nagging doubts, which Jim kept alive as long as he could. On October 3, nearly two weeks after his capture, he admitted confidentially to a reporter that he was really Cal Carter.

This fictitious revelation would have taken first place in the day's news had it not been for an event which electrified Faribault and commanded the attention of the rest of the state. On that day arrived a veritable princess of romance, nineteen-year-old Henrietta (Retta) Younger, sister of the outlaws. A schoolgirl from St. Joseph, Missouri, "tall and graceful in appearance, with features indicative of intelligence and cultivation," she had the city at her feet. Henrietta was a lady. When the Northfield photographer who had capitalized on the likenesses of the dead raiders approached her, offering five hundred dollars if she would allow him to add her features to his collection, she indignantly refused.[30]

On the day after her arrival, Henrietta — accompanied by her brother-in-law, R. S. Hall—received permission to see her brothers. They did not expect her. The sheriff arranged the visit so that she would first come upon Jim. She entered the jail, saw him, ran up to him immediately, and threw her arms around him. There was no further question of his identity.

The family reunion was affecting, and observers saw with satisfaction that all the Youngers broke down in tears. Cole, never one to waste a spotlighted moment, tenderly gave his little sister a religious work, which someone had given him. On the flyleaves he had written meditations for the benefit of himself and his sisters. Henrietta soon returned to Missouri, planning to revisit Minnesota.

It was not until November that the grand jury of Rice County brought in its formal indictment of the prisoners. It charged Cole, Jim, and Bob Younger with the murders of Heywood and Gustavson, stealing property from the bank, and assaulting Bunker with intent to kill. Woods and Howard, the Youngers' companions — that is, Frank and Jesse James — had managed to evade all patrols and presumably made their escape via South Dakota. The indictment did not name them and, in fact, Minnesota never caught up with either of them.[31]

The outlaws' trial opened on November 14, 1876, before Judge Samuel Lord. As was customary in important cases, Attorney General George T. Wilson appeared in person for the state. Three lawyers — Thomas Rutledge, Thomas S. Buckham, and George W. Batchelder — represented the Younger brothers. Interest centered on how they would plead to the charges in the indictment, for under the law passed in 1868 a guilty party could be hanged only if the jury so recommended; otherwise, the maximum penalty would be life imprisonment. Although no court had as yet interpreted the statute, lawyers and the public generally felt that a plea of guilty — which did not require calling a jury but was made to the court — meant that the court could then impose only a sentence of life imprisonment.

The newspapers repeatedly commented on this conception of the statute and attacked it in intemperate editorials and headlines, such as "Death to the Banditti" and "The Cutthroats to Escape Through the Inadequacy of Minnesota Law."[32] There was no question that journalistic Minnesota wanted hemp and blood. In this atmosphere the defendants and their counsel had to decide whether to plead not guilty — and take a chance with the jury — or to plead guilty — and take a chance that the judge would interpret the statute as it was generally understood.

Amid these deliberations, to the delight of everyone, Henrietta Younger returned to Minnesota and took her place in the courtroom. Discussion of the law was forgotten. "She is tall and graceful, and dresses very plainly in black," a reporter gushed, "and wears a cloak trimmed with fur. Her face is quite pale. . . . Her manners are very attractive." The girl again found herself the center of attention to the point of annoyance and interference with her privacy.[33]

The Younger boys managed to play a delaying game for six days without making formal pleas. Several family councils were held in which Henrietta took part. Cole read his Bible. Everyone else talked until at last a decision was reached. On November 20, 1876, Cole, James, and Bob Younger entered pleas of guilty to the indictment charging them with Heywood's murder. They had chosen to take a chance with the judge.

Their choice was sound. Judge Lord promptly ruled that he had no need to call a jury and that accordingly there was no occasion for a jury to fix the sentence. It would be life imprisonment. He passed sentence at once, saying, "I have no words of comfort for you or desire to reproach or deride you. While the law leaves you life, all its pleasures, all its hopes, all its joys are gone out from you, and all that is left is the empty shell." The brothers heard their sentences without changing expression. On November 22, 1876, they were taken to the state prison at Stillwater to begin serving their sentences.[34]

Newspaper comment on the sentence was acrid, and a bill proposing, as the paper put it, "an amendment to our Penal Statutes, in reference to the punishment for murder committed in this state, which shall not leave it optional with the criminal to escape merited punishment by simply pleading guilty" passed the Minnesota House of Representatives in its 1877 session only to die in the Senate. The 1877 legislature also appropriated three thousand dollars to pay the expenses incurred by those who took part in the great manhunt, and four thousand dollars for rewards. In addition, it tendered formal thanks to those who "resisted the attempt of the gang of brigands, commanded by Cole Younger, to rob the Northfield bank."[35]

Oratorical memorials to Heywood could not exceed that of Governor John S. Pillsbury, who declaimed in his 1877 message to the legislature: "No tale of Greece or Rome, nor the annals of heroism in any age, recount a deed of nobler personal sacrifice. Without the pomp and emblazonment which so much impel to deeds of daring, Mr. Heywood opposed gentle firmness to brutal diabolism and calmly made choice of death in preference to life purchased at the cost of its severest fidelity. In that sacrificial act he exhibited not alone exalted courage, but such attributes as attest all the nobler possibilities of human nature."[36]

Time passed. In 1881 Littleton T. Younger, an uncle of the brothers, journeyed from Missouri to Minnesota to work for a pardon for his nephews. Various Missouri citizens wrote letters detailing the Younger family's background and blaming their fate on the Civil War. On July 27, 1881, however, Governor Pillsbury declined to even consider the case. The governor remarked that "on no account, would he, for one moment, consider the propriety of pardoning any one of the prisoners or of remitting any of the sentence imposed upon them." He told Littleton Younger: "When I think of poor Heywood, the cashier, refusing with a heroism that has no parallel to forsake his trust, and when I remember how your nephews murdered him in the coldest of blood, intense indignation fills my breast, and instead of feeling that they have been punished sufficiently, I am more and more convinced that death would have been a juster and more righteous penalty." [37]

In 1884 there appeared at the Stillwater prison gates one Warren C. Bronaugh, a resident of Missouri and a former Confederate officer whom Cole Younger had aided during the Civil War. The young man, who was on his honeymoon, had a long memory, and he visited the Youngers in their cells and pledged himself to assist in obtaining their release. His visit was the first of many he was to make to Minnesota over the years in a determined effort to spring the famous outlaws. Bronaugh drew to his cause a brilliant array of notables — leading citizens of Missouri and Minnesota — among them ex-Governors Sibley and Marshall, Ignatius Donnelly, Senator Cushman K. Davis, and William W. Murphy, who had led the posse which captured the Youngers. These men insisted to successive Minnesota chief executives that the Civil War was responsible for the Youngers' criminal careers; circumstances, they said, had made the outlaws what they were.[38]

Before Bronaugh's efforts could bear fruit, however, Bob Younger died in prison of tuberculosis on September 16, 1889, thirteen years after his capture. At this time, Minnesotans once again saw Henrietta Younger, who was with her brother when he died.

No Minnesota governor wished to take the political responsibility for releasing the two remaining Younger brothers from prison, and in 1896 an amendment to the state Constitution was approved, creating a board of pardons to be composed of the governor, the attorney general, and the chief justice of the state supreme court. In July, 1897, after the legislature had prescribed the new board's powers and duties, Bronaugh returned to Minnesota with "a large leather valise, packed full" of documents, including a petition from the Missouri general assembly, and letters from many prominent citizens supporting the Youngers' pardon application. The new board, however, denied the appeal, commenting that the "character of this crime renders it one absolutely without extenuating circumstances. . . . No one claimed that there was any injustice done here, and the only reason urged for a pardon meriting serious consideration was the fact of the early environment of the petitioners and that they are now reformed." The *Northfield News* of July 17, 1897, approved the board's action, saying it "receives our warmest commendation. We would almost say that we congratulate the members of the board."[39]

Bronaugh returned to Missouri, discouraged but not defeated. Four years later he and other Younger supporters tried a new tack. In 1901 Portius C. Deming, of Minneapolis, introduced into the Minnesota legislature a bill empowering the board of managers of the state prison to parole "any prisoner . . . whether committed on a time sentence or on the reformatory plan, or for life." The terms of the carefully drawn bill made the Youngers eligible for parole. With the brothers in mind, the House amended the bill to prohibit a paroled prisoner from exhibiting himself "in any dime museum, circus, theater, opera house, or any other place of public amusement or assembly, where a charge is made for admission." The bill passed both chambers by resounding majorities — 80 to 37 in the House, 40 to 17 in the Senate.[40]

The board of prison managers then recommended that the Youngers be paroled, and their cases again came before the pardon board in July, 1001. Unable to ignore the clear directive of the legislature, the board on July 10 granted the two men conditional pardons which prevented them from leaving the state. The board explained that it had not considered "the question of the Youngers' guilt, nor whether they had been sufficiently punished. The board carried out the wishes of the legislature that passed the parole bill."[41]

Next day Bronaugh again presented himself at Stillwater prison, where he had the satisfaction of walking down the steps to freedom with the two brothers. Jim and Cole went to work in jobs approved by the pardon board, selling tombstones for a St. Paul granite company. Jim, whose speech was impaired by the wound he had received, soon suffered an accident and was forced to find other employment.

Shortly after his release from prison Jim apparently met the niece of Edward J. and J. H. Schurmeier, St. Paul businessmen, who had worked actively to obtain his freedom. The young lady, Alix J. Muller, was twenty-seven; Jim was fifty-four. She was a talented and successful author and newspaperwoman who had worked for a time on the *Pioneer Press*. They wished to marry, but the attorney general refused their request while Younger was on parole.[42]

In desperation, Miss Muller in January, 1902, wrote the following moving letter to Governor Samuel R. Van Sant in the hope that he would grant Jim a full pardon. "I know it is within your power to make Jim and myself happy," she told the governor, "and feeling that, kind as you have been, your sympathy must go out to us in our great desire to have a home and to live for one another, I cannot resist writing this.

"Of course I can hardly expect all others to know James Younger as I do, but to me — and I have lived a longer, fuller life than most women of my age — he stands as the noblest man I have ever met. To be so strong to endure, for the sake of others whom he must protect, a life of ignominy and shame, requires a character of almost superhuman strength and power, and I long for the time when the world will appreciate, and honor, this man as I do.

"Gov. Van Sant, please be merciful. You have to deal with another 'man of suffering' and in doing for him you may yet find that you have 'entertained angels unaware.' The truth cannot always remain hidden.

"As for myself, I long for health, yes — and life, so that I may brighten what few years he has yet to live. For he is sorely stricken, and I am an invalid, so that we can at best only enjoy a little peace and comfort."[43]

The governor did not respond, and Alix left Minnesota. The Younger brothers again applied for a full pardon, but the board, which met on October 13, 1902, failed to act on their application. Six days later, Jim Younger, moody, despondent, and ill, shot himself in his St. Paul hotel room. Miss Muller died of tuberculosis two years later.[44]

In February, 1903, Cole Younger was pardoned and permitted to return to Missouri. In fact, Minnesota now made it a condition of his pardon that he never return to the state which had formerly confined him within its boundaries. Once back in Missouri Cole wrote his autobiography and with Frank James joined a traveling show in which his repressed histrionic abilities could find an outlet. Later he took to the lecture platform, where he made enough money to purchase a house in Lee's Summit, Missouri, and comfortably live out the rest of his days. The last of the famous James-Younger outlaws, Cole died on March 21, 1916, of heart disease at the ripe age of seventy-two with fourteen bullets still embedded in his body.[45]

Both Frank and Jesse James had preceded him to the grave. Jesse was shot by one of his own men on April 3, 1882. Five months later Frank voluntarily surrendered to Governor Thomas T. Crittenden of Missouri. He was brought to trial in his home state and acquitted. For some years he traveled with Cole in the Cole Younger–Frank James Wild West Show, worked as a shoe clerk, and later as a theater doorman. He died on February 18, 1915.

The drubbing given a famous outlaw band by Minnesota farmers and townsmen in 1876 has appropriately been called the Waterloo of the notorious James-Younger band. It marks the end of an era of outlawry that may be without parallel in American history. It is also one of the spectacular episodes in the history of Minnesota. More printer's ink has been spilled on those five minutes in Northfield on September 7, 1876, than on any similar episode in the state's record.

The Younger boys were undoubtedly murderers, cutthroats, and brigands, but it is impossible for even the most strait-laced moralist not to admire their courage — even if grudgingly — and not to envy the free life of the highwayman — even if sneakingly. It is easy to understand how the Youngers passed into legend. Even today in the Southwest or in army camps one will sometimes hear the sad chromatics of "The Ballad of Cole Younger," as the chorus repeats:

Cole Younger, Cole Younger,
Cole Younger is my name,
And this is the song of the Younger boys,
And Frank and Jesse James.

9

A Night with French Lou

WINONA IN 1879 was a thriving upper Mississippi River town of about ten thousand inhabitants. It was a leading lumber- and flour-milling center, a busy river port, and the home of United States Senator William Windom. It also had fifty-two saloons. To step into the Winona that Edward W. Lawlor and Charles Richman knew in 1879 is to enter a society of trulls, drabs, and doxies resembling that of *The Beggar's Opera.* In the events involving these two young men, Winona's once lively demimonde roars to life in a pattern astonishingly like that of eighteenth-century London. Official histories have passed over it discreetly, but it had a robust heyday.[1]

Among Winona's recreation spots in 1879 was a bordello owned and operated by Mrs. James Reynolds, better known as French Lou. Its well-trained staff—composed of Lou's adopted sister Ella Graves, Alice Richards, and Rhoda Sanford—furnished many a tired businessman with a simple, elemental form of relaxation. The house had its comforts—a parlor where callers could await their turn, greeting acquaintances with a comradely grin. It also offered special privileges to the inner circle—meals, drinks, picnics, and the right to spend the night. Regular customers treated it as a club and were remarkably faithful patrons year after year.

In Winona at that time lived two close friends, Edward Lawlor, twenty-eight, and Charles Richman, twenty-four. Both were employed as mill hands by Laird, Norton and Company. They were unmarried. Early in their lives they had drifted to French Lou's, and by 1879 both were members of the privileged inner circle. Lawlor was, in fact, known as French Lou's lover and was recognized as such by both the staff and patrons of the house. Richman, who had been a regular caller for four years, had recently taken up with Alice Richards and was known and recognized as her lover. Their parents understandably deplored their sons' associations. Lawlor, in deference to his family's feelings but unable to quench his passion for French Lou, kept a disguise at Lou's which he wore when out riding with his light o' love. Since the disguise consisted only of a linen duster and a skull cap, he must have thought his parents extraordinarily obtuse.

Another young man about town was James Malone. He was not a patron of French Lou's, although he had heard about her. He knew Lawlor but was not acquainted with Richman. Twenty-eight and unmarried, he lived with his parents in Gilmore Valley, a short way out of town to the southwest. From his later conduct, Malone seems to have been an unpolished pearl who might have prolonged his life if he could have learned the virtue of silence.

On Saturday night, July 26, 1879, Lawlor and Richman went on one of their weekend frolics. Richman left French Lou's between seven and eight o'clock on Sunday morning, while Lawlor stayed even longer. That afternoon Lawlor still had enough energy to continue the weekend whoop-up. He found Richman and asked him to return to French Lou's for another party. Although Richman felt rather the worse for wear, he kept the rendezvous dressed in a dark suit and white straw hat. Lawlor appeared wearing a gray suit and his duster-and-cap disguise. The two friends greeted each other blearily, climbed into a rented buggy, and took the highroad to the bagnio.

There they found Lou, Alice, and Ella Graves, but Rhoda Sanford had gone out. Late in the afternoon the five sat down to a meal, probably accompanied by a potation or two, inasmuch as Richman was in a state where only the hair of the dog that bit him would help. During supper, Lou and Ella said later, the two men amused themselves by looking at firearms. An admirer of Ella's had given her a .32 caliber Smith and Wesson five-shooter, which she had lent to another friend who had just returned it. The borrower had fired three shots and returned the gun without removing the empty shell cases. For some reason Richman felt that he must carry a weapon that Sunday, and he borrowed Ella's with its three empty shell cases and two live rounds in the chambers. He put the gun in his pocket.

French Lou also had a revolver—a .32 caliber Hood. Lawlor insisted that Lou's revolver was far superior to the one Richman had borrowed, and striding into Lou's bedroom—to which he evidently needed no guide—he took the Hood revolver from under her pillow and brought it into the parlor to show it to Richman. At that time he loaded it with five cartridges. Richman took the weapon, looked it over, and handed it back to Lawlor. According to French Lou, Lawlor then gave the firearm to her and she tucked it into her capacious bosom. Richman later said that Lawlor put it in his hip pocket.

Armed and ready for a frolic, Lawlor, French Lou, Richman, and Alice Richards set out for a drive. Their course consisted of a series of beelines from saloon to saloon. By 9:30 P.M. they had managed to visit five such establishments before reaching the one operated by H. Parrhysius about a mile and a half north of Winona on the road to Minnesota City. They were all in high spirits, although Richman, saying that they had had no more than six or eight glasses of beer, later insisted, "Well we wasn't drunk."[2]

On reaching their destination, the four at once ordered beer and food, and French Lou, in the tradition of the Old West, set up drinks for the house. At about the same time, she said later, the pistol lodged in her bosom began to hurt her, and she removed it, placing the Hood revolver in Richman's pocket alongside the Smith and Wesson.

Among the people then in the saloon was James Malone. He was curious about the party, asking "ain't one of them French Lou?" Although he accepted a drink, he had already reached a stage where he was determined to make trouble, and he began uttering insulting comments about the women, "talking pretty smutty." Lou, who was not altogether unversed in this kind of badinage, answered Malone in kind. His ungrateful response to the lady who had bought him a drink was to throw beer at her. Lou did not hesitate. "There was a chair," Richman remembered, "and she jumped up on it and took a glass of beer in her hand and she swooped it over on to Malone." Saying, "There, let that shut your lip," she stepped down from the chair. Malone, taken aback by Lou's spirited defense, was momentarily pacified with another glass of beer.[3]

French Lou then began a conversation with another man in the saloon, asking him about the kind of leather in his belt. The man, whose name was George Knopp, said it was snakeskin. Lou asked if it could be rattlesnake. Before the man could answer, Malone stated that the belt was not rattlesnake. Richman joined the dispute, insisting that it was indeed rattlesnake. The belt's owner said it was not, and both he and Malone called Richman a liar. Richman was ready for a fight then and there.

Why everything became a fighting matter so fast is a puzzle and makes one suspect some unknown grudge involving Lawlor, Richman, and Malone, although there is no proof of it. The evidence indicates that Malone did not know Richman's name. Knopp once stated without elaborating that Richman said "he had a grudge against Malone," and he was going "to give it to him." The truth or falsity of this remains a mystery.[4]

Just as Richman was preparing to fight, Knopp had an imperative call of nature which took him outside the saloon. Richman decided to accompany his intended adversary and take care of the same matter himself. The two accordingly stepped outside to "tap off some beer" and talk about their difference of opinion.[5]

While they were gone, Malone's irritable temper rose again, and he repeated his remarks about French Lou and her party, saying of Richman, "If that little son of a bitch comes in again I am going to give it to him." Richman heard this statement, stormed into the saloon, walked over to Malone, and demanded, "Did you call me a son of a bitch?" Malone answered, "Yes, and I meant it, too." Richman immediately struck Malone twice across the face. Rising from his chair, Malone threw his beer glass at Richman and began to run toward the outside door. The glass hit Richman full in the cheek, staggering him.[6]

As the saloonkeeper remembered what followed, Richman and Lawlor ran after Malone; Richman had something in his hand that looked like a revolver. To the best of French Lou's recollection, Malone ran out the door with Richman close behind him. When Richman came back into the saloon, he had a revolver in his hand. Lou could not say which revolver it was. Richman said Lawlor ran after Malone, and Lawlor's memory was: "Well, just as Malone was going through the back door I sees the flash of a pistol and the flash was on the inside of the door; I could just see it."

Q. Who had the pistol?
A. I could not swear to that; Richman was there four or five feet of him.
Q. Did anybody else have a pistol but Richman; Malone didn't have it?
A. No, the flash was between Richman and Malone. . . .
Q. What was the next thing?
A. Right in quick succession on the outside I heard another shot.[7]

Knopp was still standing outside. He was later asked:

Q. Before going in did you hear any pistol shots?
A. I did.
Q. How many?
A. Two.
Q. Do you know where they [were] fired?
A. I should judge they were fired back in the saloon.[8]

Everyone agreed that Richman had come in and then gone out a second time. Alice Richards and Lawlor finally went looking for him and found him wandering aimlessly outside. They brought him in. When asked "Did you see any pistol in his hand when he went out the second time?" Lawlor answered, "I didn't see it; I saw it after I went out in the yard."[9]

All this took place about 11:00 P.M. No one in the saloon paid much attention to the pistol shots, and French Lou invoked her usual peacemaking remedy by ordering another round of drinks. Richman reportedly muttered that "If he had known the God damned son of a bitch would have struck him with a beer glass he would not have left the room," and went on drinking.[10] A half hour later the quartet decided to leave. Finishing their drinks, they piled into the buggy but went only a short distance before they had the nineteenth-century equivalent of engine trouble — the harness broke. The two men got out and began to mend it.

About the same time Knopp, who had not left with French Lou's party, had to make another visit outside the saloon. On this trip he came across James Malone lying on the ground, evidently in great pain. Malone asked feebly for "some peppermint . . . and pain killer," and to be taken into town. He had a gaping hole behind his ear and complained of severe stomach cramps.[11]

Told about Malone while they were fixing the harness, Lawlor and Richman agreed to drive the injured man into the city, but first they insisted on taking the girls home. They drove straight to French Lou's where, in Lawlor's recollection, Richman waved a revolver in the air, crying, "Yes, I am going back. . . . I am going to shoot every son of a bitch I see, to[o]; it ain't no more to shoot ten men than it is one, they will make it as bad any how."[12] This agreed with what French Lou, Ella Graves, and Rhoda Sanford remembered, and all recalled that Alice Richards was so drunk when she arrived that she had to be put to bed at once.

Lawlor and Richman returned to the saloon. Somewhat soberer, they took Malone to a doctor, who found a bullet behind the young man's right ear and another, which had entered through the back, lodged near the liver. Either would have been fatal.

In what must have seemed a very short time Richman and Lawlor found themselves cellmates in the Winona jail, charged with assault with intent to kill. There they passed a long night. In the morning the saloonkeeper was brought to the jail and asked to point out the man who shot Malone. He pointed to Richman.

Malone was still living, but sinking rapidly. On Monday evening, the day after the shooting, Richman and Lawlor were brought to Malone's bedside while officials took the dying man's deposition. The two friends were very nervous while Malone was giving his statement, although Richman gave an impression of "sullen indifference" which did not help his cause. Malone identified Richman as the man who fired the shots, saying, "Ed. Lawlor did not shoot me; he was present when the shooting occurred." Malone recalled: "The man present walked past me and hit me as he passed. I had just drunk a glass of beer and threw the glass at him after he hit me. I saw a revolver in the man's hand and turned and ran. I heard a shot fired. It hit me. I then heard another and it struck me in the back of the head. When I heard the report of the revolver first I was just out of the door. When I was hit the second time I was about fifteen feet from the door. I think he had the revolver in his hand when he hit me; he struck me an awful blow. I am positive that this is the man . . . that had the revolver." The following night, July 29, 1879, Malone died.[13]

Richman now faced a possible first degree murder charge. Lawlor was released. Both men secured counsel. For better or worse, they retained the same lawyer, James W. Dyckson, who happened to be a good friend of the Winona County attorney, A. N. Bentley. Just before the inquest Richman, alone in jail while Lawlor walked free, told Bentley that Lawlor was really the man who shot Malone. The county attorney's first move was not to investigate this charge but to call Richman's attorney — who was also Lawlor's counsel — and say that Richman had "squealed." Later when he was asked if he had told Dyckson that Richman had "squealed," Bentley replied: "No, I told him that Richman told me that he would 'squeal,' if I would bring him down. I asked him to let him [Richman] go on the witness stand, and Dyckson replied to me by saying, 'do you think I am a damn fool?' "[14]

The attorney failed to explain why he did not want Richman to testify — whether because it would prejudice Richman or because it might prejudice his other client, Lawlor. At this point he would have done better to withdraw completely from the case. On his attorney's advice, Richman remained silent during the inquest. As a result, he was held without bail until the grand jury met and duly indicted him for first degree murder.

Lawlor had promised Richman that he would work hard to secure his release, but once free he did nothing, failing even to call on his friend in jail. Later when asked about this betrayal, Lawlor — apparently forgetting that the same lawyer had first represented them both — explained that he had "heard from a good source, right here in town, that him and his attorney was plotting to put this on to me, so I wouldn't have anything more to do with them." Lawlor was then asked how this was to be accomplished, and he answered: "Well, try and have him swear that I done it, and handle these prostitutes to their satisfaction."[15]

At that time Lawlor was not charged with any crime, so it is unlikely that he was told of such a plan by the county attorney, who might have deduced it from speculating on the case or who might have learned it from his good friend, Richman's lawyer. On the other hand, Lawlor might have heard of the scheme from

Richman's counsel, who was once his own. If the county attorney disclosed it, he was betraying his public trust by giving a suspected murderer a chance to run away; if Richman's counsel revealed it, he was betraying his trust to his client. The behavior of these two members of the bar throughout this case seems very questionable.

Richman came to trial on October 27, 1879, before the Honorable William Mitchell, one of the ablest jurists Minnesota has produced. During the three-day trial, the characters in the drama — French Lou, the saloonkeeper, Ella Graves, Rhoda Sanford, and Richman's untrue friend Lawlor — took the stand and testified against Richman, telling the story as it has been related. Richman also testified in his own defense, telling a story that differed from that of the others. There was no testimony on the colloquy between Richman's counsel and the county attorney. The jury found Richman guilty of manslaughter in the second degree and on November 5, 1879, he was sentenced to six years' imprisonment. He did not appeal.[16]

On the night of Richman's conviction a party of four was holding a little celebration at a neighborhood saloon. Those present were French Lou, Edward Lawlor, Alice Richards, and a man who had supplanted Richman in Alice's affections. By coincidence the county attorney happened to stop at the saloon while the party was in progress. He told the participants that it would look better if they deferred their celebration until some other night.

While Judge Mitchell had conducted Richman's trial with all the judicial skill of which he was capable — which was a great deal — he was dissatisfied with the result. The case nagged him for nearly a year. At last on August 27, 1880, he wrote Governor Pillsbury, asking him to pardon Richman. The judge explained: "The case is one that has perplexed me a great deal both during the trial and subsequently; I have been, however, compelled to the conclusion that the Defendant is not guilty of the offense charged and that his conviction was procured largely by perjury." Surprisingly, County Attorney Bentley had no objection to Richman's pardon, writing the governor on September 1, 1880: "From the beginning of the prosecution till recently I have never doubted the guilt of the Deft. I prosecuted with that belief — But recent developments in the case have caused me to doubt the guilt of the accused and while I do not fully concur in *all* the conclusions of

Judge Mitchell yet I think the deft. is entitled to the benefit of the doubt which I cheerfully give him." Thus on September 8, 1880, Richman received a full and free pardon and was released from the state prison.[17]

Someone, however, had killed Malone. If Richman had not, officials reasoned that Lawlor must have. Events now moved swiftly and, in an astonishing reversal which makes this case unique in Minnesota's murder annals, Lawlor on October 15, 1880, was indicted for Malone's murder. His trial opened on January 19, 1881, before Judge Thomas S. Buckham, Mitchell having been elevated to the Minnesota Supreme Court. A new legal battery also appeared. Bentley had been replaced as Winona County attorney by Marshall B. Webber. Lawlor did not again engage Dyckson, instead choosing William Gale of Winona and Christopher Dillon O'Brien of St. Paul to represent him.

By 1881 the saloonkeeper who identified Richman as the killer was dead and French Lou, who supported Lawlor in Richman's trial, was in Montana. Love had grown cold. When asked why he did not call Lou to testify in his defense, Lawlor replied, "We did not think it advisable to send $250 and trust to her honesty." Even without the saloonkeeper and French Lou, however, the second trial made everything appear as if on the other side of a looking glass.[18]

From the testimony it was clear that only Richman or Lawlor could have seen the revolver fired. The victim, Malone, was running away from his assailant and only heard shots. Knopp, standing outside, thought he heard firing from within the saloon. Lawlor, who testified that he saw a muzzle flash, was obviously bent on saving his own skin. At the first trial Parrhysius, the saloonkeeper, had only recalled seeing Richman chase Malone, holding what "looked like" a revolver.

When Ella Graves took the stand, she was asked, "Have you any business or employment?" She caused a titter in the courtroom when she replied simply, "Me." She went on to admit that her testimony at Richman's trial was false and now stated that Lawlor had kept Lou's revolver and had not handed it back to her as he claimed. If both men were carrying firearms, what had really happened in the saloon?[19]

Richman took the stand and testified that Lawlor carried French Lou's revolver on the buggy ride to the saloon; in fact, during the trip he took it out several times and waved it around his head as if playing bandit. According to Richman, when Malone threw the beer at Lou, Lawlor nudged him and said, "That Irish son of a bitch will get it yet." Malone continued to make insulting remarks to the women, and, Richman recalled, "Lawlor kept nudging me," saying that Malone "would get it before he got out of the place that night." [20]

Richman admitted that he himself got involved with Malone, who threw a beer glass at him. It struck Richman in the face and stunned him for a moment, so that he leaned against a table holding his hand to his face. When he recovered and looked up, he testified, he "saw Malone running out the back door and I saw Lawlor following him." Richman began to run after Lawlor. He heard a shot fired. As he reached the door he heard two more shots.[21]

Going outside, Richman continued, he found Lawlor holding a revolver.

> A. I spoke first, I says, where is he, Ed, and he says, I guess I gave the son of a bitch enough for this time.
>
> Q. What did you understand by that?
>
> A. Why that he shot him, I saw him fire the second shot.[22]

Richman's story of the critical moment was, of course, exactly the opposite of Lawlor's. Richman admitted that he could not see Malone when the shot was fired, but this detail was unimportant. He was positive that he saw Lawlor chase Malone, firing a revolver as he did so. After their colloquy outside both young men returned to the saloon and remained there calmly imbibing until they drove to French Lou's place.

At French Lou's, Richman said, Ella Graves had opened the door and let them in. Richman went into Alice's room for a moment. Lawlor then asked Richman to give up the revolver he was carrying because there might be trouble, and after some discussion Richman gave it to Alice.

Ella Graves continued the story by saying that French Lou—rather than Alice—had been so drunk on arriving that she had to be put to bed. Just after Lawlor and Richman left to get Malone, Alice came into the parlor holding a revolver. She then disappeared for a moment. Two shots were heard. Alice returned to the parlor, swinging the weapon over her head and saying, "I hurt my finger firing off that pop." [23] Rhoda Sanford confirmed this, as did a customer who had seen it while waiting in the parlor.

Soon, Richman went on, he and Lawlor were put in jail together. During the long, sleepless night, they had ample time to talk. Richman recalled that Lawlor began the conversation saying, "Charley, by God . . . don't go back on me; I says Ed. it will put me in a terrible position if I keep my mouth shut, and he says I may have the luck to get out, and . . . the minute I get out I will skip the country altogether and get both of us clear; I says Ed. if you will promise to do that I will do it under that condition." This, Richman explained, was why he had kept silent when Malone's statement was being taken.[24]

After the saloonkeeper visited the jail and identified Richman as the man who shot Malone, the two friends had another talk. Richman testified: "I says to Ed. you can see how it is now, a man came up here and thought I done the shooting, you see it is putting me in a nice fix; he says don't be alarmed, he says it will be all right if I get out; I says, all right Ed. you stick to your word and I will stick to what I said." [25]

Lawlor, released, did nothing, and Richman was shocked when his friend failed him.

> Q. You believed in Ed Lawlor?
>
> A. I believed he was true, yes.
>
> Q. And as long as you did you was perfectly willing to stand up to it?
>
> A. Yes.[26]

Richman, deceived, underwent his trial alone. His onetime friend, not content with escaping indictment himself, fortified the prosecution's case by coercing witnesses.

At the second trial Ella Graves revealed some of the pressures that had been imposed upon her. Lawlor and French Lou literally forced her, she said, to testify that when the party returned to Lou's "Alice was so drunk she didn't know anything at all. . . . and not to say anything about the two shots that was fired off that night." After Richman's conviction, Ella had told an acquaintance that she did not believe him guilty. In some way this got back to Lawlor. One night at French Lou's, Ella said, "he picked up the revolver off from the table and he says you will go out some night and Ella Graves will turn up missing; and he shook the revolver at me and he says it would not take me long to do it now." Ella testified that Lawlor continued to make her life miserable, so miserable that she actually attempted suicide in 1880. During the entire time between the two trials she had stood in fear of him:

> Q. Did he ever make threats at any time?
>
> A. Yes, sir; he said several times that shooting me with a revolver was too good for me and it was a good job for other parties around here.
>
> Q. What did he mean?
>
> A. That he would give them a good job to do, I suppose, and pay them well for it.
>
> Q. Any other threats that the defendant made that you have not testified to?
>
> A. He was sitting playing on the piano and Lou was on the sofa and he said I would like to see that carcass under the ground, referring to me by the way he nodded his head.[27]

Rhoda Sanford told the court that she, too, had been subjected to pressures and threats to make her testify "that Alice was so intoxicated she didn't know what she was about." [28] She had been warned, she said, not to say anything about Alice emptying Ella's revolver. Perjured testimony by these terrified prostitutes had helped convict Richman. The second trial not only amply brought out the fact of perjury but also revealed publicly for the first time those ethically questionable discussions which Richman's lawyer had with the county attorney.

The jury, having weighed all the contradictory testimony given by witnesses who admitted having perjured themselves earlier, this time decided to accept Richman's version of how the killing took place: that Lawlor carried French Lou's revolver to the saloon, chased Malone holding it in his hand, fired it at Malone three times, gave Malone two fatal wounds, and spent considerable time and effort manufacturing evidence to convict Richman. He did all this for love of French Lou and in anger at Malone's insulting her. On January 21, 1881, the jury found Lawlor guilty of manslaughter in the second degree — the same crime of which Richman had been convicted. This time, however, the jury recommended mercy. A month later on February 24 Lawlor was sentenced to five years in prison.

Within the next month he appealed to the Minnesota Supreme Court, which affirmed his conviction on August 1. The court said: "Lawlor testified that he took no pistol with him on the ride, and had none at the saloon where the homicide was committed. With the testimony thus conflicting, and much of it from such sources, and delivered under such circumstances as were not calculated to inspire confidence, it was plainly the province of the jury to sift and weigh it, and determine its effect; and we are of [the] opinion that there is no ground disclosed by the record for disturbing their verdict."[29]

For probably the first time in Minnesota history two men had been convicted of a crime which only one of them committed. This anomalous result suggests that Anglo-American methods of judicial inquiry could use more refined mechanisms for sifting conflicting evidence, and that juries snatch at inferences unsupported by clear facts.

What really happened? One fascination of this case is that the evidence bears several interpretations, none of which gives an exclusive answer. Consider the witnesses. At the first trial those who gave important testimony were French Lou, Ella Graves, Rhoda Sanford, Edward Lawlor, and the saloonkeeper. The first three were prostitutes, beyond the pale and under the necessity of lying every day. Lawlor, in dread of being accused of the crime himself, was guarding his own interests. Only the saloonkeeper seems to have been disinterested. Even the county attorney and Richman's lawyer appear to have been biased. At the second trial French Lou and the saloonkeeper were not available. Ella Graves and Rhoda Sanford had not changed their occupations and admitted having perjured themselves at the first trial. Richman, who was the chief prosecution witness, was immune from further charges by reason of his pardon and could not be expected to resolve any point in favor of the man whose testimony had sent him to prison for a year.

The vital questions were: (1) who had firearms, (2) what happened at the saloon, and (3) what happened afterward at French Lou's. There was no question that bullets from Lou's Hood revolver killed Malone. Considerable testimony on this point was introduced at the second trial, including that of a qualified gunsmith. In reviewing Lawlor's conviction the Minnesota Supreme Court noted: "The testimony for the state tended to show that Richman borrowed, at the house of Lou Reynolds, before the party started for the ride, a pistol of Smith & Wesson manufacture, having grooved or rifled barrels, only two of which, out of five, were loaded, and that upon the return of the party to the house the same evening, after the homicide, this pistol was restored by Richman with the two barrels still loaded, which were then discharged; that the defendant [Lawlor] obtained a pistol at the same house, before the ride, of a different manufacture, having its barrels grooved only at the muzzle; and generally there was testimony tending to show that the bullets taken from Malone's body could not, from their appearance, have been shot from the Smith & Wesson revolver, but might well have come from the other."[30]

Who fired Lou's revolver? Richman admitted having a weapon but denied firing it. At the first trial French Lou and her two associates confirmed Lawlor's statement that he did not take Lou's revolver, and Lou said that she placed it in Richman's pocket at the saloon. Ella and Rhoda, who confessed that they had been lying at the first trial but averred that they were telling the truth at the second, said Lawlor had Lou's revolver. Richman swore that Lawlor had taken Lou's gun and waved it in the air during the buggy ride to the saloon.

The dying Malone pointed to Richman and exonerated Lawlor. On the day following the shooting Parrhysius, the saloonkeeper, pointed unhesitatingly to Richman as the man who shot Malone, and he so testified at the first trial. He also said that both Lawlor and Richman ran after Malone. At each trial Lawlor said that Richman chased Malone immediately after Malone struck him. Richman testified that Malone's blow stunned him, and that only Lawlor chased Malone at first. Lawlor claimed to have seen the muzzle flash of a revolver in Richman's hand, while Richman asserted positively that he saw Lawlor fire his second shot.

Everyone except Richman testified to hearing two shots; Richman heard three. Knowing that the revolver which he carried had only two usable shells may have affected his hearing, but similar knowledge may have affected the hearing of others who swore they heard only two shots.

At the first trial the testimony showed that Lawlor and Richman simply took the girls to French Lou's and left. Alice Richards was said to be drunk and had to be put to bed. At the second trial, witnesses who had earlier perjured themselves confirmed Richman's statement that Alice Richards had fired two shots from the revolver which Richman carried all evening, and that it was French Lou who had to be put to bed. On this point, an independent witness confirmed Alice's story of firing the revolver. There was no question that the revolver carried by Richman had only two live rounds in it.

Where is the truth? The dying Malone and a disinterested witness implicated Richman, but another disinterested witness said that the revolver carried by Richman still contained two live rounds when Richman returned from the saloon. Lawlor said he saw Richman shoot. Richman said he saw Lawlor shoot.

It seems probable that both men carried weapons and that Richman did not fire his. Both men very likely chased Malone, but there seems slightly greater reason to believe that Lawlor did the shooting. Both were undoubtedly intoxicated and their memories of that catastrophic evening would be blurred. Lawlor did not deny having threatened and coerced Ella and Rhoda, and their stories at the second trial may have been true. On the whole the more satisfactory solution is that reached by the jury in the trial of Edward Lawlor. But enormous doubts surround every controversial item.

The quality of mercy was also extended to Edward Lawlor. On October 23, 1882, Governor Lucius F. Hubbard commuted his sentence to two years, and on April 21, 1883, he received a full pardon. It is unlikely that he picked up the threads of his old friendship with Richman. For these young men and their associates, it had been a very expensive night with French Lou.

10

Two Affronted Ladies

IN NINETEENTH-CENTURY AMERICA the feminist cause led many women across barriers into preserves once limited to males, but the jury box remained secure against female infiltration. Had lady agitators of a later day been wiser, they would never have dreamed of subverting this masculine citadel, for the all-male American jury furnished the true stronghold of women's liberties, making it possible for the fair sex to enjoy the freedom to remove some inconvenient mortal from this world without having to take the consequences. It helped if the feminine defendants were young and beautiful, but neither youth nor beauty was essential. The following random duet will show representative reactions of nineteenth-century Minnesota to feminine peccadilloes in the homicidal line.

BERTHA HEGENER

According to contemporary accounts, in 1887 Bertha Hegener was young and beautiful. Born Bertha Augusta Thom at Bernstein in the kingdom of Prussia in 1863, she came to the United States with her family in 1865. Charles Gotthelf Hegener was also born in Bernstein in 1861 and came with his parents to the United States four years later. The two families probably knew each other and very likely emigrated together, inasmuch as both finally settled in Watertown, Wisconsin, in 1873. Among their acquaintances was John Murphy, a young man about Bertha and Charles's age.

It does not appear that Hegener and Murphy were rivals for

Bertha's hand; if they were, Hegener prevailed, and Charles Gotthelf took Bertha Augusta as his lawful wedded wife at Milwaukee, Wisconsin, on August 18, 1882. The couple moved to Minneapolis, where Hegener opened a barbershop. In 1883 they had a daughter, Louisa, and in 1885 a son, Charles.

By 1887 Charles Hegener was the proprietor of an apparently flourishing shop in downtown Minneapolis. His brother, Richard, worked as one of the barbers, and was also Charles's confidant. Another barber in the shop was Charles's old friend from Watertown, John Murphy. Hegener was fond of Murphy and insisted on having him live in his home. The master barber appeared to know not of Lancelot and Guinevere, Tristan and Isolde, or even his contemporaries, Parnell and Kitty O'Shea; he had to learn in the school of experience.

Murphy was about twenty-five, handsome, and had a reputation of being, in the idiom of the day, a "masher." He promptly set out to make a conquest of Bertha. Living in the Hegener household gave him a rare combination of propinquity and opportunity, and he used his best efforts to push his advantages. It was shortly common gossip among the barbers in Charles's shop that Murphy was in ardent pursuit of Bertha Hegener.

It is not clear whether Bertha really spurned his advances or finally let her wrath fall upon him who kissed and told. She doubtless felt herself irresistible and pursued. Murphy doubtless felt himself irresistible while pursuing. At any rate, Murphy bragged that he had conquered the fair Bertha and, on April 4, 1887, went so far as to make this statement in the presence of her husband and one of the other barbers. Bertha did not suffer this astounding audacity quietly. She promptly drew a revolver and shouted, "If Jack don't take back the scandalous reports about me I will shoot him!" The other barber had to step in and disarm her.[1]

The scene upset Charles Hegener and later that day he convened a curious sort of private tribunal, consisting of his sister, some friends, and himself. This court was to hear accuser and accused and presumably — for it is hard to imagine why he wanted outsiders to hear all this — judge the truth or falsity of the accusations and advise him what to do. Murphy coolly repeated his story; Bertha swore it was false and became very angry, as well she might. It is impossible to see why Bertha, who later proved herself a cool customer indeed, submitted to such nonsense. The upshot of the hearing was that Charles dismissed Murphy, who immediately moved to St. Paul. Presumably Mr. and Mrs. Hegener then had a private talk.

That night John Murphy sat down and wrote Charles Hegener a long letter. In it Murphy took all the blame upon himself, insinuated that he was a bit of a Don Juan and that it would not be unusual for ladies to fall into his arms, but assured the irate husband that Bertha had, nevertheless, remained immune to his extraordinary appeal. "I've got the blackest heart of any man on earth," he wrote. "I had it in for your wife all winter. . . . But don't doubt Bertha. She may be a little wild, but she is true to you." With this faint praise he purported to vindicate the reputation that he alone had called into question.[2]

On the following day, however, Murphy wrote another long letter, this time to Richard Hegener. In the second epistle he recanted his generous admissions of the day before and outlined in detail a series of intimacies with the beautiful Bertha calculated to make all males envious and the abused husband bloodthirsty. He concluded with the amazing advice that Charles Hegener should not go on living with his wife because she was unfaithful to him! Richard Hegener gave the letter to Charles, as Murphy had surely intended he should; and Charles, whose urge to proclaim his family's transgressions to the world seems pathological, discussed both letters with his barbers.

The outcome was a deadly pact between husband and wife. Charles handed Bertha a .32 caliber revolver, and she, a veritable Brünnhilde in panoply and courage, set out to avenge the family honor while her spouse preferred to remain at a rear-guard post. With a lady friend, Bertha stepped aboard a train in Minneapolis and soon descended at the St. Paul depot. It was the afternoon of Wednesday, April 6, 1887.

Bertha and her friend made their way directly to the Winona House, where Murphy was staying. He had somehow heard of the visit and was ignobly hiding, having about the same love for combat as Hegener. When the women asked where Murphy was, the hotel clerk recognized impending trouble and lied to them. "I don't know," he said, "he went away from here." As Bertha turned to investigate for herself, Murphy, realizing the jig was up, came out from behind the stove. Muttering that he had only written the truth about her, he slithered rapidly through the front door. Bertha followed him.[3]

Many witnesses saw them walking along Sibley Street arguing their separate points of view. Bertha demanded that Murphy retract his slanderous words and restore her honor. Forgetting that she had shown herself handy with side arms only two days earlier, Murphy made the error of refusing. A reporter for the *Pioneer Press* of April 7, 1887, reconstructed the scene: "The two appeared to be very much excited and to be quarrelling. The woman was apparently urging the man to do something. . . . They had gone on this way some time when suddenly the man turned as if to dare his companion. At that instant she drew a revolver concealed in her dress, and raising it, fired directly at him. Without speaking the man fell on his face on the pavement, shot through the head."

Bertha's highly accurate shot entered Murphy's skull behind his left ear. As he lay bleeding on the sidewalk between Third and Fourth on Sibley Street, a police officer hurried to the scene and asked, "Who did this?" Bertha answered, "I did." She was still holding the revolver, which the officer took from her. After arranging to have Murphy sent to a hospital, the policeman took Bertha to the station.[4]

The wounded man lingered for several painful hours. The bullet had scarcely touched the base of his brain, but it had severed an artery, causing massive hemorrhage. Although conscious, he was unable to speak because blood poured from his mouth, and he answered questions only by shaking his head. In this way he denied having said that Bertha was unfaithful but asserted that she, in fact, was. He died about 11:30 P.M., six hours after being shot.

The St. Paul police now turned their attention to the woman who admitted shooting him. She had not yet retained counsel and withheld nothing. Her remarkable soliloquy, as reported by a newspaperman who must have been a melodrama devotee, told her side of the story. "Scarcely had he [Murphy] entered our home before he began to make violent love to me," she said. "He begged me to elope with him, but I refused. He loved me. Everything that he could do he did to win my affections. . . . Oh, the wretch! Heaven alone knows how I despise him! He swore that he had stayed with me. . . . Once he walked into my room when I was sleeping, and then walked out, so as to be seen by my husband. Sometimes he would ask my husband what he would do should he discover that I was faithless to him. Said my husband: 'I would at once drive her with her children from my door, and never allow her to return!' Oh, God, but I was persecuted! He followed me everywhere with his repugnant attentions. All of this time I did not dare to say a word to my husband, because I dreaded his jealous disposition."

The newspaper then quoted Bertha as saying that Murphy "boasted that it would only be a question of time when he would win me. Once he almost choked me to death in an attempt to kiss me. . . . Oh, but he was playing a deep, black, treacherous game. . . . It was yesterday that his foul, black, lying, slanderous letter from St. Paul, besmirching my character came to the hands of my husband. He read the letter, calmly for him, and then showed it to me. Said he 'Mary, you see this letter containing these charges against your character. There is but one way in which you can prove your innocence. Either you must kill that man or I will cut you in pieces.'" Bertha said she then took the train to see Murphy. When he refused to retract his statements about her, Bertha stated, "I then drew my revolver and shot him. I shot him! I am guilty of the shooting, and did it because the villain tried to blackmail me. But, as God and heaven are my witness, I am innocent of the charges which he made."[5]

This is obviously not the language of an unschooled woman who emigrated from Germany, but the conventions of the day accepted it as such, and one must overlook such a minor error as the narrator referring to herself as Mary when her name was Bertha! Perhaps her husband did say Mary. There is always the precedent of Mrs. Watson, wife of Dr. John H. Watson, Sherlock Holmes's immortal associate, who once mysteriously addressed her husband as James.[6]

Acting speedily on the information furnished by Bertha, the police arrested her husband as a principal in the murder. The coroner's jury found correctly that "the said John Murphy came to his death at about 11:30 P.M. April 6, 1887, caused by a pistol shot fired by Bertha Hegener at or about 5:30 P.M." On April 8 Bertha and her husband were both formally charged with manslaughter; James J. Egan, Ramsey County attorney, probably felt that enough provocation existed to reduce the charge from murder. At the preliminary hearing observers said that Bertha "was neatly dressed, wore a heavy veil and acted as if she were perfectly at her ease. Her self-possession was remarkable." Her aim had also been remarkable.[7]

Meanwhile, there was a body to dispose of. When Murphy's mother was notified of her son's death, she first telegraphed tersely, "Cant come. Sick myself. Bury him there." Later she had a change of heart and sent a brother-in-law to take the remains to Watertown for burial. On his arrival the relative pronounced owlishly, "There has been some crooked work in this matter."[8]

Both Charles and Bertha were released on bail and spent nearly a year in the comfort of their home awaiting trial. One cannot help wondering what Hegener's customers thought while being shaved by a man about to be tried for manslaughter. Almost anyone — particularly those melodrama enthusiasts who knew of Sweeney Todd, the demon barber of Fleet Street — might be uncomfortable under the circumstances.

The two asked for separate trials; the judge assented, and gallantly set Bertha's trial first. It opened on February 28, 1888. Representing her was William W. Erwin, renowned criminal lawyer of the day, known for some reason as the "Tall Pine Tree of the Northwest." On that day "Mrs. Hegener was dressed in a neat costume of blue cashmere with brown jacket and hat, and her face indicated more than ordinary intelligence. Her husband, despite a bulldog cast of countenance, is a fair specimen of the German workingman."[9]

The prosecution did not press Bertha very hard. The testimony for the state, completed in one day, consisted chiefly of admitted facts — what the police officer saw and what Bertha had said at the time of the shooting. A beautiful tableau was presented when Louisa and Charles, the two Hegener children, entered the courtroom "with bright faces and neatly dressed."[10] While this parade was an open appeal for sympathy from the jury, the county attorney did not object, and the children remained, to behold with their own eyes an event which would ever occupy a prominent place in the annals of their family.

Bertha took the proceedings calmly. "That Mrs. Hegener is

confident of an acquittal," the *Pioneer Press* of March 1 commented, "was evident yesterday by the way she laughed and talked while on her way from the hotel to the court room, with her little girl trotting along by her side, while her husband carried the other child." She was also aware of her charms, for the reporter went on to say: "As she entered the court room, she removed her brown jacket and appeared in a neat tight-fitting dress of navy blue."

The defense planned to show that Mrs. Hegener was temporarily insane when she shot Murphy and accordingly incapable of committing a crime. This defense was, even then, sarcastically known as *dementia Americana* because of its use in American criminal cases. The actual testimony for the defense did not go much beyond what Bertha had already told the police. Charles Hegener testified, disclosing his habit of talking over his wife's virtues with his friends and employees. Family friends dutifully recounted how wild and distraught Bertha had looked and acted on the day she boarded the train for St. Paul to carry out her mission. Bertha herself took the stand and described Murphy as a fiend who tried to isolate her from her husband so that she would be forced to turn to him. The portrait she painted was of a woman driven to despair, unable to think, incapable of reasoning. She overlooked her uncanny skill in hitting a moving target using a weapon notoriously difficult to aim.

The case went to the jury at 4:30 P.M. on March 2, 1888; at 5:42 P.M. the jury returned with the expected verdict of not guilty. Bertha "hid her face in her hands, tears of joy streaming thick and fast from her eyes." [11] The county attorney promptly issued a nolle prosequi in Charles's case, and husband and wife went free.

Anyone familiar with this case must wonder whether John Murphy really recognized the core of steel in this remarkable little woman, and what he would have had on his hands if he had won her. Very probably her husband treated her with a high degree of respect forever after.

PEARL WILSON

Like the famous Harriette Wilson who adorned Regency London, Pearl Wilson was a Cyprian, adroit in her profession and well known in certain Twin Cities circles. She was an enigmatic figure, and never more so than when she was involved in a famous shooting which nearly cost her life. Confusing her business and her emotions, the courtesan fell in love—with deplorable consequences.[12]

It was on Wednesday, August 15, 1888, at 11:30 A.M. when Mrs. Jennie Harris, the proprietor of a Minneapolis rooming house, heard three shots fired in rapid succession in room number six. She ran to the door at once. "Come to me," a woman's voice called faintly between moans. "Are you alone?" the proprietor asked suspiciously. "Of course I am," the voice replied wearily. Nevertheless the proprietor did not enter. Instead she went outside, found a police officer, and led him to the locked door of number six, which he broke open.[13]

On the bed lay James Scanlan, wearing only his underclothes, with one hand under his head and the other loosely clutching a handkerchief. He seemed to be enjoying quiet slumber; his lips were parted in a half-smile; but a raw wound in the left temple near his ear was grim evidence that no one could awaken him from that last sweet sleep.

Pearl Wilson lay on the floor, clad in a nightgown, stockings, and a pair of diamond earrings. Near her right hand and about eight feet from Scanlan was a .38 caliber revolver containing three empty shells. A stream of blood trickled down her cheek from a bullet wound in her right temple.

Room number six was in disarray. A nearly empty quart bottle of whisky and a half-full bottle of beer stood on a cluttered bedside table, and clothes were scattered about carelessly. A box of snuff, a pack of cards, a lady's collar, a trunk, and a gold-handled umbrella—the last two items labeled *P. Wilson*—were also visible. A small, whining terrier, the mute and only eyewitness, crouched beneath a sofa.

What had happened? A man whose room was two doors down the hall heard no quarreling. The proprietor remembered only that Scanlan arrived the previous evening, requesting a room for himself and his wife. He paid a week's rent of five dollars in advance. The man and woman had then gone out, returning about midnight. The case probably would have been written off as an obscure tragedy if someone had not identified the survivor as Pearl Wilson, "a well-known St. Paul sporting woman." It then became a matter of great public interest.[14]

At first Pearl was reported to be dying. At 3:35 P.M. the same day, however, she regained consciousness and was able to talk. On the following morning she was taken to a hospital where it was announced that she would live. The bullet had entered her right temple, lodging in the brain, but a doctor was able to probe the wound, remove several skull splinters, and two pieces of the bullet. The woman was strong enough to survive even her medical attention. One chronicler was forced to admit that "Notwithstanding her dissipated life, she possesses wonderful vitality."[15]

Pearl Wilson was no ordinary harlot but a puzzling mixture of personalities — on the one hand brawling and riotous, on the other calm, shrewd, and intelligent. Tall and slender, with dark hair and large, bright, gray eyes, she was strikingly attractive. She dressed soberly but elegantly. When she smiled, dimples showed in both cheeks with charming effect. She spoke in a lovely, low voice. Yet this woman had been arrested repeatedly for taking part in public brawls. She used opium; she drank constantly and heavily; she could match any profanity or obscenity; and she had an ungovernable temper.

In 1886 her rage led her to strike a saloonkeeper in the chest with a hatchet, and she seems to have provoked disturbances for the pleasure of watching them or taking part in them. Yet hers must have been a joyless life. She tried to commit suicide by taking heavy doses of opium, morphine, or laudanum, and once while under arrest she had tried to hang herself in the Minneapolis Central Police Station. It was as if a sober other self watched with detachment the imbroglios into which a riotous alter ego was thrown.

Scarcely fifteen years before the shooting, Pearl Wilson had been Betty Sawcer, a young girl in Louisville, Kentucky. She became a prostitute while still in her teens and was notorious in that city of dissipation in the 1870s under the name Bertie Tesser. In 1880 she met and married a gambler named William Helwig in Hot Springs, Arkansas.

During that era St. Paul provided facilities for dissolute conduct equal to those of most contenders, and it was to this Minnesota city that Mr. and Mrs. Helwig went shortly after their marriage. Helwig saw no reason to limit his stake to what he could win from gambling, and he allowed, even perhaps encouraged, his wife to continue her career under the name of Pearl Wilson. Minnesota's advanced social legislation in that day probably had the effect of attracting misfits and malingerers, and before long Pearl brought her mother to the North Star State. There, mad as a March hare, Mrs. Sawcer lived contentedly in the state's first insane asylum at the Minnesota Valley town of St. Peter while the people of Minnesota paid the bill.

Upon arriving in St. Paul, Pearl obtained work in a local sporting house. With her ambition and business acumen, however, she soon had her own establishment on Jackson Street between Seventh and Eighth. She acquired a reputation for being dissolute and was once called "an outcast even among the social pariahs among whom she passed her life." [16] This could have been a pose assumed for its business value, since competition was keen in St. Paul those days and the impression one gets in reading about this woman stresses her unusual intelligence and poise.

In 1885 James Scanlan, a twenty-three-year-old fellow who was "always identified with the gambling and sporting fraternity," also went to St. Paul. Formerly he had lived in Louisville, where he may or may not have been acquainted with Pearl. His only known employment while residing in St. Paul was as an assistant bartender. The greater part of his income may have come from his gambling winnings, but it is more likely that he lived on the earnings of prostitutes. By 1888 Scanlan and Pearl Wilson had become well acquainted, and Scanlan concentrated on wooing Pearl. As early as February, 1888, he announced in a St. Paul sporting house that he was going "to have her or kill her." Pearl was flattered and yielded. She sold her established house for four thousand dollars and became free from daily police shakedowns and pay-offs. She and Scanlan then settled down to the serious business of spending the money.[17]

Pearl's husband, Bill Helwig, took unkindly to the association. When he saw them riding together in a hack on the Fourth of July, he took a shot at them, but succeeded only in hitting Scanlan's hand. Despite this dramatic evidence that Helwig wished them anything but Godspeed, Pearl felt that her husband deserved the courtesy of being informed of her plan to go with Scanlan to California. The two lovers actually traveled no farther than North Dakota. Possibly finding each other less romantic than anticipated when thrown completely upon themselves, they were back in Minneapolis by August 13. Two days later Pearl and Scanlan were found in the Minneapolis rooming house.

Lying in the hospital, Pearl sent for her husband, who came at once. He must have been an unusually forgiving spouse. They talked at length, but not about Scanlan. When Helwig left, Pearl became confused; she could not understand how she got the wound in her head. Swarms of curiosity-seekers called at the hospital hoping to see the notorious woman. Police investigating the case also watched her for signs of improvement because they were now ready to charge her with James Scanlan's murder.

On September 2, Pearl Wilson was taken from the hospital to court, where she heard herself charged with first degree murder. It was an era of great crimes; only two days later the newspapers were full of the murder in England of Mary Ann Nichols — the third victim of Jack the Ripper — another in the grim series of Whitechapel Horrors.

Pearl again appeared in court on September 20 in order to plead to the charge of having murdered James Scanlan. Now she was represented by William Erwin and his partner, Cyrus Wellington, who had so capably steered Bertha Hegener into calm waters. Upon arraignment, Pearl made her not guilty plea in a firm tone that won the reluctant admiration of newsmen. "She was dressed entirely in black," reported the *Minneapolis Evening Journal* of September 20, 1888, "and except for her rather slow and uncertain step and pale face there was no sign of her sickness, but her slender, emaciated form appeared supernaturally tall as she stepped up to the bar to make her plea."

Her trial began on November 15, 1888. When Pearl entered the courtroom, her look was described as "inscrutable." This appearance must have been especially difficult to maintain when Frank F. Davis, Hennepin County attorney, for reasons best known to himself, perched a human skull on the counsel table throughout the proceedings.[18]

In quiet contrast to her lurid reputation, Pearl was neatly attired in a dark silk dress with a dark broadcloth jacket and black gloves. A large yellow plume in her black hat was the only dash of color in her costume. Spectators, craning their necks to see her, could find no visible trace of her head wound. The defendant was as much at ease as if she were merely a spectator, looking serious when the testimony covered weighty matters, and laughing heartily at anything funny.

The prosecution brought out little that was not already known, but it takes ingenuity combined with extraordinary luck to prove which of two people in a locked room fired first. In substance, Attorney Davis showed that someone heard pistol shots, that others later found Pearl with James Scanlan in room number six, and that a .38 caliber revolver with three empty shells lay on the floor near Pearl and six to eight feet from Scanlan. Medical testimony indicated that the wound in Scanlan's left temple would have paralyzed him at once, so that he could not have tossed the revolver consciously or through reflex action. No one tried to explain where the third bullet had gone.

The most damning evidence was the testimony given by a policeman who talked to Pearl in the hospital. "She said her head pained her," the officer testified, "and wanted to know what was the matter. I described the wound in her head to her. Then she asked where Scanlan was. I said, 'I guess you know that he is dead.' She began to cry then and said, 'To think that I shot him with his own gun.' And she added: 'Well, Jim has got a big hole in his head, too.' "[19]

The defense challenged the prosecution's evidence, asserting that nothing in it showed Pearl guilty of a crime. Pearl's counsel also called the doctor who supervised her case during the entire time that she was in the hospital. The physician testified that Pearl was delirious throughout the period.

Another important defense witness was the doorkeeper and bartender in a Fargo, North Dakota, house of joy who was reluctant to admit her occupation. "What kind of a house was that?" she was asked. "I can't exactly tell," she responded at first. When the truth was coaxed from her, she broke into a violent speech of self-vindication, shouting that she, too, had to earn her living and that she could judge how best to do it. "All this seemed very funny to Pearl," an observer wrote. "She smiled and dimpled and could scarcely restrain herself from laughing outright." When the amused courtroom spectators were quieted, the witness proceeded to give valuable testimony. She was an old acquaintance of Scanlan and could confirm that he was left-handed. When he and Pearl had taken their trip West, they stopped in Fargo where Scanlan, making it something of a busman's holiday, visited the house where the witness worked and had a long conversation with her. At that time he said that he wanted to return to Minneapolis, but Pearl insisted on going back to St. Paul. "I believe Pearl is going to skip me," Scanlan said, "and go back to Bill Helwig. If she does I shall kill her."[20]

Pearl herself appeared as the last witness in her own behalf. Giving her name as Betty Helwig, she spoke clearly and with dignity. On August 13, she said, the day of her return to Minneapolis from Fargo, she went to St. Paul to see her husband. When she got back to Minneapolis, she told Scanlan about her visit. His reaction to her report came on the fatal morning. She testified: "'So you have decided to go back to Bill Helwig, have you' he said. I said I had, and to stay. . . . I was sitting on the edge of the bed, and as I rose to step away from the bed I felt something strike my head. . . . I did not shoot James Scanlan. Of that I am positive."[21]

After only two days of trial, the case went to the jury at 6:00 P.M. on November 16, 1888; within a half hour the jury brought in a verdict of not guilty. Pearl calmly and politely thanked each juror individually. Then after saying good-by to the sheriff and the jailer, the tall, pale woman walked out of the Hennepin County courthouse to freedom.

Who killed James Scanlan? The answer to this depends upon the man's temperament. Is a man who lives from the earnings of prostitutes likely to fall so deeply in love with one of them that he will kill her and commit suicide if she leaves him? It seems doubtful. Yet, from Scanlan's remarks in St. Paul and Fargo, it is just possible that he had such an infatuation. He could have killed himself. He was left-handed and died from a wound in his left temple. Whether or not he could have thrown the revolver eight feet was perhaps more open to dispute than the medical testimony indicated.

Pearl could have killed him. The revolver lay close to her right hand. She certainly had the iron nerve, but she seems to have had no motive. She had seen her husband; he was anxious to take her back and was solicitous during her convalescence. Although Pearl had suffered fits of depression in which she attempted to kill herself, a suicide pact is quite different from doing away with oneself in solitude. Moreover, there was seemingly no reason for Pearl to consider suicide at that time.

The jury may have been right in believing that Scanlan, bitterly jealous, saw his beloved about to vanish, and like the dog in the manger, attempted to see that neither he nor anyone else should have her. At this date it is a plausible view, but the facts will also support other interpretations. And one is left wondering about the possible meanings of the half-smile on the dead man's face.

11

High Stakes and Green Goods

ON THIRTEENTH STREET at Hennepin Avenue in Minneapolis stands the Bellevue Hotel, a five-story building now faded and smudged. It has, as it did in 1894, a narrow ground-floor lobby leading to an elevator. Although the place has come down in the world, its rooms are spacious, and a beautifully carved handrailing testifies to its former elegance. In 1894 this edifice was two years old; its red brick was bright and undimmed. Known as the Ozark Flats, it was owned and managed by William W. Hayward, whose sons, Harry T. and Adry A., lived there and occasionally helped in the office. Claus A. Blixt, who occupied a basement apartment with his wife, was the janitor and off-hour elevator operator.

Many residents of the Ozark Flats ate at a boardinghouse on Thirteenth Street across from the apartment building. There in January, 1894, Harry Hayward, twenty-nine and unmarried, met Katherine Ging, also twenty-nine and unmarried. Their acquaintance ripened, and in November Miss Ging and Louise Ireland, her seventeen-year-old niece, moved to a fifth-floor apartment in the Ozark Flats.

Hayward was a professional gambler, a ne'er-do-well, and an associate of petty crooks. He had never learned a trade or taken part in a legitimate business, since he had at the age of twenty embarked on his lifelong career of gambling. His father once gave him a building, the only capital asset he was ever known to have, which he sold in order to finance his predilection for the gaming tables. Ironically, he received his first stake from a puritanical old family friend and wealthy property owner named Levi M. Stewart. This money, too, he frittered away. It was said that Hayward's success at faro "gave the professionals a scare," and he claimed that he had $9,500 in cash at the end of 1894. In reality, however, he was probably losing to the law of averages and was in financial hot water with debts in excess of his assets.[1]

Harry saw himself, however, as a great man, a genius of hypnotic power who moved among his companions as though he were Haroun-al-Raschid probing for a night the secrets of Baghdad. He was handsome; he had good manners; and he moved in levels of society acquainted with evening dress — one of his best pictures shows him wearing it. His usual company, however, was the social set which congregated in saloons, billiard parlors, and gambling houses.

Katherine Ging was handsome rather than beautiful. She had abundant black hair, gray eyes, and good teeth. Standing slightly over five feet seven inches tall and weighing a hundred fifty pounds, she was more commanding than petite. She was born at Auburn, New York, and moved at an early age to Syracuse. Later she went to Minneapolis — to escape a persistent suitor it was rumored — and at once took up dressmaking. In 1893 she became engaged to a St. Paul man but broke the engagement within the year. Kitty kept the diamond ring she had received, however, and ever afterward carried it in a little chamois bag worn in a corporeal area decorously described as "inside her corsage."[2]

The fact that Kitty kept the valuable engagement ring may offer a clue to her secret ambition which, like that of many people who have never had a great deal, was somehow to get her hands on money. Her worship of mammon became more fervid after she met Harry in 1894, and it may explain her rather curious association with him. She was not too scrupulous about the means by which her future wealth was to be obtained. She gave Harry sizable sums to gamble, which he promptly lost; she listened eagerly to his plans for buying stolen jewels at huge discounts below their resale or loan value; and she had no hesitancy about peddling "green goods" (counterfeit money). To further her principal ambition, she could be persuaded to meet strange persons in out-of-the-way places at unusual hours. She liked the flashy and sporty Harry, liked him well enough to promise to marry him, Harry said, although Kitty never admitted this, and in 1894 she was frequently seen in St. Paul and Minneapolis with other men.

On Monday, December 3, 1894, Kitty Ging went shopping in the late afternoon. She met a friend who invited her to dinner but Kitty declined, saying that she had a business engagement with Mr. Hayward that evening. She then went to the West Hotel, an elegant establishment that was the first such million-dollar operation in Minneapolis. There she ordered a buggy for 7:00 P.M. from Henry Goosman, the agent for his father's livery stable. It was to be delivered to her not at the Ozark Flats but at the West Hotel. Kitty had previously driven a quiet, gentle, buckskin mare named Lucy, and she specified that this horse be given her for the evening. At 7:08 P.M. Kitty appeared at the West Hotel, climbed into buggy number twenty-seven, which was waiting for her, stirred Lucy into motion, and drove away. She was wearing a sealskin sack over her dark blue skirt and striped shirtwaist. To accent her costume she wore a jaunty sailor hat and woolen mittens.

The night of December 3, 1894, was brightly moonlit until 8:30 P.M., when the moon sank below the trees. Near Lake Calhoun passersby could hear the voices of skaters as they called to each other and joked back and forth. Just as the moon disappeared, a man walking home along Excelsior Boulevard from the streetcar stop at what is now West Lake Street paused to look at something lying in the middle of the road. He had very nearly stepped on the still-warm body of a woman sprawled on a carriage robe. A pool of blood had formed beneath her head, which was dented, her clothing was bloodstained, her left eye hung out of its socket, and a bloody spot appeared behind her right ear. The man at once telephoned a doctor and the police. The doctor arrived first and found the woman dead. A policeman came somewhat later and removed the body to the city morgue.

Meanwhile at 9:10 P.M. the mare Lucy had returned to her stable with buggy number twenty-seven — empty. The horse was cool and gave no indication that it had run away. An observant stableboy noticed bloodstains in the buggy, and further examination disclosed particles of what later proved to be brain tissue. The boy immediately notified Henry Goosman. After checking the register to see who had hired the rig, Goosman telephoned the police department and was told that an accident had been reported but that details were not yet available. The livery agent then went to the Ozark Flats, where he also lived, and asked the policeman on the beat to call headquarters for more information on the accident. The call was made from the second-floor phone at the Ozark about 10:40 P.M. Once more the caller was told that the full story was still not known.

About 11:00 P.M., while Goosman and the policeman were still talking, Harry Hayward arrived at the Ozark. Entering, he probably heard voices in the hallway above, but took the elevator to the basement and came up five minutes later to join in the excited discussion of the accident. The buzzing residents of the building feared that the victim may have been Miss Ging. "I have been expecting that they would do her up!" Hayward blurted to the group. "My two thousand dollars is gone to hell!" He continued: "It is nobody but Miss Ging. She has not been hurt in any runaway accident; she has been done up for her money." When the policeman cautioned him that he could not be sure of this, Harry replied positively, "I am sure — I have reasons for it." He excitedly told how Kitty recently displayed some two thousand dollars in currency while eating in a restaurant. Taking a revolver from his pocket, Harry snarled, "Anyone that comes to do me up will get the contents of this." [3]

Hayward then talked with the livery stable agent who told him that this was the third time Miss Ging had gone out alone in a rented buggy. Harry exclaimed, "I wish I had known it. They are trying to do me up for my money. . . . God damn it, $2,000 gone to hell. What a fool I have been." He took out his wallet and began to remove some papers which he said were promissory notes Kitty gave him that day, but Goosman was not interested and suggested they go to the police station together. "As we were leaving the [Ozark] block," the livery agent recalled, "Harry asked me whether I thought life insurance was good in case of murder, and I told him I didn't know. He said she had been done up for her money. He seemed to be nervous and somewhat excited." [4] Harry had not yet seen the body, nor had he heard any official report.

At the Central Police Station a jailer was able to describe the clothes worn by the dead woman found near Lake Calhoun. Hayward unhesitatingly pronounced them to be those of Kitty Ging.

According to an officer on duty, Harry said that "the woman's name was Miss Ging; he knew it was her; that there was no question, but that she had been killed and killed for her money." [5]

The dead woman was indeed Katherine Ging; she was soon identified by markings on her underclothing. A round, ragged wound a quarter-inch in diameter, two inches behind her right ear, and surrounded by blackened skin where the hair was burned off, marked the point where a bullet had entered her head. The projectile had crossed the skull diagonally, severing the internal carotid artery, and finally lodged in the protruded eyeball where it was found. Death was instantaneous. Other injuries to the body indicated that it had fallen or had been struck. Kitty's nose was broken and turned to the left; her lower lip was cut; and her skull was fractured in three places.

After the positive identification was made, several detectives appeared at the Ozark to tell Louise Ireland that her aunt was dead. While looking for Kitty's apartment on the fifth floor, these policemen met Harry, who asked to have someone else break the news to Lou. Accordingly, the investigators called a lady in the adjoining flat to awaken Lou and bring her into the room. As soon as Harry saw Kitty's niece, he began to ramble on about his missing money. "Lou," he broke in, "you know she has worked me; you know I have given her money." The detectives took the girl into another room. When they returned, Harry continued, "She has a vault at the Minnesota Loan & Trust Company, and if the money is not there, I have been worked." He continued in this vein, speaking somewhat incoherently about $2,500 which he had advanced to Kitty, and which she was supposed to repay before he lent her another $7,000 to enter the millinery business. A police officer then asked Hayward "who he thought suspicion pointed to, and he said, suspicion pointed to him more than any man in the world, but he could tell where he was." [6]

The next day news of Kitty Ging's murder created a sensation in Minneapolis and made life miserable for people caught in the investigation. "It is known," said the *Minneapolis Journal* oracularly on December 4, "that she had lately been receiving attention from a certain man, but seems to have exerted herself to having kept her acquaintance with this man from the knowledge of her friends. Undoubtedly this was the man who accompanied Miss Ging on her last ride. Young ladies do not take long drives at night on winter evenings alone."

As a result of this journalistic hint, Frederick I. Reed, valued employee of St. Paul's Golden Rule Department Store, underwent some wretched hours. It was he who had been engaged to Kitty Ging and bought her the ring which she carried in the chamois bag securely pinned to her corset. Upon investigation he was found to have a perfect alibi and was discharged.

The police next looked into the abrupt departure from Minneapolis of Miss Lillian Allen, "a pretty, petite brunette, well known in certain circles." The inference was that these circles included those in which Pearl Wilson and her associates had moved. It appears that Lillian and Kitty once tangled over Mr. Reed's affections, after which Kitty wrote anonymously to Lillian's landlord advising him "to harbor her no longer if he wished to maintain the high standard of the house."[7] As luck usually handles these things, Miss Allen came across the note and recognized Kitty's handwriting. Lillian had packed her trunks on December 4 and vanished from Minneapolis. Her flight looked suspicious until she reappeared after visiting friends and explained satisfactorily that she had taken her belongings because she was moving to St. Paul.

Harvey Axford, a former traveling salesman who had known Kitty for seven years, then came under fire. The police found that on the day she died Miss Ging received a note reading in part, "I cannot marry you," which so agitated her that she tore it into bits.[8] The messenger who brought it thought that a man five feet seven inches tall, with a florid complexion, gray hair, and a moustache, sent it. The description fitted Axford, who admitted sending Kitty a note three weeks before but denied doing so on December 3. He undoubtedly could not have married Kitty since he already had a wife. By good fortune other people living in his rooming house heard Axford and his wife talking on the night of Kitty's murder. After the police inquiry, Axford was left to the mercies of his own fireside tribunal.

Although he was not above suspicion, Harry Hayward was the one person who looked completely innocent of Katherine Ging's murder. On the afternoon of December 3 he had gone with his friend, Thomas A. Waterman, to a cigar store. From there the two men threaded a tortuous course to a saloon, to the Dime Museum, to another saloon, to a shooting gallery, to a saloon, and to yet another saloon. There a slight interruption, best described by Waterman, delayed their onward motion. "Met a lady at Hofflin's drug store on First avenue south and Washington," said Waterman. "Went up stairs with the lady over a saloon . . . on Fourth street. Mr. Hayward left us at the bottom of the stairs. He came up in fifteen minutes or so."[9]

The men resumed their wanderings about 4:00 P.M., visiting an office and a jewelry store. By five o'clock they were playing billiards at the West Hotel. Although Kitty went there about that time to order a carriage, she and Harry do not seem to have met. At 5:45 Hayward and Waterman left the hotel and returned to the cigar store which was their starting place. At 7:08 Kitty dashed into the night in a hired buggy drawn by the horse Lucy.

If Harry Hayward had a business appointment with Kitty that evening, he apparently forgot about it. A few minutes before eight he arrived at the home of Mabel Bartleson, an attorney's daughter, and by 8:30 he and Mabel were sitting in the Minneapolis Grand Opera House watching a recent hit, Charles Hale Hoyt's *A Trip to Chinatown*. The musical show lasted until 10:30 P.M., long after the time Kitty's still-warm body was found. But Harry's financial ravings aroused suspicion, and the police became even more curious when they learned that he was the beneficiary of two insurance policies on Kitty's life totaling ten thousand dollars.

Hayward was questioned extensively. He answered queries, was open and unevasive, and co-operated fully with the police. At the request of William H. Eustis, mayor of Minneapolis, Harry underwent a medieval sort of ceremony confronting the corpse. According to the *Journal* of December 5, "The lid [of the coffin] was thrown back, and there the once beautiful but now terribly marred face was exposed to view. The side of the head which had been pierced with the murderous bullet had been turned so that it could be seen plainly. It was a sight to try the strongest nerves." Harry reportedly asked, "You gentlemen think I'm guilty? — God knows I am not!" As the undertaker closed the coffin, Harry spoke again. "Leave it open," he said, "I like to look at her." Again the coffin lid was removed and in a trembling voice Hayward said, "Oh, my God, if she could only speak!"

After passing this test, Harry was released, while the police investigated other suspects and the thousand and one rumors begotten by such a murder: that some married man was responsible, that a man with a gray moustache killed Kitty, and other equally misleading theories.

On December 5, two days after her death, Katherine Ging was buried. Harry attended her funeral and carried flowers to the church in his arms. Louise Ireland later accompanied the body of her unfortunate aunt to Auburn, Kitty's last resting place.

Investigations into the murder went on. Hayward continued to co-operate, meeting the police and the mayor and talking without reserve. On December 6, 1894, Attorney Charles J. Bartleson, the father of Harry's friend Mabel, burst into a conference in which Hayward was holding forth at length to the mayor. Bartleson told Harry sharply that he should have better sense and, furthermore, that the time had come for him to get a lawyer. That afternoon Harry and his brother, Adry, were arrested and charged with first degree murder. The following day, December 7, Claus Blixt, the Ozark Flats janitor, was also arrested and charged with firing the shot that killed Kitty. Without recourse to fingerprints, instruments of scientific analysis, or crime laboratories, the Minneapolis police found their murderer in four days.

With Harry a prime suspect, the press began to scrutinize his relations with Kitty. The *Journal* of December 7 described her as Hayward's "paramour" and referred to the "now admitted fact of the liaison between Hayward and Miss Ging — an admission borne out by the results of the autopsy." Later, in a reverse twist, the *Journal* of December 10 called Kitty a "pure girl," for whatever that was worth. It is impossible to say with certainty whether or not Kitty was Hayward's mistress. Contemporary accounts attest to her shrewdness and to her canny, suspicious nature. It is, moreover, an enterprise of singular difficulty to carry on a satisfactory affair while living in a small apartment with a seventeen-year-old niece in a preautomobile era. Kitty seems to have been interested in Harry largely for his money and financially valuable underworld connections. It was Harry who spoke of marrying, not she.

Hayward's murder plans, as they came out during the months that followed, proved to be a curious mixture of cleverness, braggadocio, and carelessness. In spite of his aptitude for the work, he violated nearly every canon in a useful murderer's handbook: he was closely connected with the victim; he gained from insurance policies on her life only recently taken out; he could not keep his mouth shut; and, like Nathan F. Leopold and Richard Loeb in the famous Chicago case of 1924, he could not keep from taking part in the police investigation. In choosing associates — who would necessarily hold his life in their hands — he made the egomaniac's error of picking easily influenced, weak men, and believing that a hypnotized rabbit can do a lion's work.

It all began in 1894 when Harry Hayward decided to murder someone. In July of that year he asked a hack driver if he would consider guiding his buggy into Lake Calhoun with someone in it. The hackie replied that he was no swimmer and took a long look at Harry.

After this unsuccessful experiment, Harry turned to his older brother, Adry. A pathetically dependent man of thirty-two, Adry would have liked nothing better than to have Harry for his confidant and guide through life's devious mazes. But Harry was contemptuous, and Adry turned instead to Levi Stewart, the family friend who had inadvertently given Harry his first stake. Harry tried to test Adry's courage by offering him a hundred dollars to go out and shoot someone, anyone. Adry refused. Later, according to Adry, Harry then "said I could make some good money if I was not too particular about it. He asked me finally if I would kill a woman for two thousand dollars if he would get her out somewhere; take her out driving, or something like that." Various plans were suggested: take her out in a hack, shoot her, and then shoot the hack driver; take her out in a boat and drown her; take her for a ride and have her buggy hit a boulder; or take her for a ride, get her hand tangled in the reins, and provoke the horse to run away. Adry refused to have anything to do with murder.[10]

Although irritated by Adry's lack of co-operation, Harry was nevertheless determined that murder should be done. From his reference to killing a woman, it seems that he had chosen a victim, but he still had to find an executioner. He turned to Claus Blixt. The janitor was not an ideal accomplice. An immigrant of low intelligence, he had been fired once as a dishonest bartender and twice as a dishonest streetcar conductor. Lacking strength of character and easily influenced, he was a willing tool but hardly the man to withstand the pressures which follow attempts to conceal murder. Harry tested Blixt by having him set fire to a barn. The janitor passed the test, and early in November, 1894, Harry jubilantly told Adry that the instrument of his scheme had come to hand.

Kitty Ging was to be the victim. Hayward now concentrated on outlining his plan and setting it in motion. Having shrewdly assessed Kitty's psychology, Harry tailored his scheme to fit it. He first lent her a large sum of money, nearly all in counterfeit bills. He next began building a picture of Kitty as a woman who carried substantial cash with her and displayed it carelessly in public. Hayward told Blixt, "I am going to take her to the restaurant and have her show this two thousand dollars, and then I will remark that she is awfully careless to show around so much money, and she will be killed for it." [11] The following week Harry did take Kitty to a restaurant, where she duly displayed a roll of bills while Harry loudly told the waiter that it contained two thousand dollars and Kitty was foolish to carry so much money. How he persuaded her to undergo this peculiar ritual is unknown.

Under Harry's guidance, Kitty unknowingly executed a second phase of his plan in November by taking out two life insurance policies in face amounts of five thousand dollars each, naming Harry as beneficiary. These were supposed to serve as security for Harry's loans to her, although they were worthless as collateral until her death. Harry told Blixt about the transaction, saying "he was going to kill her, and he thought he was going to make about ten thousand dollars on her." [12] When Kitty took out the second policy, Harry asked the issuing agent whether it would be good if Kitty were murdered — a question he later asked the livery stable agent on the night of Kitty's death — and he was told that it would be.

Throughout November Harry held a series of conferences with Blixt outlining various methods of carrying out the murder. Adry was present at several meetings, although he had refused to take part in the plan. Harry apparently viewed Adry with such contempt that he thought speaking before Adry about desperate ventures had no more effect than speaking before animals in a zoo.

By the end of the month Hayward finished his preparatory

schemes. He told Blixt and Adry that the dressmaker must die on the first possible occasion. Harry had already spent a good deal of time trying to find a spot where a buggy could be dashed against rocks, making the murder seem an accident, but the place was not to be found. On December 1 Hayward attempted a variant plan: he would take Kitty for a buggy ride, hit her over the head with an iron rail, and leave her body in the street near a manhole so that it would look as if a runaway horse had overturned the buggy. Harry and Kitty went riding, using the very buggy number twenty-seven in which she was to die two days later. The Saturday night crowds, however, made things unpropitious for murder, and Harry returned to the Ozark Flats, explaining in disgust to Blixt, "You need not ask me any questions. I could not kill her. I could not make it an accident. It was not possible." [13]

The following evening Harry suggested to Blixt that someone might leave the elevator shaft gate open, hit the girl over the head as she left her apartment, make it appear that she had fallen with her head inside the elevator shaft, and lower the elevator, cutting her head off. The gruesome idea was shelved as too difficult, but Hayward was getting impatient. "Every time I go up to her room," he told Blixt, "she puts her arms around me, and I would like to put a knife into the God damned bitch. . . . if there was a dog and her, I would rather shoot her and let the dog go." [14]

The next day Harry Hayward decided that Kitty Ging must die. In preparation, he told her with an air of mystery to meet him at some secluded point shortly after 7:30 P.M. He hinted that at last he had arranged for her to meet some of the gang's key men who would discuss ways and means of handling merchandise passing through unlawful channels.

Harry spent the day in studied idleness. After leaving his friend Waterman, he returned to the Ozark Flats about 6:30 P.M. and went immediately to the basement. There he confronted Blixt and told him that he must kill Kitty that night. Handing the surprised janitor a full bottle of whisky, he said, "Drink it all, damn you. You haven't nerve enough for this job without it." [15]

Blixt wanted to back out, but Harry told him coldly that his refusal meant his life and that of his wife. "He fixed me with his eyes," the wretched janitor said afterward. "I couldn't say no when he looked at me that way—nobody could." Trying to nerve his wavering accomplice, Harry said reassuringly, "Do you know when I make a plan it is so deep down that the smartest detectives can't get at it." Blixt was also promised two thousand dollars of the insurance money.[16]

In a sort of hypnotic trance, Blixt took Hayward's .38 caliber Colt revolver and cartridges and heard Harry tell him to clean the weapon and replace the empty cartridges after using it. Hayward finally reduced the terrified janitor to a quavering automaton by saying "that there was twenty in his gang in the green goods, and if I should ever say anything one of the gang would shoot me before I had time to walk two blocks."[17] With his mind already whirling, Blixt drank the entire bottle of whisky and awaited further orders.

After this conversation, which alternately nerved and unnerved Blixt, Harry ran to join two friends for supper at the boardinghouse in order to be seen going through his normal daily routine. It was noticed, however, that he arrived late, consumed little, and left precipitately. It was then about 7:08 P.M., and Kitty was getting into buggy number twenty-seven at the West Hotel.

From the boardinghouse, Harry returned to the Ozark Flats to make three rapid calls. The first was at his parents' apartment. The second was at Kitty's flat, where he made a good deal of noise, apparently to call attention to himself when told that Kitty was not at home. The third call was made on Adry to tell his brother that the crime would be committed that night. Adry tried to dissuade Harry, who shook him off impatiently and departed.

It was then 7:30 P.M. Getting the almost stupefied Blixt started, Harry, followed at a safe distance by his accomplice, walked quickly to a point near the present corner of Kenwood and Bryant avenues. The walk took about ten minutes, and the two men found Kitty waiting in her buggy. Telling Blixt to get in, Harry explained to Kitty that the janitor worked at the Ozark only as a disguise. "This man is one of the gang," he lied. "He is in it, too." Hayward then told them to "drive around to Hennepin, and go around Hennepin boulevard, around to Lake street, and follow around the west side of Lake Calhoun and I will meet you, and when you meet the two horses, you exchange with me." The exchange of horses would, he said, confuse anyone trying to follow them. Kitty doubtless listened with eagerness, thinking that here at last was the real thing.[18]

Blixt and Kitty drove off into the night. By now it was 7:40 P.M. The Opera House curtain rose at 8:15 and Harry was nearly a mile from the home of Mabel Bartleson. He managed to reach her house before eight o'clock and was seen running down Hennepin Avenue in order to do it. Unbelievable as it seems, while he planned to see Miss Bartleson that evening, he had not planned to attend the theater. It actually appears that Harry Hayward set up this essential part of his alibi on the spur of the moment, and risked spending a secluded evening when his scheme required being seen in public.

Harry and Mabel left the Bartleson home at eight and took a streetcar to the Opera House. Hayward had to buy tickets at the box office, and the curtain had risen before the two of them were seated. They remained at the Opera House until the program ended at 10:30.

Meanwhile Kitty Ging came to her death. For fifteen minutes she and Blixt drove in silence. Kitty's last speech revealed a pathetic belief in the reality of her mysterious rendezvous and its hope of illicit wealth. "She asked if it was green goods Harry was after," Blixt later reported, "and I said I did not know." Kitty was nervous, looking for Harry to follow; Blixt was nervous, trying to work up his courage. "She kept looking around," Blixt said, "and if I had wanted to I could have killed her ten times, but I could not, it was fighting with me and I tried to raise my revolver and I could not. At last I got too far, and she stuck her head out like this, and I raised the revolver and shot. I never looked when I shot, but it just happened that I shot her where he first told me to shoot her . . . behind her ear or in the forehead." Kitty's great calf eyes, as Blixt described them, became forever dim. It was eight o'clock.[19]

Blixt had held the revolver less than a foot from Kitty's head. When she was shot, she threw herself back in the buggy and lay still, making no sound. Placing the carriage robe against her, Blixt drove another mile and then pushed the body from the vehicle. The corpse struck the front wheel and the body rolled on its side; a wheel passed over it. Blixt drove on. After a while he got out and let the horse return alone.

He took a devious route back to the Ozark Flats where, upon arrival, he went straight to Harry's flat, removed the used cartridge from the revolver, cleaned the weapon, replaced the spent round, and, as instructed, put the pistol under Harry's pillow. He then went to his basement apartment. There he was astounded to hear from his wife that the horse had already returned to the stable, and that something had happened to Miss Ging. Blixt said nothing and went to bed.

He was awakened about 11:00 P.M. when Harry rushed downstairs to see him. They exchanged an agreed signal indicating that Blixt had carried out his assignment. Mrs. Blixt saw them together and thought her husband seemed terribly anxious to tell Hayward that Miss Ging had been hurt while out driving. "What, did she get hurt very bad?" asked Harry, catching his cue, "I guess I will go up and see." Harry went upstairs and then to the police station. Between three and four in the morning, he returned to Blixt's apartment, where he complained about the money he had lost with Kitty and commented, "I don't know whether I better go down in the morning and notify the insurance companies or not." [20]

From Blixt's bedroom Harry, excited and wide awake, went at 3:30 A.M. to his brother Adry's apartment. There he announced that "Miss Ging has been murdered; she has been found way out beyond Lake Calhoun stone dead." He asked Adry to step over to his rooms, where Adry watched Harry clean and oil his revolver and throw the dirty cleaning patch into the toilet. As he cleaned the gun Harry said to Adry, "It is just like picking up money." [21]

On the morning of December 4 Hayward was smug in the success of his murder project. He was sure his associate, who did the actual killing, would not speak out, and his brother would keep silent out of fear or family loyalty. All three men withstood tough police grilling on December 4, 5, and 6. Yet by December 7 the entire plot was known and all the principals were under arrest. Something in the elaborate plan had gone wrong.

Troubled, Adry had gone to Levi Stewart on November 30 and told him that Harry planned to murder Kitty very soon. Stewart refused to believe it, but when he learned that the murder had taken place, he wrote the county attorney, who told the police. They arrested Blixt and Harry at once. Adry was also arrested, but at first admitted nothing that would incriminate Harry. When confronted by Stewart, however, who told him sternly to tell the truth, the miserable Adry broke down and, crying that Harry had managed to hypnotize him as well as Blixt, revealed the entire plot.

In the meantime the police had learned from Mrs. Blixt that her husband had been away from home between the hours of seven and ten on the evening of December 3. Blixt first told the police a fictitious story that Hayward had accompanied him and done the shooting. Later, faced with Adry's statement and after experiencing a religious conversion, the janitor accurately described how he had killed the girl.

Harry Hayward and Claus Blixt were indicted for murder in the first degree on December 13, 1894. Both entered pleas of not guilty. Adry was not charged. The court set Blixt's trial for the following January 7 and Harry's for January 21, but as it turned out, the prosecution shuffled the trials. Since Blixt was the only eyewitness to the killing, Frank M. Nye, Hennepin County attorney, undoubtedly feared that if the janitor were tried first and found not guilty, it might be impossible to convict Harry Hayward. In order to avoid that possibility, Hayward came to trial first, on January 21, 1895, while Blixt's trial was postponed indefinitely.

The Hayward trial lasted 46 days, during which 136 witnesses testified. William Erwin, who had appeared for Bertha Hegener, Pearl Wilson, and others who strayed beyond the purlieus of the law, conducted Harry's defense.[22] The first nine days of the trial passed slowly in impaneling a jury, which was finally sworn on January 30. From that point the prosecution went on rapidly to outline Hayward's plans to murder someone, his search for accomplices, his choice of a victim, his finding of Blixt, and his acts and those of the janitor on the evening of December 3, 1894.

The testimony of Adry and Blixt was essential to the prosecution, which was bound by the legal rule that uncorroborated testimony of an accomplice will not sustain a conviction of crime. Only through Blixt, who was beyond doubt an accomplice, could the prosecution show who did the deed and at whose instigation. Adry's testimony was needed for corroboration. When Adry Hayward took the stand, Harry's counsel at once objected to his competency "upon the ground that he labors under a delusion and is in fact insane upon the subject." Judge Seagrave Smith, however, in an offhand comment — which the Minnesota Supreme Court had ultimately to rule was not prejudicial but which doubtless came from the judge's heart — snorted, "Well, I don't see that he is any more insane at the present time than the attorney is." In spite of repeated defense efforts to interject the issue of Adry's sanity, the court would not allow testimony on it. Adry then told his story without interruption as it has been related above.[23]

A choice example of how Harry managed to smother everything with mystery came out when Emma Goodale, a "Trance Medium" known as Madam Peterson, testified that Harry had brought Kitty to her for advice. "Whatever I tell them is told in a trance condition," the medium told the jury. "My charges are from two to five dollars. For the whole past and future it is five dollars. For just one part it is two." Madam Peterson testified that Hayward surreptitiously asked her to give Kitty some specific gambling advice which he furnished; the medium, doubtful, asked her husband about the wisdom of doing it. The husband was a wise soothsayer's mate and advised playing it straight.[24]

The defense then took over. In trying to confuse the jury about Harry's movements on that fatal evening, defense witnesses recounted a series of specific incidents occurring at critical times which, if true, would have made it impossible for Harry to meet Kitty before going to the Opera House. One of them went so far as to remember seeing a woman dressed like Kitty drive off at 7:10 P.M. with a man who looked neither like Hayward nor Blixt. Unfortunately for the defense, cross-examination brought out the fact that the witness had a long record of arrests and convictions, including the genuinely rare crime of sending indecent letters through the mail to his divorced wife. Hayward's parents testified that Harry had not left their apartment until 7:48 P.M. and that they thought it rather late to start for the theater. Since Harry himself admitted that he made a spur-of-the-moment decision to attend *A Trip to Chinatown*, his parents' story is obviously wisdom after the event.

Doctors for the defense, all Civil War veterans with extensive gunshot wound experience, testified that Kitty's skull fractures might have taken place before death, suggesting that Blixt's bullet did not kill her. But doctors for the prosecution — the chief of operative and clinical surgery at the University of Minnesota and his assistant—insisted that the lack of extensive bleeding proved the skull injuries had occurred after death.

The great star of the courtroom drama was the defendant playing the role of Harry Hayward, a part into which he threw himself with relish. He was expert in it, delivering an unruffled stream of eloquent perjury. Although Kitty had been "a true and noble girl," he said, she had borrowed a total of $9,500 from him and then, to his shocked surprise, had displayed a huge roll of bills at a restaurant where anyone could have seen her and made plans to rob her. Hayward did not chide her for this, he said, because she "was a very dear friend of mine, and I would not want her to think I was suspicioning her." [25]

Hayward testified that he finished dinner at 7:22 P.M., then called on Adry, and reached Kitty's apartment at 7:30, only to find that she was out. "I had time to sell then," he said, so simply strolled in the neighborhood until "twelve or fourteen minutes of eight," when he decided to call on Miss Bartleson and take her to the theater. When he returned to the Ozark Flats, he was surprised to hear of Miss Ging's accident.[26] Never, he insisted, did he discuss anything with Blixt, and never did he clean a revolver. Adry always needed money, Harry said, and might have killed Kitty to get it. In essence Hayward merely denied everything, forgot a certain ten minutes in which he met Blixt and Kitty, and insinuated that Adry was the murderer.

After much forensic eloquence on the part of counsel, the case went to the jury on Friday, March 8, 1895, at 11:30 A.M. By 2:15 P.M. the jury had returned, having eaten lunch and held its formal meeting. "We, the jury," the verdict read, "find the defendant, Harry T. Hayward, guilty of the crime of murder in the first degree." On Monday, March 11, 1895, the court sentenced Hayward "to be hanged by the neck until you are dead." At that time the law required a three-month interval between sentence and execution. This meant that Harry would probably swing some time after June 11, although the governor would fix the actual date.[27]

On May 20 Governor David M. Clough issued his warrant directing the sheriff to execute Hayward on June 21. On June 19, while carpenters' hammers resounded as the gallows went up in the Hennepin County jail, Hayward's attorneys appealed to the Minnesota Supreme Court and asked a stay of execution pending the appeal. The stay was almost denied; Justice Thomas Canty opposed it, but a majority of the court agreed to grant it. Months later on November 20, 1895, in an opinion written by Justice Canty, the supreme court affirmed Hayward's conviction. The high court's mandate directing that the sentence be carried out reached the Hennepin County District Court on December 3, exactly one year after Kitty Ging's death. On December 7 the governor issued a second warrant for Hayward's execution, setting December 11, 1895, as the date. Harry's parents secured an interview with Governor Clough and tearfully begged for mercy, but he refused any commutation.[28]

The death sentence had little effect on Harry, who continued to joke, maintain a gambler's indifference, and enjoy life as well as one may under confinement. At first he had special privileges and was allowed callers, but after he tried to escape he spent the rest of his time in unprivileged isolation. During his year in prison, the smartly turned out rogue of 1894 had become a heavier, more indolent man who let his beard grow and wore prisoner's garb. He still kept his gambler's pose, saying when told the date of his execution, "A damned long time to wait for a railroad train." And to the workmen putting up the gallows for a second time he yelled, "Go it!" He even asked that the gallows be painted red, and it was done. Keeping cool to the last, Harry continued to joke about his dim future. "It will be all over soon enough," he said. "I'll just give a sigh and drop with a sickening thud, ha, ha, ha! . . . I don't think it will hurt much. Say, doctor, before you begin to cut me up . . . just prick me a little with the knife at first. Try several places, so as to be sure that I am dead."[29]

During the months when his appeal was pending, Harry had gradually ceased to be an item of news. With the denial of his appeal and a definite date set for his hanging, he again sprang into a dominant position on the front pages of the local press. In fact, the prison fairly buzzed with reporters eager to record the last events of Harry's life.

He consented to give a lengthy final interview to a newspaperman and a court reporter on the evening before his death. The text of this conversation is an extraordinary, rambling tale of an immortal Hayward, coursing the byways of this world and twisting its supine inhabitants to the requirements of his will. During the interview Harry finally confessed, reluctantly admitting that he had indeed planned Kitty Ging's murder. He revealed, too, that he had lent Kitty only counterfeit money; he had given Blixt a Colt .38 revolver; and he had parted from Blixt and Kitty at 7:40 P.M. on the evening of the murder. Then, in a flash of pride, he refused to admit that he was an unsuccessful gambler, insisting that when Kitty died he still had nearly ten thousand dollars in cash.[30]

As the interview ended, Adry came in to say good-by. Harry admitted that all his accusations against Adry were false. He apologized and the two brothers shook hands. Adry and the other visitors departed. Harry Hayward remained alone in his cell, awaiting his summons to the hangman.

It came at 2:00 A.M. Harry put on the traditional black robe and black cap — over a fashionable cutaway coat and pinstriped trousers — and walked to the gallows. Asked if he had anything to say before he died, he chatted almost gaily for several minutes before the rope was placed around his neck. His last words were those of a gambler: "Pull her tight; I'll stand pat." The drop fell at 2:12 A.M. Death was not merciful. His neck was not broken and he thrashed, strangling, until he died. The man was pronounced dead at 2:25 A.M.[31]

An autopsy performed at the morgue disclosed that Hayward's brain weighed fifty-five ounces, which is substantial. Criminologists carefully examined and measured his skull according to the then popular theories of Professor Cesare Lombroso, an Italian psychiatrist who believed that criminals were a distinct anthropological type with definite physical and mental stigmata. They found that three of the four Lombrosian stigmata — "symmetry of skull, brain and face; the protrusion of the front teeth, and the narrow and sharply arched palate" — were present in Hayward, labeling the dead man a degenerate biological phenomenon somewhat below the savage and above the lunatic.

Later that day, funeral services for Harry Hayward were held at Lakewood Cemetery in Minneapolis. A vast mob of curiosity-seekers attended and watched Harry's mother become hysterical as she threw carnations upon her son's coffin and seemingly heard her dead boy's spirit speak to her. Addressing Adry she said in a semblance of Harry's voice, "Tell him I've forgiven him, mother." The gambler's body was stored in a vault at Lakewood, and two weeks later it was taken to Illinois for burial.

After Harry's death it was found that two enterprising Minneapolis citizens had smuggled a recorder into his cell and made phonographic transcriptions of many of his statements, including his last words. These cylinders were later reproduced and sold, and if any still exist, they would be of interest as some of the earliest examples of such records. Legend would have it that more than Harry's recorded voice survived the hangman's noose. After his funeral, rumors persisted that Hayward did not die but was resuscitated by a secret organization. So persistent is this legend that the writer heard it repeated in 1962. In the modern version, the Masons were credited with reviving Harry. The story is typical of the usual moonshine that surrounds a spectacular execution, and one has no reason to believe that, short of the last resurrection of the flesh, the human body can withstand both dissection and burial.

And what of Claus Blixt? The story of his life from 1894 on is as dull as the man. He pleaded guilty, and the court sentenced him to life imprisonment. Never granted a parole, Blixt spent an uneventful thirty years in the state prison, becoming quite insane before he died there in August, 1925, at the age of seventy-two.[32]

The Ging murder, springing from avarice on the part of planner, murderer, and victim, is probably Minnesota's best-known, carefully planned crime. The case lives on in that half-twilight of the ballad singer. Here, in "The Harry Hayward Song" is the last requiem for the soul of the greedy dressmaker: [33]

> Minneapolis was excited,
> And for many miles around,
> For a terrible crime committed
> Just a mile or so from town.
> It was a cold and winter's eve,
> And a villain did reply
> Tonight she takes that fatal ride,
> And she shall have to die.

CHORUS

The stars were shining brightly
And the moon had passed away
The roads were dark and lonely
When found dead where she lay.
Then telling the tale of a criminal
She was his promised bride
Just another sin to answer for
Another fatal ride.

When for pleasure she went riding
Little did she know her fate,
That took place on the lonely night,
On the road near Calhoun Lake.
She was shot while in the buggy,
And beaten ('Tis true to speak!)
Until all life had vanished —
Then was cast into the street.

He was at heart a criminal
But a coward of a man!
And so he sought another
To execute his plan.
It was a cold and bloody plot
It was a terrible sin
To take a life so kind and true
As she was then to him.

12

The End of the Rope

AT THE END of the nineteenth century Americans looked upon their handiwork and called it good simply because it was one hundred per cent American. Railroads spanned the continent, gas and even a few electric lights had replaced candles, the telephone had been invented, and everywhere the mechanization of life went on in a highly satisfactory way. In the early 1900s, however, citizens of the United States became self-conscious and self-critical. The crankiness of nineteenth-century New England reformers began to permeate the whole nation. Upon analysis some practices of the last century, such as hanging criminals, seemed archaic, while others — the placid acceptance of municipal corruption, for example — challenged the citizen to act. It was the heyday of the muckraker; moral earnestness was fashionable, and, to paraphrase Alexander Pope's "Essay on Man," a motto for the times might have been:

> Imperfect Man, proclaim thy new-found Norm,
> Whatever is, is wrong and needs Reform.

During such an era, Minnesota could almost be said to await a sensational criminal case from which a moral object lesson could be drawn. William Williams furnished just such a case.

At one o'clock on the morning of April 13, 1905, a haggard and disheveled man pounded on the door of Mrs. Emma Kline's apartment at 1 Reid Court in St. Paul. Mrs. Kline was awake. Sounds of gunfire and a fall in the Keller apartment overhead had just jolted her abruptly from sleep. Going to the door, she admitted the man whom she saw to be William Williams, an acquaintance of the Keller family and an occasional visitor at the apartment. Williams was greatly agitated. After blurting out that the Keller boy had been shot, he asked Mrs. Kline to go upstairs to look after Mrs. Keller and her son. Then he disappeared as suddenly as he had come.

Mrs. Kline ran up the steps. She found Mrs. Mary Keller seated in a chair, bleeding profusely from a wound apparently in her back. Mrs. Keller muttered faintly, "Bill shot my boy and nearly killed me, too. You take the lamp and see if my boy is dead." With some reluctance Mrs. Kline tiptoed into the next room where she found Johnny Keller lying on his side in bed, facing the wall. Although the sixteen-year-old boy was still alive, he had two bullet holes behind his right ear. Feeling "scared," as she later put it, Mrs. Kline stayed only a short time and then scurried away.[1]

Meanwhile the same haggard and disheveled man had appeared suddenly at the St. Paul Central Police Station. Speaking to Lieutenant William Hanft, Williams said excitedly that he had shot someone and asked the police to send a doctor to Reid Court at once. Hanft questioned the man who said he did not know why he had done it. Williams then rambled through an incoherent story about a quarrel with the boy's mother—the reason and details of which he could not tell—and an explanation that he wanted the youth to go away with him but he would not go. Questioned about a weapon, Williams said that he had a revolver which was in the Keller apartment. He was placed under arrest while a police detail sped to Reid Court and found the two injured people. Williams' revolver was lying on the floor. That afternoon Johnny Keller died of his wounds; his mother died eight days later.[2]

What led to this dreadful affair was the mortal passion of love, which takes so many forms. William Williams, the protagonist in the drama, was an immigrant from St. Ives, Cornwall, who was twenty-seven years old in 1905. He was uneducated but not unintelligent. He had been in the United States for about seven years. During that time he had served in the army, spending a portion of his enlistment in the guardhouse for attempted mutiny. He had also served a two-year term in the St. Cloud Reformatory for being too ready with a knife. Later Williams had worked as a miner and as a common laborer. He finally seems to have settled on the steam-fitter's trade but never stayed long in one place, remaining a rover and an intermittent workman.

Williams met Johnny Keller two years before the shooting when both were suffering from diphtheria and were thrown together as patients in the St. Paul City and County Hospital. A handsome lad of good reputation, Johnny was then fourteen and working as a bellboy at St. Paul's Windsor Hotel. His father, John Keller, was a not-too-successful cook, whose efforts to earn a livelihood took him away from St. Paul and obliged him to leave his only son in his wife's care most of the time. Mary Keller, Johnny's mother, also worked to supplement the family income — which was obviously meager — and it had been necessary for Johnny to find a job at an early age.[3]

When the two were released from the hospital, Johnny Keller, who had been a model son, defied his parents and went to live with William Williams, first at a rooming house and then at a hotel. The older man developed a tremendous passion for Johnny, which the boy apparently reciprocated. They were inseparable companions. Young Keller, who previously had to work for a living, now found himself supported by an adoring protector. How the youth could have been attracted to Williams puzzled their contemporaries, for the man was apparently an ugly "tough-looking customer." He is described as a "square-shouldered, sallow . . . young man" with a "capacious forehead," bluish-tinged cheeks, and "frowning brows, small, black eyes, short upper lip, wide mouth, and the protruding down-curved lips that are his most notable feature." Although he seemed an unlikely man to attract a good-looking youth, there was no doubt about what attracted Williams to Johnny Keller. It was, as writers of that and other days expressed it, "an unnatural attachment."[4]

In 1904 Williams was working as a steam fitter near Winnipeg, and he took Johnny to Manitoba with him. The two, however, soon returned to St. Paul. Williams explained their leaving Winnipeg by saying that the sleeping accommodations were not good enough for Johnny — which may have been a way of saying that the two of them either met criticism or could not find privacy.

During this time the boy's father violently opposed his son's association with Williams but, working outside St. Paul and unable to exert any direct influence, he was forced to let the relationship go on until he could act. By December, 1904, the boy appeared to be tiring of his companion and seemed ready to obey his parents; at least, for the first time, he left Williams in Manitoba to join his father at St. James, Minnesota. He did not stay long.

About a week later, on December 26, Williams — unable to bear the separation — abandoned his job and followed Johnny to St. James. There he had a violent argument with the boy's father, who said that he would put Johnny in reform school before he would let him go back to Winnipeg with Williams. But the man's strange hold on the boy was not yet broken, and Johnny again trotted after Williams. The two were soon in Winnipeg once more. It must also be reported that in spite of his storm and bluster, John Keller — in the manner of fathers-in-law who have married their offspring to persons in better circumstances than themselves — wrote Williams to ask for a loan.[5]

In spite of Johnny's disobedience in December, the bonds of the William Williams and Johnny Keller relationship were loosening. When Mary Keller sent her son a railroad ticket in February, 1905, the youth obediently left Winnipeg and went back to his parents' apartment in St. Paul. Within three days Williams again threw over his job and returned to the capital in pursuit, but he did not stay. On February 13 he departed for St. Louis, where he found employment and tried to save money so that he and Johnny could go back together.

During his absence in Missouri, Williams wrote Johnny a remarkable series of letters, usually signing them "Your loving friend, Bill." The burden of this correspondence was that Williams believed Johnny had thrown him over, and that if so, Johnny had better reconsider before something drastic happened to him. On March 3, 1905, Williams wrote: "You have been playing with me long enough now, Johnny; so it is time you tried something else for a change. Keep your promise to me this time, old boy, as it is your last chance." Ten days later he wrote more ominously: "I cannot believe you have gone back on me, and have good reason to think that others are doing this, not you. If I really thought it was yourself, I would see you so quick as the train would get me there, and you know what would happen." On March 18, almost in phrases of a lovesick schoolboy, the man said: "I told you all about my past, and gave you a true account of it, too. I did not think you would care for me after, but you told me then that you cared more for me then than you did before."[6]

At last Williams came to believe that Johnny had made a final decision never to return to him. On April 12, 1905, after riding a freight train from St. Louis, Williams reached the Kellers' St. Paul apartment in a nervous and emotional state. Only the day before John Keller had told his wife that he was going to shoot Williams if he did not leave the boy alone. Thus when Williams appeared at the apartment, Mrs. Keller questioned him coldly, asking what he was doing where he was not wanted. It is probable that she also told him of her husband's threat, for Williams apparently knew about it and armed himself. He did not, however, know that Johnny's father had again left St. Paul. After talking to Mrs. Keller, Williams departed and did not return to the apartment until eight o'clock that night. He found Mrs. Keller and Johnny alone. What then happened cannot definitely be known, but two deaths were the result.

Williams was charged with first degree murder almost at once. Moving with commendable speed, County Attorney Thomas R. Kane was able to bring Williams' case on for trial by May 11. District Judge Olin B. Lewis presided. Francis H. Clarke and James Cormican represented Williams. In an exchange that had prophetic overtones, "County Attorney Kane succeeded in having excluded one or two [jurors] that might otherwise have proved acceptable, on the score of having scruples against the infliction of the death penalty," reported the *St. Paul Dispatch* of May 12, 1905.

The prosecution opened its case on May 16. Mrs. Kline told the court about Mrs. Keller's dying accusation that Williams had shot her and her son. Officer Hanft testified that Williams had admitted shooting someone at 1 Reid Court, that he said he had an argument with Mrs. Keller, and that Johnny Keller had refused to come away with him. Other policemen testified that upon searching the apartment after arresting Williams they found a revolver belonging to him from which the fatal shots had been fired.[7]

Medical experts testified that Johnny Keller had a bullet wound in the back of his head and another in his neck. Both were blackened and singed, indicating that the weapon had been fired at close range. The boy's body had lain in bed, they said, in a natural pose. He was not dressed. With such wounds, the experts stated, he could not have moved after being shot. The medical men also told the court that Mrs. Keller had been shot from the front. The wound in her back, which Mrs. Kline had observed, was in fact one of exit.

Much to the jury's enlightenment the county attorney introduced in evidence — and had read in full — all Williams' letters to Johnny, written from St. Louis during March and April, 1905. And to complete its case, the prosecution called the slain lad's father, who testified fully about the strange passion which for a time bound his son to William Williams in defiance of a father's opposition, revealing the whole odd tale of Johnny's wanderings with Williams, the arguments the association provoked, the boy's wavering, and Williams' impassioned pursuit of Johnny when his parents did succeed in separating them.

After this distasteful chronicle had been spread before the jury, Williams took the stand in his own defense. Trying to follow the classic course used by women defendants of his day, he claimed to have no recollection of what happened during the critical time and felt that he must have been temporarily insane. As soon as he arrived in St. Paul, the defendant testified, he sped to the Keller apartment. Finding Mrs. Keller in a cross mood, he stomped out and went to several saloons where he drank heavily until he returned to the apartment about eight in the evening. He then had to submit to another scolding from Mary Keller. Williams admitted that he had been armed but described a curious ritual which he claimed to have followed in handling his weapon. He took the revolver, he said, emptied the shells, and gave it to Johnny; Johnny put the firearm in Williams' trunk, which was at the Kellers', locked the trunk, and gave his mother the key.

Continuing his story, Williams said that he and Johnny then went to bed together while Mrs. Keller sat in the next room and kept up such a steady stream of angry and provoking conversation that he found it impossible to sleep. Mary Keller's tongue-lashing, Williams said, finally provoked him to violent anger. This, on top of what he had drunk made his mind go completely blank.

He remembered getting up and he vaguely recalled some sort of struggle, but his next clear recollection was of standing in the room holding a smoking revolver. At the police station, Williams claimed, he told Lieutenant Hanft that someone had been shot, not that he, Williams, had shot someone.

In substance the defendant admitted visiting the Keller apartment armed, admitted being present when the shots were fired, admitted holding the recently fired weapon immediately after Johnny and Mrs. Keller were shot; and admitted that his revolver did the shooting. John Keller's testimony and Williams' letters gave ample evidence of motive. The only question appeared to be whether or not Williams' defense of temporary insanity would be successful. Unfortunately for the defendant the medical examiners found him quite sane.

Nothing more could be said for the prisoner and on May 19, 1905, the case went to the jury. Not long after retiring to deliberate the jury returned to ask the trial judge, "If John Keller was shot by defendant in the heat of sudden passion, on the spur of the moment, immediately following a scuffle with Mrs. Keller, with intent to kill, but without previous intention, would that be murder in the first degree?" Not answering directly, Judge Lewis reread his charge on first and second degree murder and manslaughter. After five hours of deliberation, the jury again returned, this time with its verdict: guilty of murder in the first degree. Williams' defense by reason of insanity had failed.[8]

After the verdict was announced, the county attorney moved for immediate sentence, which the court granted. When asked if he had anything to say, Williams replied quietly, "No, judge. If I must die, it might as well be now as later." He was then sentenced to be hanged by the neck until dead. The *Dispatch* of May 20, 1905, reported that the man "heard his awful fate with composure."

By 1905 it was almost routine for criminal cases involving a man's life to be appealed to the state supreme court. Williams' counsel followed this course, but on December 8, 1905, the Minnesota Supreme Court affirmed the lower court's decision. Justice C. L. Lewis dissented. He argued a hopeless cause by trying to persuade his colleagues that Williams' letters to Johnny Keller did not hint at a homosexual relationship or contain threats against Johnny's life. Shortly after the decision was handed down, Governor John A. Johnson issued his warrant for Williams' execution, setting the date of his hanging as February 13, 1906.[9]

While awaiting his death, Williams found new dimensions in his life; from a vicious man seeking only self-gratification he became contemplative and kindly. On February 2 he joined the Roman Catholic church. Fortified by a new calmness, he was able to face death without fear, to joke about his predicament, and to enjoy life. He even plunged avidly into a series of checker tournaments which continued until the night of his execution.

On February 13, 1906, after a simple meal of steak and fried potatoes which he ate with relish, Williams walked to the scaffold dressed in a new suit, shirt, collar, and necktie. He put on the black cap and cloak without hesitation. As he stood on the trap he made a dignified final statement, asserting that he was innocent of killing Johnny Keller, the best friend he ever had, and that he was dying a victim of judicial murder. Then he turned to the priest attending him and said simply, "Good-by."[10]

The sheriff released the drop at 12:31 A.M. Williams fell through quickly, but there was an immediate shout from the spectators: "He's on the floor!" The rope was six inches too long. Three deputy sheriffs immediately ran to the platform, hauled on the rope, and held the unfortunate man's feet off the floor for the fourteen and a half minutes it took him to choke to death. As soon as Williams was pronounced dead, spectators seized the rope and cut it into small pieces for souvenirs.[11]

As it was explained later, this cruel fiasco resulted from overlooking the grim but elementary law of physics that if weight is applied to a rope and to a human neck, both will stretch. The rope had stretched eight inches; Williams' neck, four and a half inches. The sheriff, who on the previous day had tested the rope with weights in order to avoid its breaking, neglected to allow for expansion factors. The public took these things and pondered them in its heart. Williams was dead but his influence went marching on, to such unforeseeable destinations as free speech and criminal law reform.

As had been true from earliest days, a first-rate hanging was a first-rate newspaper story. The St. Paul papers — the *Pioneer Press*, the *Dispatch*, and the *Daily News* — pounced upon the scandal of Williams' execution and followed newspaper tradition by giving the story the space and treatment it deserved. A great deal of gush was poured over Williams' admittedly exemplary last days and a good deal more splashed on his last hours — his walk to the scaffold, his final words, and his death. The *Pioneer Press* of February 13, 1906, described the execution but did not go into the gory details of the bungled hanging. The other two newspapers did — extensively, in detail, and with diagrams. This was not pleasing to the Ramsey County authorities.

Eighteen years earlier the execution of Nels Olson Holong in Little Falls had drawn attention to the methods by which hangings were carried out. The sheriff had followed the usual custom of having the gallows built outside the jail surrounded by a fence which did not completely hide the proceedings from the spectators. All the other sheriffs in Minnesota were invited to watch inside the enclosure. The execution was, in fact, almost public and was thoroughly described in the newspapers. Perhaps as a result, in 1889 a reforming legislator from Minneapolis named John Day Smith — who tried unsuccessfully to get Harry Hayward to pray with him on the evening of Hayward's hanging in 1895 — sponsored a bill which passed almost without opposition. It provided that executions must take place before sunrise — they had often been held at midday — and within a jail if possible, limited the number of spectators, and also stated explicitly: "No account of the details of such execution, beyond the statement of the fact that such convict was on the day in question duly executed according to law, shall be published in any newspaper." [12]

The John Day Smith law, as it was known, took effect on April 24, 1889, but the section dealing with newspaper reports of executions had never been enforced. From the hanging of Albert Bulow on July 19, 1889, through that of Claud Crawford on December 5, 1905, Minnesota journals openly gave their readers full and gruesome details of the rope dances which took place during that period. Apparently no attempt was made to invoke the law even in 1891 when the newspapers reported that the rope had broken in William Rose's execution on October 16.[13]

The Ramsey County officials, however, seem to have been thin-skinned. On March 2, 1906, seventeen days after Williams' death, the county attorney who successfully prosecuted Williams secured an indictment of all three St. Paul newspapers for violating the John Day Smith law. The papers pleaded not guilty, asked for separate trials, and finally agreed to have the *Pioneer Press* case tried and to be bound by that decision.[14]

Chosen to represent the entire St. Paul journalistic world, the *Pioneer Press* demurred to the indictment; that is, it admitted publishing the details of Williams' execution, while arguing that no violation of law occurred because the law which punished such publication was unconstitutional. If the court sustained the paper's view, the case could be disposed of without going to trial. The argument was not successful, however, in the district court, which overruled the demurrer on April 16, 1906. The case was then appealed to the Minnesota Supreme Court, which handed down its decision on February 21, 1907. The high court's opinion was written by the same Justice Lewis who dissented in Williams' appeal. Whether the assignment of the case to Lewis was by design or chance, the jurist, whose humanitarian opinion in Williams' case found no allies, might yet strike an indirect blow for the hanged man.[15]

The *Pioneer Press* based its demurrer upon the argument that the John Day Smith law muzzled a newspaper, violating freedom of the press as guaranteed by Amendment XIV of the federal Constitution and by Article I, section 2 of the Minnesota Constitution. The case is of special interest to lawyers because counsel in 1906 used a legal argument then novel — that Amendment XIV kept state authorities from interfering with rights which Amendment I protected against federal interference — later used effectively and successfully in the free-speech cases of the 1930s.[16]

Justice Lewis and his colleagues on the state supreme court were neither ready to adopt novel legal views nor to concern themselves much with newspapers. What, they inquired, is this freedom of the press supposedly protected by constitutional provisions? Going back to the eighteenth century, they found their answer in a paraphrase of Lord Mansfield's famous decision in the Dean of St. Asaph's case as interpreted by New York's Chancellor James Kent: "The liberty of the press consists in the right to publish with impunity truth with good motives and for justifiable ends."[17] English law states it more accurately as the right to publish anything without securing previous license, but subject to all consequences attached by law. In other words, no one may censor a newspaper before publication, but its publisher is subject to punishment if he violates any law. This now seems a restrictive view, but it is still the law; in 1906 it fitted the newspaper's situation in the Williams' hanging to the letter. A distinct and positive statute forbade such publication. The editor published his account in spite of it.

Following this authority the supreme court saw no reason to interfere with the legislature's judgment that publishing details of hangings could have no justifiable end. Justice Lewis wrote that "if, in the opinion of the legislature, it is detrimental to public morals to publish anything more than the mere fact that the execution has taken place, then, under the authorities and upon principle, the appellant was not deprived of any constitutional right in being so limited." [18]

As a result of this ruling — that the John Day Smith law did not infringe constitutional freedom of the press — the demurrer was overruled, and the *Pioneer Press* had to stand trial. The sequel was anticlimactic. On March 17, 1908, the case was called; the newspaper pleaded not guilty; the trial took place the next day; the journal was found guilty and fined twenty-five dollars.[19]

The supreme court's decision was unpopular among those favoring freer expression of opinion, because it seemed to bless a simple way to suppress freedom of the press completely: the legislature had only to declare publishing certain types of material to be a crime and to impose stiff penalties. Nine years later, in 1917, after Minnesota had abolished capital punishment, the statute was repealed. It had been a dead letter in all instances except this one, but sparked by Williams' execution it had served to arouse concern over a classic freedom threatened with restraint.

Although the St. Paul newspapers were found guilty of misdemeanors in doing so, they had brought the bungled execution to public attention, hinting at a parallel to Inquisition tortures of the Middle Ages, and Minnesota was shocked. Since the state's creation in 1858, Minnesotans had harbored uneasy feelings about hanging criminals. Under the spur of the Ann Bilansky trial, the state's second legislature in 1859 had considered the abolishment of capital punishment. In 1868, as we have seen, the legislature enacted a sort of compromise, which provided that the death penalty would not be inflicted unless the jury should recommend it. Fate then took a hand and a series of difficult cases followed the enactment of the law, which proved so unsatisfactory that it was repealed in 1883 when hanging was restored as the mandatory penalty upon conviction of first degree murder. The 1883 law stated that persons guilty of first degree murder "shall suffer the punishment of death" unless the trial judge certified compelling reasons for not imposing it.[20]

By 1906 social reforms of all kinds were in the air throughout the United States and penal reform got its share of attention. Minnesotans had before them the example of the neighboring state of Wisconsin, which had done away with capital punishment in 1853 and apparently had not suffered in consequence. The brutal details of Williams' execution underlined the very specific and nonabstract nature of the death penalty: a human being is killed, very often painfully. Although the effect of the Williams' hanging on popular thought can only be guessed, persons concerned may well have been jolted into taking action. For whatever reason, Williams was the last man legally hanged in Minnesota. Even though the death penalty remained on the statute books for five years after he died, successive governors consistently commuted death sentences to life imprisonment. On April 22, 1911, the reformers carried the day and Governor Adolph O. Eberhart signed the law making first degree murder "punishable by imprisonment for life in the state prison." On April 20, 1911, the day the bill passed the legislature, the *Minneapolis Journal* printed a front-page cartoon, showing on one side the old hempen halter with the caption, "This necktie will not be worn in Minnesota hereafter," and on the other side the striped prison garb with the statement, "While this suit will be worn a little longer." [21]

To read of William Williams' crime is not an ennobling experience. There is no question of his guilt, and the sordid tale of his epicene romance offers nothing to mitigate his crime. By coincidence, however, his death seems to have been instrumental in doing away with capital punishment in the state. There is something fascinating about the beginning and ending of a historic era. Ann Bilansky began the state of Minnesota's "capital punishment era"; William Williams' fame lies in the fact that he brought it to a close.

13

Six Women Who Kept a Secret

THREE MAY KEEP A SECRET, Ben Franklin said, when two of them are dead, but six St. Paul women once kept a fearful secret so well that it has not been disclosed to this day.

In 1909 Louis Arbogast, a well-to-do St. Paul butcher, lived with his wife, Mina, and four of his five daughters — Louise, Ida, Minnie, and Flora — in a large residence on Seventh Street not far from his shop. The fifth daughter, Emma, was married to a young man named Lawrence Ulmer and lived not far away. Louise, the eldest girl, was twenty-three and beautiful. She was betrothed to Henry A. Spangenberg, a young butcher who had a shop near that of Louis Arbogast. At one time Arbogast had opposed the marriage but later gave his consent. Ida was twenty-two; Minnie, eighteen; and Flora, better known as Babe, was only sixteen. All were unmarried and not affianced. Emma, the married daughter, had two small children whom she often brought to visit their grandparents and aunts. The girls appear to have lived normal lives for their ages and backgrounds. They were sociable and gregarious, and seemed fond of their parents but not dominated by them. Their mother, however, was so quiet and self-effacing that she had to be introduced to a close neighbor. In outward appearance the Arbogast family was united and happy.[1]

On May 12, 1909, the family spent a placid evening. Louise was at home, having just returned from a visit to Eau Claire, Wisconsin. Ida, Minnie, and Babe went out but came back early. William Manteuffel, an old family friend, called to see Louis, whom he found in jolly spirits. Shortly after 10:00 P.M. Manteuffel left, and the household settled down for the night.

A few minutes after 4:00 A.M. the agonized screams of women in the Arbogast house jolted the neighborhood awake. People living nearby ran to help, and they were soon joined by policemen and firemen. Those who arrived first found Louis Arbogast lying crosswise on a burning bed, naked, and covered with blood and feathers. The back of his skull had been completely smashed. He was still gasping, alive but clearly beyond help. The bed was in flames, having been drenched with gasoline, the fumes of which were apparent in the room. Rescuers smothered the flames and rushed the man to the nearest hospital. He died en route.

Meanwhile, police examined the Arbogast house and yard. They found the house completely closed and locked with two exceptions: a bedroom window was open but covered by a locked screen, and a basement window, while open, was covered by an obviously undisturbed cobweb. When firemen arrived, a large watchdog met them; the dog had roamed the yard all that night. Police learned from Louis Arbogast's son-in-law that the family had a spaniel, a bulldog, and a rat terrier, all of which might be outside at night. A little later the police located a streetcar watchman who walked the tracks in Arbogast's neighborhood to keep them free of obstructions. The man had begun work at midnight. He had seen no strangers in the vicinity; he had, in fact, seen no one at all until after he heard the terrible screams around four o'clock.

These facts, which were never contradicted, justified Ramsey County Attorney Richard D. O'Brien in stating that "the crime had been committed by some one in the house." [2] But by whom? Obviously Louis Arbogast did not kill himself. With the best will in the world he would have found it difficult to pound his head "to a pulp," as the *Pioneer Press* of June 2, 1909, described it. Only Louis, his wife, Mina, and his daughters, Louise, Ida, Minnie, and Flora, had been in the house. Who among these, singly or jointly, could have committed the crime?

From the beginning the family seemed to be withholding some secret and gave no help to the investigation. After making their first excited statements just after Louis Arbogast was found upon his flaming bed, they became evasive, noncommittal, or silent.

Employees were told to say nothing. A stableboy engaged in tearing to pieces the burned mattress upon which Arbogast had lain — why the police did not forbid this is another mystery — was told, in the presence of newspaper reporters, to say nothing. Photographers were chased away. When one of them tried to snap the watchdog's picture, a member of the family even ran out and took the dog inside.

Secrecy extended to in-laws and prospective in-laws. Henry Spangenberg, Louise's fiancé, had nothing to say. Although he lived nearby and reached the house in moments when summoned, he insisted that he knew nothing about the murder or even about conditions in the household. Emma's husband knew equally little. Both he and his wife had satisfactory alibis for the night; beyond explaining his whereabouts Lawrence Ulmer was silent.

Louis' brother, Henry, visited the Arbogast house after the murder and was interviewed by a newspaper reporter. He, too, spoke ambiguously and revealed nothing helpful to the police. "I speak only to my brother," he said. "As I go to work I pass by in front of his shop and wave my hand at him. I never come here. I do not care to say what the trouble was. I must not say anything. You see the house is locked. The murder could not have been committed by any one on the outside. But about the murder I cannot say anything." [3]

When the entire family remained tight-lipped, it is little wonder that the newspapers hinted darkly at "testimony of a very disagreeable character," "peculiar conditions in the family previous to the murder," and affairs "of a character not yet related." As a matter of fact, to the irritation of both contemporary and later investigators, no such information — if any existed — was ever disclosed. The baffled county attorney could only say in disgust, "I am satisfied that the entire Arbogast family is holding something back. They could clear this whole matter up in a minute if they wanted to." [4]

The facts were few. There was no doubt that Arbogast's "frenzied daughters, half clad and disheveled, awoke the peace and quiet of the early morn with their frantic shrieks for help for the stricken victim." [5] Help had come. Louis died. His wife, Mina, was badly burned. Treated and bandaged, she was taken to a hospital. The house was locked and guarded by watchdogs all night. On the second floor the police found an empty gasoline can, which still had a strong odor, indicating that it had been emptied recently. Casual inspection of the basement disclosed a bloodstained ax half hidden in a trash pile. The ax was normally kept in a woodshed some distance from the house. Further checking brought to light a bloodstained nightgown and two bloodstained women's undervests lying in a bathtub where someone had apparently tried to wash them.

Just as the fire engines left, an employee in Arbogast's meat market ran up to the house. He met Louise, who exclaimed, "Papa is dead. The gas jet fell down on him and burned him." At this time Louis was still alive and on his way to the hospital. When the employee entered the house, Mrs. Arbogast told him, "The gas fell down and burned him, and I am also burned." The man then rushed off to get the family doctor but was unable to find him.[6]

When this same employee returned to the house after his unsuccessful mission, Louise spoke excitedly: "Papa has a hole in his head," she said. "They say Papa shot himself, but I know he didn't. Papa wouldn't do such a thing. When Ida screamed out I came down stairs, and when I came back again I saw the man who did it. He was standing pressed up against the wall on the stairs. He was just about your height, with tousled hair, and had a cap on and his eyes looked straight at me, and I flew upstairs, and when I looked around again he was gone. That's the man who did it." After this recital she cautioned the employee not to tell anyone what she had said.

To the butcher shop manager, who came to the house when Louis did not appear at his usual time, Louise shrieked hysterically, "Papa is dead and there is something wrong with the gas." Since she said nothing more, the manager got the impression that Arbogast had suffocated. While these conversations were taking place, no one as yet knew definitely that Louis Arbogast had died. As the day wore on, Louise became increasingly hysterical and was taken to St. Luke's Hospital.

Mrs. Arbogast parried all questions and was thought to be shielding an insane daughter, who was hinted to be Louise. Two days later Mrs. Arbogast was not so reticent. She was now ready to give the police a purportedly complete statement. Feeling ill, she said, she had arisen and gone into the bathroom. When she returned to her bedroom, she saw the bed ablaze and Louise standing in the doorway watching the flames. Mrs. Arbogast ran into the room and threw herself on the bed to smother the fire. Ida, hearing the noise, rushed in and dragged her mother away, but not before Mrs. Arbogast was seriously burned. The younger children, Minnie and Flora, then ran outside for help. In response to a direct question, Mrs. Arbogast replied, "Yes, I think Louise did it." [7]

Attention then focused on the beautiful Louise. The *Pioneer Press* of May 18, 1909, reported that when the police reached the Arbogast home they found Louise in her room "praying hysterically for aid from Heaven." Three days earlier the police and county attorney let themselves be quoted as believing the murder was the work of an insane person. This supposition also seemed to point toward Louise. She had been so hysterical that she had to be hospitalized on the day of Louis Arbogast's murder, and some people thought her conduct strange when she refused to look at her father's face as he lay in his coffin.

As the days went by other curious stories about the good-looking girl came to light. She was said to have had a series of nervous ailments which for years sent her to various parts of the country in search of cures. It was rumored that she spent Christmas of 1908 in a sanitarium. In March, 1909, two physicians were reported to have told Louis Arbogast that unless confined in a sanitarium Louise would kill herself or someone in the house. These medical men supposedly found Louise "insane" and "repeatedly warned [her parents] for their own safety." Going further back into her past, someone recalled that she once fell from a bicycle and suffered severe head injuries. In an interview, Dr. Arthur A. Sweeney, an alienist, made the flat statement: "Miss Arbogast was hopelessly insane two months ago when I saw her at St. Luke's Hospital," and added that she was not cured when she was released.[8]

The trip to Eau Claire from which Louise returned only four days before her father's murder was said to have been connected with her efforts to regain mental health. After her return to St. Paul she was rumored to have roamed the Arbogast home at night, "pacing up and down the hallways, moaning and wailing and muttering ghastly and unearthly things." Mrs. Arbogast revealed several of these stories, and also let it be known that Louise had become quite violent a few days before the murder and attacked her mother with a hammer. If these accusations were not enough, Louise was also said to have frequented fortunetellers and clairvoyants who filled her mind with thoughts of violence, blood, murder, and the "strange things that were to come to her through the murder and violent death of someone very dear and close to her." [9]

Mother and daughter had a dramatic confrontation scene at the hospital where both were confined. Mrs. Arbogast said accusingly, "It's between you and me, Louise, and God knows I did not kill your father," to which Louise was reported to have replied, a bit cryptically, "It isn't me who did it, and the spirit of my father will come down from heaven to say it was not you." [10]

Fortified by Mrs. Arbogast's direct accusation and the sensational information about Louise's private life, the police arrested her on May 17, 1909, four days after the murder. She was charged with having caused the death of Louis Arbogast. When she was advised to retain counsel, she replied, "I did not harm my father. I need no attorney." By May 20, however, she had retained eminent counsel indeed: William D. Mitchell, a prominent St. Paul lawyer who was to serve as attorney general of the United States from 1929 to 1933. Mitchell appeared on her behalf, entered a plea of not guilty, and waived a preliminary hearing.[11]

Louise was ordered held pending action by the grand jury. Informed speculation hinted that either the grand jury or the police would order an inquiry into the girl's sanity. If the probate court found her insane, she could be committed to an institution; public opinion and the police could assume tacitly that she killed her father in an insane fit; there would be no need to prosecute anyone; and the puzzling Arbogast case would be closed. Louise seemed to accept this disposition, saying, "I did not commit this deed, but I am willing to spend several years in an asylum for the sake of my people." [12] While such a course would have saved face for the police — who had made no progress in solving the case — the trouble was that people who called to see Louise at the county jail found her intelligent, clear-spoken, and even shrewd.

If mad, Louise was, like Hamlet, mad but north-northwest. Quite early in the investigation she told County Attorney O'Brien:

"They say I did this because I'm insane. I want to tell you that I'm as sane as any person that ever lived, and I tell you honestly and candidly, I did not do it. . . . And I'll tell you more, Mr. O'Brien, my mother had nothing to do with my father's death." Trying to encourage further talk, O'Brien asked, "Now, Louise, taking it for granted that what you say is the truth, whom do you think killed your father?" Louise went white, paused, and then answered slowly, "You know, it might sound funny, but Ida and I used to always fight about Dutch collars and who ironed the last shirtwaists."[18]

During the latter part of May and the first week of June, the Ramsey County grand jury met to hear what presumptive evidence of guilt the police had been able to amass. Although these hearings were secret, enough leaked out to suggest that the police were still groping and fumbling. Ida and Minnie Arbogast testified; Flora was also summoned but could not appear because she was ill with scarlet fever. Whatever the evidence presented, it was at least convincing enough for the grand jury to return two indictments. On June 3 Louise was charged with first degree murder. "At the same time," said the *Pioneer Press* of June 4, "a secret indictment was returned, which, it is rumored in police circles, is against the mother." Two days later, the newspaper announced: "Mrs. Arbogast . . . has been indicted on the same charge as her daughter." It seems probable that the indictment was not immediately made public because of fear on the part of officials that Mrs. Arbogast might take her own life. She was reported to be very depressed, with nurses in attendance twenty-four hours a day to prevent her from harming herself.

On June 29, 1909, Louise Arbogast entered a formal plea of not guilty and, to the astonishment of all, waived an insanity hearing. She would stand trial without trying to insist she was *non compos mentis*. As early as June 10, a friend of Louise's told the *Pioneer Press* that it looked as though the Arbogast family had made Louise a scapegoat. She was in effect to admit killing her father while insane, and the prosecution would then be dropped, much to the relief of other members of the family. Louise's spirited individual defense swiftly ended that speculation. On July 2 Mrs. Arbogast pleaded not guilty to the indictment charging her with the murder.

Nearly two weeks later, on July 14, Louise was released from the Ramsey County jail on twenty-thousand-dollar bail. To County Attorney O'Brien, who had not opposed her request for release, Louise said effusively, "Oh, sir, I can never tell you how much I appreciate your kindness; the only thing I can do is to thank you, and I do thank you from the bottom of my heart." She planned to spend a quiet summer with friends and to keep in touch with the county attorney.[14]

The next criminal term of the district court would not be held until October, allowing the public ample time to speculate on what the trial might bring out in the light of the many newspaper reports and rumors. Exhaustive questioning had turned up only two additional lines of investigation, neither of which promised very much: (1) Louise had been her father's favorite, which did not make her the most likely murderess; (2) just before his death Louis Arbogast had contemplated a trip to the Klondike, which his family strongly opposed. It was rumored that he planned to sell his prosperous business and go to the Arctic with Louise and William Manteuffel, both of whom had chatted with him on the night of his death.[15]

Louise was known to be fond of her father and had acted as cashier in his meat market. Because of their close association, the *Pioneer Press* of May 25, 1909, reported: "The authorities have been reluctant to charge the murder against the daughter on account of the manifest friendship that existed between her and her father. She was known as her father's favorite. She was most intimate with his business affairs." The account was meant to carry overtones, and a reasonable inference could be that Louis Arbogast was, as some fathers are, so unduly fond of his eldest daughter as to cause anger and jealousy in his spouse and other children. At one time, a family friend disclosed, the father set aside two thousand dollars for Louise to buy a home after her marriage; this move caused a violent squabble among the others. "The Arbogast family was not so harmonious as many have supposed," the friend said, "and I would not be surprised if the murder was the result of an imaginary wrong felt by some one."[16]

It was also reported that on the night before his murder Louis Arbogast told his family that he would leave shortly for the Klondike, taking Louise with him. This statement was said by the

Pioneer Press of May 25 to be "the real key to the motive that lashed to an ungovernable and insane fury that caused the sleeping man to be struck over the head with an ax." Since Louise was twenty-three, even her father could not force her to make the trip. If she wanted to go, she would not be likely to show "ungovernable and insane fury" at the announcement. Someone else must have taken violent exception to the proposal. Was Louis Arbogast displaying too openly his affection for his eldest daughter? Was he murdered to keep him from making the trip?

All these speculations, well aired in the newspapers, kept public interest in the case alive until the trial opened on October 18, 1909. The defendant stood accused of first degree murder, an offense still punishable by hanging in Minnesota. The defendant was Mrs. Mina Arbogast. Over the summer the prosecution had time to analyze its evidence and had concluded to try Mrs. Arbogast first —possibly in the hope that testimony in her trial might produce additional evidence useful in the case against Louise. The trial was, in fact, to bring several surprises as well as information contradicting that which fed the summer speculations.

Wearing a black veil and accompanied by Patrick J. McLaughlin, her counsel, Mrs. Arbogast took her seat in the courtroom before Judge Grier M. Orr. As counsel examined prospective jurors, the defendant was seen to shudder whenever the customary question was asked: Do you oppose capital punishment? Louise was present, wearing "deep black and . . . a jaunty looking picture hat, without a veil." All the Arbogast girls attended the trial regularly.[17]

It took the better part of three days to draw a jury, after which the case proceeded rapidly. Introductory testimony showed that ambulance and fire calls at 4:30 A.M. on May 13, 1909, brought police and firemen to the Arbogast house, where they found Louis Arbogast lying on his bed, covered with blood and feathers, and bleeding profusely from a large head wound. The two mattresses on his bed had been on fire; a pool of gasoline lay between them. Before he could reach the hospital, Arbogast died from several heavy blows on the head.

In trying to advance beyond preliminary matters and, in fact, throughout the trial, the county attorney was hampered by an evident agreement among the Arbogast girls to reveal as little as possible about anything, and to say that only after protracted questioning. Rarely in the history of Minnesota criminal law has a prosecutor undertaken such a difficult and exasperating job as that which fell to County Attorney O'Brien in the Arbogast case.

He began his attempt to elicit critical testimony by calling Ida Arbogast. At this, said the *Pioneer Press* of October 21, 1909, a "care-free slip of a girl, with a very young-looking face, dressed in deep black, tripped from her chair" to testify. On the evening of May 12, Ida said, she visited her dressmaker but returned home at 9:30 P.M. There she found her father, her sister Louise, and William Manteuffel talking in the dining room. Minnie, with whom she shared a room, and Flora were already in bed. She did not see her mother that night. On cross-examination Ida admitted this to be unusual, since she customarily kissed her mother good night.

At about four in the morning, Ida continued, her mother's screams awakened her abruptly. Rushing into her parents' room, she found them both in bed; her father's side of the mattress was ablaze. The girl seized her mother's nightgown and dragged her from the room; then she tugged at her father's arm but could not move him. Returning to her mother, Ida took her downstairs. Minnie was close behind. Ida said she ran into the street to get help, then went to the house of Mrs. Mary A. Garvey next door and remained there until she returned home in the company of policemen. At eight-thirty or nine o'clock that morning someone told her what had happened to her father. Although Ida said that she ran outside for help, she could not recall whether it was then daylight. This difficulty in remembering occurred each time she was asked a question which she obviously did not want to answer. She "became purple whenever the county attorney pressed her for answers," commented the *Pioneer Press* of October 21, "and her countenance was almost blue when she was forced to admit that after she did come home, four hours after she had dragged her mother from the burning bed where her father lay writhing in agony, she did not go near her mother."

Minnie Arbogast next took the stand. The passage of time since the events of May 13 seemed to have numbed her recollection also. On the night before the murder, Minnie said, she visited a friend but came home about nine o'clock and went directly to bed.

She heard the voices of her father and Mr. Manteuffel downstairs and thought that her mother was with them. She did not see her mother. Like Ida, she admitted this was unusual since she, too, customarily kissed her mother good night. In the morning, Minnie said, someone's screams awakened her. She rushed from her bedroom and saw Ida and her mother hurrying down the stairs. For a moment, Minnie added, she looked into her parents' room, where she saw the bed on fire but did not see her father. Her last recollection was of running out the front door and later awakening on a bed. At no time had she seen a stranger in the house.

Flora Arbogast followed her sister to the stand. She was a very unwilling witness and, although only sixteen years old, displayed the wisdom of Eve. "There is nothing childish about her," commented the *Pioneer Press* of October 22, ". . . and she took her own sweet time answering questions she did not like." The county attorney had to pry all answers from her, and she never replied without looking at her sisters and family friends in the courtroom. Her characteristic response seemed to be, "I forget." Babe testified that she visited a friend on the evening of May 12, came home at 10:00 P.M., and went directly to her parents' bedroom. There she found her mother talking with Louise. Flora could hear her father and William Manteuffel conversing in the parlor downstairs. At approximately 10:10 P.M., Flora said, her father came upstairs and joined the three of them in conversation. Flora could not recall what had been said, except that her father spoke of taking a Masonic degree. Then, looking at his watch and winding it, he told Louise and Flora that it was time to go to bed. Heeding their father's suggestion, Flora said, she and Louise retired to the room they shared. Louise was first in bed. "There was no quarreling in the house that night," said the youngest Arbogast girl, "and everybody was good friends as far as I know."

Babe's memory failed her on several critical points. She could not recall what kind of nightgown her mother wore. She would not admit that anyone talked about the proposed Klondike expedition that evening, but she did say that her father had planned to leave for the Yukon on June 3, 1909, three weeks from the day on which he was murdered. According to Babe, both she and her mother were to have accompanied him.

Minnie Arbogast, recalled to elaborate upon the morning's

events, now testified that she wanted to help her father, got a rug, and tried to put out the fire. When asked how she knew he needed help, she could only answer in Arbogast fashion, "I don't know." In a similarly forgetful way she remembered seeing a red gasoline can in the house but could not recall exactly where she had seen it. The fatal ax was also familiar to her, but she could only remember giving it to her brother-in-law when it needed a new handle. "I never heard father and mother quarrel," she concluded, "although mother scolded sometimes."

A police officer testified that when he reached the Arbogast house he found Henry Spangenberg, Louise (who was only partly dressed), Mrs. Arbogast (who was barefoot), and a hysterical younger girl. Louise and the younger sister ran aimlessly about the house, the officer said, while Mrs. Arbogast quietly strolled through room after room, alone. In the kitchen the officer found the range still hot with remnants of recently burned cloth smoking inside it.

Henry Spangenberg, "a clean-cut business-like young man," now stepped forward to testify. Spectators who were watching Louise, his fiancée, were surprised that she showed no emotion when he was called. At 4:28 A.M. on May 13, Spangenberg said, he heard Ida running up and down the street crying "Fire! Fire!" and "Save my poor father, he is burning up." He ran quickly to the Arbogast house where he saw no one else outside. Someone was standing in the hallway, and Minnie was in the sitting room. Without pausing to talk, Spangenberg ran upstairs, where he found Isadore Abrahamson, a newsboy who had also come to help after hearing Ida scream. The two young men put out the flames. While they were doing so, Spangenberg said, someone, probably a member of the family, stood in the doorway watching them, but Spangenberg was too busy to notice who it was. When the fire was out, Spangenberg called an ambulance. At about 8:00 A.M. he learned that blows on the head had killed Louis Arbogast. Asked specifically, Spangenberg testified that he did not use a rug to smother the flames, that he had not seen Minnie or Babe in the blazing bedroom, that Minnie did not come and throw a rug over the fire while he was there, and that he saw no rugs on the floor or bed.

The most clearheaded witness was the sixteen-year-old newsboy, Isadore Abrahamson, who had been passing the Arbogast house when he heard Ida scream "My poor papa!" and "Won't some one please help my poor papa?" Minnie was also outside on the steps, screaming, said Abrahamson, but ran inside as he hurried toward the house. By the time he entered, Louise, Minnie, and Flora were all standing in the hallway, crying and screaming about their father.

Abrahamson dashed up the stairs. As he did so, he met Mrs. Arbogast, wearing a nightgown, coming down. Brushing by her quickly, he ran into the bedroom to find Louis Arbogast lying on his flaming bed, his body actually burning in several places. There were no bedclothes on the bed, but Abrahamson found a sheet on the floor, grabbed it, and began to smother the fire. At this point Henry Spangenberg joined him and the two finally put out the blaze. Like Spangenberg, Abrahamson was positive that a woman stood calmly in the doorway watching their efforts. He had seen Ida elsewhere, barefoot and wearing only a nightgown. Going to a window, intending to open it and let the smoke out, he found it already open, but covered by a locked screen.

After putting the fire out, Abrahamson continued, he ran down the back stairs. There he found a blazing roll of feathers and cloth — he could not tell whether it was clothing, or a rug, or something else — which had set fire to the woodwork. Seizing this firebrand, he threw it into the yard and then put out the blaze in the wood. By this time, he said, firemen had arrived and had taken charge.

The county attorney then recalled Babe Arbogast to the witness stand and succeeded in dragging from the reluctant girl some account of her experiences on that shocking May morning. She saw her father in bed, she said, and saw that the bed was on fire. She thought a spark from the gas jet must have lighted it. Crying, "Papa, wake up," she tried to drag Louis from the bed but could not. She then ran downstairs where she found Louise, whom she could not remember having seen upstairs, her mother, and Minnie. After this, Babe said, she went to her sister Emma's. She stayed there all day, and someone later told her that her father was dead.

Emma Ulmer, whom the *Pioneer Press* of October 26, 1909, described as "a delicate looking little thing," followed her sister to the stand and outdid all the Arbogasts in nervousness and forgetfulness. Her chief responses were "I don't know" and "I don't remember." The prosecution conceded that she was not in the house when the murder was discovered, but brought out that she did visit it later. All Mrs. Ulmer was willing to remember of her visit was that she wiped up some feathers downstairs.

Mrs. Mary Garvey, who lived next door, testified that she first learned of the occurrence early in the morning when she saw her daughter and Ida Arbogast leaving the Garvey house; Ida was wearing one of the Garvey girl's dresses. Mrs. Garvey's son ran in to say Ida told him that her father had been burned. Hearing this, Mrs. Garvey immediately started for the Arbogasts. From her back porch she could hear Louise asking her father if he did not know her. As she entered the Arbogast house, Mrs. Garvey saw some of the girls in the upstairs hall; Minnie was moaning loudly. Louise put her head over the upstairs banister and said, "Mrs. Garvey, my father is dead." At this time Mrs. Arbogast was standing at the head of the stairs, about four feet from her bedroom. She did not know Mrs. Garvey and Louise had to introduce them. Mrs. Arbogast said: "Mrs. Garvey, I'm badly burned," and added, "My night dress has been all burned off." The nightgown, said Mrs. Garvey, was made of flannel; it buttoned down the front, and had a spot of blood near the neck.

Mrs. Arbogast asked her neighbor to rub some lard on the burns, and the two women went into the sewing room. There Mrs. Arbogast said, "I was in the kitchen when the fire started." She explained that she had been getting breakfast. When her neighbor asked if 4.00 A.M. was not rather early for breakfast, Mrs. Arbogast answered that "papa had to be at the shop at 6 o'clock." Mrs. Garvey remembered clearly that Mrs. Arbogast did not explain how she got burned, and replied, "I heard Ida crying" when asked how she had known about the fire.

Mrs. Garvey testified that Mrs. Arbogast was clearly not at her ease while being cared for. She seemed nervous and did not like her neighbor's questions. She was badly burned on her back, neck, and left arm, and had a cut on the left side of her head which was still bleeding. While Mrs. Garvey was applying lard to the burns, Louise and Babe were in and out of the room. Louise brought her mother some underwear and a clean gown. Mrs. Garvey took the bloodstained nightgown, rolled it in an old bedspread, and left it in the bathroom. The nightgown was properly identified and introduced in evidence.

Called to the stand, Mrs. Garvey's daughter said she also had gone to help after hearing Ida scream, "Our house is on fire and papa is burned," and heard Mrs. Arbogast say that her other nightgown had been completely burned off.

A cleaning woman, whose husband drove a wagon for the Arbogast market, then testified that on the morning of the murder she had burned some bloody feathers as well as a number of Mrs. Arbogast's garments which she found upstairs. She added that the Arbogast girls positively shunned their mother that morning. Mrs. Arbogast, lying down and in pain, called several times for Ida, who refused to go to her, and the other girls were in no hurry. Ida then left, the woman said, and did not return from the Garvey house until noon.

Babe Arbogast was recalled a second time to identify a bloody undervest and handkerchief found in a closet by Lawrence Ulmer on the morning of May 13. After resisting questioning as long as she could, Babe admitted that the garments belonged to her mother. In spite of Babe's identification, the court would not allow this clothing introduced in evidence because Ulmer found it a few hours after the murder. The passage of a few hours, ruled the judge, destroyed any probative value the clothing might have had because no one could show it in any immediate connection with the crime. Here, it may be respectfully submitted, the learned district judge was wrong.

Although one of his discoveries was not used, Lawrence Ulmer's identification of an ax he found in the basement was willingly accepted by the court. The handle, said Ulmer, had been sticking out of a refuse heap; the blade had been lying on fragments of a broken wine bottle. The blunt edge was smeared with clotted blood; the sharp edge was clean. "The daughters of the accused woman gazed with horrified fascination upon the weapon that had killed their father," said the *Pioneer Press* of October 28, "and even Mrs. Arbogast appeared to be transfixed by the sight of the ax." It was admitted in evidence.

The street railway watchman testified that he spent the hours between midnight and 4:00 A.M. in the Arbogast neighborhood. He saw no one, but around four o'clock he heard a girl screaming. Going to the Arbogast house, he found Minnie, standing barefoot in the hallway, holding in her hand a blazing piece of what looked like straw matting. He told her to throw it away and ran to turn in a fire alarm. When he returned to the house, he found the girl standing in front, pulling her hair. He told her to be quiet, that firemen were on the way.

A driver for Arbogast next related that on the afternoon of May 12 he used the ax to chop firewood and then replaced it in the woodshed. Needing the ax again at 4:00 P.M., he went to the woodshed, only to find the tool missing. The obvious inference was that someone had taken it inside, preparing for a bloody night's work.

Police officers told of finding an empty red gasoline can in the second-floor back hallway, and described how blood had stained the bedroom floor, walls, and ceiling. Bloody footprints led from the room down the back stairs to the basement. This testimony seemed to indicate that the murderer left a visible trail as he carried his bloody weapon to its hiding place. To follow the line of thought, the county attorney recalled the newsboy who had been the first to answer Ida's calls for help. Abrahamson now revealed that his shoes had been bloody when he descended the back staircase. Asked by the disgusted county attorney why he had not said this before, the boy replied simply that no one had asked him.

Testimony by various policemen continued. When he arrived, one officer said, Mrs. Arbogast told him she had arisen early to take a bath and was in the bathroom when the fire was discovered. Another stated that Mrs. Arbogast said she found the bedroom afire when she returned after taking a bath. She told him she rushed to put out the flames and was badly burned. Ida came in while she was there. When the officer asked Mrs. Arbogast how she burned her back without getting her nightgown burned, she did not answer. He remembered that she did not complain at all until questioned about her husband's death, at which time her burns began to pain her severely. A policeman also corroborated the cleaning woman's statement that Ida Arbogast did not want to see her mother on the morning of the murder. In searching the house, the policemen said, they found a charred blue calico bathrobe and a white corset cover in the bathtub. These items were admitted in evidence.

The family washerwoman testified that she had come across a

skirt covered with bloody feathers but laundered it along with the other washing. A doctor testified that Louis Arbogast could not have lived more than an hour after sustaining the head blows he received.

The last witness called by the county attorney was Louise Arbogast. She answered the first few perfunctory questions — name, address, age, and occupation — and then refused to testify further. Since she herself was under indictment for the same crime, she was within her rights in refusing, but it was, as the *Pioneer Press* of November 2 said, "a hard blow to the state."

With this, the state rested. The defense immediately asked for a dismissal because the prosecution had brought out nothing showing that Mrs. Arbogast committed the crime. This was denied. After further consideration, counsel decided not to introduce any evidence for the defense, and the defense rested. Court adjourned for the day.

Immediately after adjournment, Louise Arbogast ran to the county attorney, exclaiming, "Don't blame me, Mr. O'Brien. I was willing to tell everything I knew, but they would not let me." It was doubtless small solace to the prosecutor that Louise had only complied with her attorney's advice.[18]

On the next day, November 3, 1909, counsel for both sides presented their arguments to the jury, after which the district judge gave the customary charge on the law. Motive, he said, was not an essential element of the crime. At 4:35 P.M. the jury retired. During the course of its deliberations, it once returned to ask the court if Mrs. Arbogast could be found guilty of some crime other than first degree murder. Judge Orr said the evidence showed that someone committed first degree murder and the issue was whether or not the defendant committed it. "That or acquittal should be your verdict," he stated. Nearly twenty-four hours later, at 2:10 P.M. on November 4, the jury returned with a verdict of not guilty. Mrs. Arbogast was free.

The result was anything but satisfactory to the public, the prosecution, and the *Pioneer Press*, which ended its account of the case on November 5 with an editorial entitled, "Police Stupidity in the Arbogast Case." Having shot his bolt and missed the target, County Attorney O'Brien dismissed the indictment against Louise Arbogast on December 3, 1909, and the case became history.

Who killed Louis Arbogast? From the established facts, a woman living in the Arbogast house must have committed the crime. Its bloody nature suggests premeditation and revenge for some serious wrong. But what serious wrong? The prosecution failed to show any motive whatever, although both the county attorney and the police had hinted at possible "testimony of a very disagreeable character" about "peculiar conditions" in the household," leaving the mind free to range over all sorts of possible family complications from incest to irritation at slamming doors.

The trial brought out only some vague comments on a proposed trip to the Yukon. The Klondike story, at first glance, does not seem of enough substance to provoke murder. If it is considered, however, as the last in a series of affronts—if these were known—it might do very well as the detonator which finally set off an explosive charge. But what was the root of the trouble?

Women usually murder for personal reasons. Jealousy and money are perhaps the commonest motives. Money seems to be irrelevant here. Louis Arbogast's fortune, although rumored to be extensive, actually amounted to about sixteen thousand dollars.[19] The ferocity of the murder rather suggests jealousy. That hell hath no fury like that of a woman scorned is an ancient aphorism tested in the crucible of time. But which woman? And how scorned?

It is a police truism in murder cases to look first for the spouse. Since murder is seldom undertaken lightly, it most often arises from close personal contact, and history shows that no other human arrangement provides so great a mixture of propinquity and irritation as matrimony. Does circumstantial evidence lead to the spouse in this case? Flora's testimony places Mrs. Arbogast as the last person seen with her husband. A bathrobe and corset cover belonging to her were found partly burned, and a servant admitted destroying other clothing of hers. Mina Arbogast's own stories of her activities that morning conflict: she was in the bathroom because she felt ill; she was in the kitchen preparing breakfast; she was in the bathroom taking a bath. Each version, however, concluded with Mrs. Arbogast rushing to the bedroom, seeing the flames, and being saved by Ida, who dragged her away. Ida, however, testified that she heard her mother scream. Upon running into her parents' bedroom, she found the bed ablaze on her father's side, and her mother still in bed. The stories of rescuer and rescued do not agree.

Immediately after news of the crime became public, someone made consistent efforts to show Louise insane. Upon examination, these stories about insanity, violent conduct, and soothsayers appear to have come from Mina Arbogast, who also told the police that when she returned to the bedroom she saw Louise standing in the doorway, hands upraised, watching the fire. Why Louise? She was known to be her father's favorite. Could her mother have been jealous of her?

It seems highly probable that Mrs. Arbogast and her five daughters knew exactly who killed the late Louis and why, but those coming after them are faced with a secret which all six women refused to divulge. Behind the murder lay the fact that something odd had been taking place in the Arbogast household. Henry Arbogast had hinted that all was not well in his brother's family, but he was not called as a witness. No one can say exactly what was wrong, but the reticence of every member of the family circle suggests that something was amiss. Very likely it had to do with the girls. Whatever it was, it aroused jealousy and hatred which led to violence.

Psychologically, there may have been reasons for jealousy on the part of Mrs. Arbogast. If Mina Arbogast saw one or more of her daughters gradually displace her in their father's affections, she may well have felt jealousy and anger, consciously or not, to the point that such an apparently unrelated act as going to the Klondike could make an unbearable situation explosive. The same reasoning, moreover, could apply to one of the girls becoming jealous of a sister.

A possible reconstruction of the crime, quite at variance with the jury's verdict, is that Mrs. Arbogast rose early, dressed, sprinkled one side of the bed with gasoline which she stored in a second-story closet, took the ax from the same closet, where she had concealed it the preceding afternoon, bashed her husband's head in, took the ax to the basement, returned to the bedroom, and set the bed on fire. Gasoline accidentally splashed on her clothes and they caught fire, burning her rather severely. She ran into the bathroom, threw her flaming clothes into the bathtub, put on a nightgown, returned to the bedroom, lay down, screamed, and was discovered by Ida. She was the last person to see Louis at night, and the first in the morning.

She probably meant to rush upstairs from the kitchen, where it would be logical for her to appear fully dressed, but when her clothing caught fire she had to change her plans. Her clothing would also have been splattered with blood; the wound in Louis Arbogast's skull had caused blood to spurt all over the bedroom. After the discovery, Mrs. Arbogast's excited daughters called upon the neighborhood for help — early and disrupting the premeditated plan. All this is possible, but the jury said it did not happen.

Did any of the Arbogast girls commit the crime? Their stories are curious. Louise told the market manager that a gas jet fell and burned her father. She told a driver that someone accused her father of having shot himself, and went on to say that she saw the man who really committed the crime. To the driver, and to Mrs. Garvey, she said her father was dead, although he was still living when the ambulance carried him away and positive news of his death did not arrive until later. These things, however, may be explainable. Flora also testified that she thought a gas burner caused the fire. Mrs. Arbogast mentioned this once, and the girls may have adopted it as their explanation. The mysterious assassin Louise thought she saw could have been Isadore Abrahamson, the newsboy. In the moment's excitement, seeing her father badly injured and gasping for breath, Louise may have thought him dead as he passed into the coma preceding death.

But many things are not so easily explained. Minnie was seen holding a burning wisp of straw matting. Why? No one knows, and the county attorney did not ask her about it. Similarly no one was questioned about the burning cloth bundle which the newsboy found on the rear staircase. Mrs. Garvey heard Louise asking her father if he could recognize her; no one seems to have explored this.

None of the Arbogast women ever revealed anything further about the case. For what it is worth, the Ramsey County records do not show that a marriage license was ever issued to Louise Arbogast and Henry Spangenberg. The evidence, official and unofficial, has been recounted. Here are the materials. Now, reader, who killed Louis Arbogast?

14

The Case of the Convenient Cliff

AMONG THE FOUR THINGS said by the compiler of Proverbs (30:18, 19) to be "too wonderful for me" was "the way of a man with a maid," or in this case the way of a bounder with a lady. On October 2, 1908, Mary Fridley inexplicably joined herself with Frederick T. Price to live with him unhappily but not forever after. She was the twenty-one-year-old daughter of David Fridley, a well-to-do pioneer for whose grandfather the Minnesota city of Fridley was named. Fred was twenty-eight, an ex-convict and a wastrel, separated from a former spouse without the formality of a divorce. Although Mary knew Fred had been married before, she believed him to be divorced. She probably felt that her Fred had been mistreated and that she could succeed where her predecessor had failed.[1]

Mary did not know, however, about a woman living near her in Minneapolis who was quite as indifferent to Mary as Mary probably was to Fred's earlier wife. The woman was Carrie Olson, Fred Price's mistress. Carrie knew that Fred was married, but she ignored this trifling impediment. She went riding with him, accepted money from him, and told people that she was engaged to Fred and would marry him in the near future.

In 1914 Fred and Mary had lived together for six years. Although Fred worked as a traveling salesman for a printing house, he resented having to work at all, since Mary's father was rich. "The old man has a lot of money," Fred remarked. "I need the money and will get it." David Fridley was well aware of his son-in-law's attitude, saying bluntly that Fred's chief interest was "to get into his bank roll."[2]

Fred needed a substantial bank roll to support his extracurricular activities. He had given Carrie a trip to Norway in May, 1914, and on her return to Minneapolis in October found that she was most willing to accept additional financial donations. As any married man knows, attractive young females often set a steep market price upon their endearments.

Although he knew that Mary would eventually inherit substantial property, Fred chafed at having to wait until David Fridley died. In September, 1914, he discussed the problem with Charles D. Etchison, a former employee and an old acquaintance who was substantially in debt to him. Etchison, who worked in Washington, D.C., was visiting in Minneapolis at the time. He later said: "Price reached over and touched an electric button on the wall. 'I wish that three persons you know were electric buttons like these, Charlie,' he said. 'I wish that David Fridley was the first electric button here, that Louise Dye [*Mary's sister*] was the second, and that my wife, Mary, was the third. Do you know what I would do? I would first press out David Fridley, then I'd press out Lou Dye, then I'd press out Mary Fridley Price.' 'You wouldn't do that, Fred?' I said. 'I would, too,' he said."[3]

Fred was anxious to grasp any money within his reach and began to press Etchison for his loan, saying that Etchison must either repay it or help Price get money elsewhere. He convinced Etchison to leave his position in Washington and return to Minneapolis to help Price's financial projects.

Fred and Mary had no children. One of Mary's few outlets for her affections was her dog, Chum. David Fridley, knowing his daughter's loneliness and no doubt assessing Fred Price at his worth, tried to comfort Mary with gifts. He had already given Mary and her sister Louise substantial lands and identical diamond rings, which each daughter had agreed should go to the survivor when either of them died.

Late in 1914 Mary's father decided to make her an additional gift. On November 25 Fred Price told a friend that David Fridley was planning to give Mary a substantial amount of money and that he, Fred, intended to get it for himself. Two days later her father did make the gift by transferring to Mary ten thousand dollars in cash and railroad bonds, which she at once put in her safe-deposit box. On the next day Mary discussed with her brother-in-law, William M. Dye, the possibility of making a will giving a large sum to a home for children or aged women, but she reached no definite decision. Fred Price, who was aware of this move, could not support such visionary uses of money.

Charles Etchison was Price's everyday confidant, listening to his stories about the Fridley family, hearing accounts of Carrie Olson, and riding in Price's handsome 1913 Cadillac touring car while Fred scrutinized various localities and commented now and then, "There is a good place for an accident."[4] Etchison knew Mary and often visited the Price apartment. On November 27, the day Mary's father gave her the bonds, Etchison joined in plans to lunch with the Prices next day and to attend the theater with them.

At the Price household the following morning of November 28, 1914, Fred and Mary quarreled over the familiar subject of money. The dispute ended by noon when Mary, Fred, and Etchison lunched together at the Price apartment, after which they drove to the Metropolitan Theater in Minneapolis to attend a matinee of *The Prince of Pilsen*. The operetta proved to be excellent entertainment. Mary enjoyed it particularly and laughed throughout.

When the musical drama ended at five o'clock, Price suggested that since it was still early they should drive to St. Paul to look at some portieres he had noticed advertised as bargains. Mary was reluctant to go driving on a raw November day, but she wanted new draperies for her apartment and was interested in seeing what St. Paul offered.

On the way to St. Paul, thoughtful Fred stopped at the apartment to pick up Mary's dog, Chum. The group then crossed the Mississippi River on the Franklin Avenue Bridge and drove south along the East River Road. As they approached the steepest bluffs near the Town and Country Club, Price stopped the automobile abruptly, saying, "The car is not working right, the engine needs some adjustment."[5] Both Price and Etchison got out, raised the hood, and began to tinker with the motor.

At first Mary stayed in the car because she thought the weather too cold for her to get out. As Price later recounted events, she soon asked, "How long are we going to be here?" Price replied, "Oh, five or ten minutes maybe." Hearing this, Mary said, "Well, I guess I will get out and exercise the dog." She stepped out of the car and Chum followed her. The men continued to inspect the engine, Price recalled, until they heard the sudden cry, "Fred!" Price and Etchison ran to the edge of the bluff. They saw Mary lying at its base, moaning slightly. The two men scrambled down the precipice. Price knelt by Mary, while Etchison stayed a short distance away. She had no visible outward injuries. Price told Etchison to get help and then call Mary's relatives at Fridley. Fred remained with Mary. Etchison climbed up to the road where he succeeded in flagging a passing motorist. He then started Price's Cadillac without difficulty and drove to Fridley to get Mary's sister.[6]

Passersby carried Mary to the street level. After making an emergency examination, a doctor said that he could do nothing. Commenting that she had not broken her neck in the fall, the doctor pointed to a huge indented fracture, over three by four inches in size, on the left side of her skull. Although she was still alive, this injury, he said, would inevitably cause her death. In a few moments an ambulance arrived, and in spite of the doctor's objections, Price insisted on accompanying Mary in it. During the ride to the hospital as she lay unconscious and near death, he kept shaking Mary violently, crying, "May [*sic*], speak to me!" until the ambulance surgeon threatened to throw him out bodily if he did not stop.[7]

Mary was dead on reaching the hospital. Price and Etchison told the examining surgeon the version of the accident already related. The doctor did not understand how Mary could have died from the fall without breaking her neck, but he accepted the account given him by the two men. A police officer soon brought Mary's dog to the hospital. Chum was found not far from Mary; his hind legs were badly injured and he had to be shot. The policeman listened to what the men said about Mary's fall, accepted it, and left the hospital.

Etchison had brought Mary's sister, Louise Dye, and her husband to the hospital. Fred repeated his story to Louise, who heard it with greater skepticism than had the doctors and police — such is the way of in-laws between whom not much love is lost. In telling Louise about the accident, Price showed her Mary's ring, from which the diamond was missing, and said that Mary's hand must have struck a rock with enough force to tear the diamond from its setting. Fred also showed Louise the gloves Mary wore that day. Louise noticed that while the left one was intact, the right one had a long tear in the third finger. Mary always wore her ring on the third finger of her left hand. When Louise called this to Price's attention, he growled, "Some day you people will try to make trouble for me about this."[8] A few days later he took Louise's husband to the accident scene, where Dye found the missing diamond with suspicious ease.

On the evening of Mary's death, Mr. and Mrs. Dye sadly left the hospital and returned to Fridley. Price spent the night with Carrie Olson. So far as the police and public were concerned the accident happened as Price said. A headline in the *Minneapolis Journal* of November 29 stated: "Fear for Pet Costs Her Life." The accompanying report alleged that a sudden stop had stalled the automobile engine and said briefly: "Mrs. F. T. Price, 1335 Spruce Place, was killed late yesterday in a fall over the river cliff near the Town and Country club. Her pet dog had jumped from an automobile in which Mrs. Price and her husband were riding, and had run near the top of the cliff. Mrs. Price feared the dog would plunge over the cliff and ran to head him off. She missed her footing and fell to her death."

Mary left an estate valued at slightly more than twenty-three thousand dollars, a substantial sum at that time.[9] Under Minnesota law all property of a spouse goes to the survivor if there is no will and if the couple has no children. Mary had neither will nor children. Fred Price moved quickly to exercise those invaluable rights which he felt the law gave him as surviving spouse. In the first week of December, 1914, he demanded the funds in Mary's savings account and was seriously annoyed to find that he must first have himself officially appointed administrator. At another bank he had better luck; on December 8 this institution advanced him five hundred dollars pending his appointment. As usual, he needed the money. Within ten days after Mary's death he and Carrie had set up housekeeping in a new apartment.

In quest of additional finances, Price in October, 1915, began a civil suit for $7,500 against the Minneapolis Park Board, alleging negligence in failing to erect a guardrail where Mary fell. Counsel for the board advised resisting the claim and the case came on for trial. Both Price and Etchison testified, telling the same story they had given the doctors and police when the accident took place. On the issue of negligence, the board admitted that only a single-strand wire fence ran along the bluff.

It soon appeared, however, that the case was bringing up hotter issues than negligence. A park board expert testified that he made an investigation of the area. Mary's body was found, he said, forty-two feet below and twenty-seven feet beyond the outermost cliff edge. Some propulsion other than a mere fall, he testified, would be necessary to bring her to that place, since she weighed less than a hundred pounds. Midway in the trial Price abruptly dismissed his lawsuit. He later insisted that he merely changed his mind, although circumstances suggest that his effort backfired. When asked whether he withdrew the suit because "the battle got too warm," he replied, "No, sir." [10]

After Price's negligence case came to its jarring termination, nothing more was done publicly, and Mary's death was seemingly forgotten. David Fridley, however, had not forgotten. Doubting Price's story, he had retained an old friend, John P. Hoy, a former police detective who now operated his own agency, to investigate the case. Hoy is probably the first private eye to take an important part in a Minnesota murder case. Looking into Price's background, Hoy found that Fred had performed certain maneuvers to separate himself from his former wife but was not legally divorced. This meant that Mary had never been Price's lawful wedded wife.

Meanwhile Price succeeded in having himself named administrator of Mary's estate. He swiftly transferred all Mary's land to his sister, who lived in Wisconsin, and all Mary's cash and securities to himself. In December, 1914, he gave his friend Charlie Etchison a personal note for $7,000; in April, 1915, $1,500 in cash, and in June, 1915, an additional $1,150 in cash. David Fridley bided his time.

Fred and Carrie Olson had been living together since the night of Mary's death, representing themselves as husband and wife. On one occasion an inquisitive friend asked when they were married. "Price fidgeted, turned red," and finally asked Carrie. Cleverer in such matters, Carrie replied, "It was Christmas eve, have you forgotten so soon?" "That's right," Price said in relief, "I got her as a Christmas present." At Kansas City on July 12, 1915, the two went through a formal marriage ceremony which had no greater legal validity than Fred's espousal of Mary Fridley.[11]

While the public considered Mary's death a closed question, Detective Hoy continued to investigate throughout 1915. On December 1, believing that he had enough evidence, he went before the grand jury of Hennepin County. The jury heard the evidence and visited the fatal cliff. On that day Fred Price and Charles Etchison were indicted for murder in the first degree. Price screamed, "This is persecution, not prosecution," when he was arrested and held.[12]

As soon as the grand jury returned its indictment, David Fridley made his move. He asked the probate court to revoke its decree assigning Mary's estate to Fred. Price was never Mary's husband, he said, and was not entitled to her property. This proceeding was successful. The Fridley family eventually recovered those assets which Price had not squandered, although it took further investigation by Detective Hoy to uncover the securities Price had secreted.[13]

As the only person who accompanied Fred and Mary on the fatal day, Charles Etchison obviously held a key to the puzzle. He was arrested on December 2 in Washington, D.C., and set out with his wife under police escort for Minneapolis. In Chicago they were met by the assistant Hennepin County attorney and two Minneapolis policemen eager to obtain advance information. These men questioned Etchison for two days but drew from him only the same account of Mary's accident to which he had testified in the lawsuit against the Minneapolis Park Board. Finally, after the questioners pressed him repeatedly, Etchison hesitated. Turning to the investigators, he said, "Gentlemen, give me time to pray to my God for strength." Kneeling in a corner with his wife, he prayed, "O God, give me strength, strength to tell the truth." He paused dramatically and blurted, "Price killed the woman." Mrs. Etchison slumped to the floor in a faint.[14]

From then on Charles Etchison held nothing back. The murder had been planned months in advance, he said, and Price chose the exact spot at least six weeks ahead of time. For his help in corroborating Price's story, Etchison was offered $3,500 in cash and was released from a $1,200 debt. Charles explained that since Fred spent eighteen months in prison in 1894–96 for assault with intent to kill, Price felt that his account would not be believed without a witness. As early as November 6, 1914, Etchison said, Fred divulged his plans, saying that he must have money and that Etchison must help him kill his wife to get it. Although Charles refused to take an active part in the murder, his elastic conscience allowed him to give perjured testimony to conceal the very fact of the killing.

Etchison was much like Claus Blixt, and Price resembled Harry Hayward in his blindness toward his chosen human instrument. When Price was near, Etchison did his bidding well and faithfully. Away from Price, Etchison told everything. Like Hayward, Price recognized only his own power over a weak-willed servant. Neither Hayward nor Price realized that a slave would yield to any strong influence.

When Price read Etchison's statement, he stormed, "He must be having an hallucination." Later he said: "Etchison has made his statement and it may look black for me, but I will make a statement in the next day or two that will make Etchison's hair stand up. . . . I don't claim to be a saint, just an ordinary fellow, but Etchison is laying it on pretty thick under the circumstances." [15]

Two can play at the game of exchanging greetings through the newspapers, and Etchison was given space to reply. "Well, I never posed as a saint, either," he said in the *Journal* of December 8, 1915, "and if Price can tell anything that will cause me more trouble than he has already gotten me into, why let him go ahead." After delivering this verbal missile to a reporter, Etchison returned to reading his Bible, which was his solace during confinement as it had been Cole Younger's nearly forty years earlier.

Mrs. Etchison proclaimed that she would stand by her husband. Carrie Olson, who was located by an enterprising sleuth at the home of Price's sister in Neenah, Wisconsin, then went to Minneapolis and likewise announced to an incredulous world that she, too, would stand by her husband. "My heart goes out to her in sympathy," Mrs. Etchison said, patronizingly approving Carrie's stand. "No real woman would marry a man she believed had killed another wife, and no real woman would desert her husband afterward because he happened to be charged with a crime." [16]

Carrie did not acknowledge the compliment, but gushed about her Fred: "I wouldn't believe him guilty—not if he should tell me with his own lips. . . . It may be only intuition . . . but I can't conceive that Mr. Etchison has made a voluntary confession. Anybody who knows Mr. Price as I know him could not believe him capable of killing a woman. . . . Openhearted, openhanded, generous and sympathetic. . . . I guess Mr. Price never posed as a saint . . . for if he had been one I don't suppose I would have been his wife. . . . Mr. Price has the heart of a child."[17]

Fred intruded into this exchange of symbolic hair pulling and face scratching long enough to say of Carrie: "She is the best little woman in the world. I knew she would stand by me, no matter if all the others should turn against me. I am going to repay her by a lifelong devotion."[18] He also protested to the newspaper against what he regarded as the false image of himself being built by innuendo. To a *Journal* reporter on December 14 he said that "on the whole I have been a pretty decent fellow, a human being and a domesticated animal, not the gorilla that the state is going to try to prove me to be."

Preparations for the imminent trial put an end to these compliments. On December 29, 1915, Mary Fridley's body was exhumed from its grave in Lakewood Cemetery, and an autopsy was performed the following day. Experts for both sides readied themselves for inevitable questioning in court.

The Fred Price trial opened on Monday, January 3, 1916, in the presence of an overflow crowd. The defendant tried to appear nonchalant, saying, "Why should I worry? I am innocent. I shall be acquitted and I am already planning what I shall do when I am liberated."[19] It was noted, however, that his eyes showed tremendous strain, and that he looked ill at ease when the judge had to dismiss thirty-six successive jurors who admitted they believed him guilty of murder. He tried to avoid the gaze of an old man dressed in a blue flannel shirt and an inexpensive suit who sat in the front row of spectators, never taking his eyes from Price. The patient, relentless man was David Fridley, Mary's father.

When the jury was finally chosen, its members were taken to see the cliff where Mary met her death. The prosecution then opened its case. "Frederick T. Price met a stenographer with whom he fell in love," George W. Armstrong, the assistant county attorney, began. "He found married life burdensome, but he did not want a divorce. Divorced husbands get no alimony in this state. He wanted money sufficient to pay the fiddler. He murdered his wife to get it."[20]

The testimony then began. Etchison was, of course, the state's principal witness. As he described it, Mary's death had occurred this way:

> A. Mrs. Price backed down out of the car stepping out backwards and stepped down on the ground right by the side of the car naturally, and as she cleared the car, Price put his arm in front of her, reached right in front of her and caught me by the right arm and jerked us both right over by the river bank, and as he did that he released his hold on me and shoved his wife right under the wire and she fell off the cliff.
>
> Q. Did you see how she went?
>
> A. She went backwards.
>
> Q. She went backwards?
>
> A. Yes, sir.
>
> Q. Did she make any noise or outcry?
>
> A. Just a slight noise, kind of cried as she was in,—just as if something had frightened her a little. She didn't make a loud noise.
>
> Q. Then what happened?
>
> A. Price looked down and he heard her moaning at the bottom of the cliff. I stood there and I could hear the moaning. And he said we have got to get to her quick.[21]

Etchison said that Price next threw Chum over the cliff, after which both men scrambled down the bank to find Mary. She was lying on the ground. Etchison saw her turn slowly on one side and draw her legs up under her. Price straightened Mary's legs and told Etchison to go for help. At that moment, Etchison said, "I saw him stoop again, and I turned away. Then I heard the crunch of rock against bone, and the woman was still." Thus Mary Fridley died.[22]

At the hospital Price told Etchison that Mary was dead. "Did the fall kill her?" Etchison asked. "No, it didn't," Price replied.

Later that evening Price called at Etchison's hotel room. When Charles spoke of the afternoon's events, Price said impatiently, "Oh, don't worry about it, keep your damn mouth shut and everything will be all right, there is no jury in the world will convict me with you as a witness." His only expression of remorse was, "There's only one thing I am sorry about, that I had to hit her on the head." Then Fred Price went off to spend the night with Carrie Olson.[23]

For salutary reasons the criminal law does not allow convictions based upon the uncorroborated testimony of accomplices. The prosecution accordingly had to produce additional evidence to show how Fred had killed Mary. This consisted of medical testimony using as its object Mary Fridley's pitifully crushed skull, which had been exhumed and was formally introduced in evidence for the scrutiny of jurors, the public, and her sorrowing family. Two doctors agreed that Mary could not have died from the fall. Both said that a violent blow caused the extensive skull fracture which killed her. The doctor who performed the autopsy further testified that so far as he could tell from the body in its existing state of preservation the woman had sustained no internal injuries. His reasoned opinion was: "The object that came in contact with the skull must have been of a flattened or blunt character," lending support to Etchison's accusation that Price seized a handy rock and bashed in Mary's skull.[24] When the prosecution rested, it had presented a convincing case.

A medical defense expert tried to insinuate that Mary might have fractured her skull before falling over the cliff. This exculpatory effort was feeble, however, and the defense did not urge it forcefully. Price himself took the stand to refute the prosecution's story. Calling him proved to be a mistake, for he was not a particularly good witness. On direct examination he repeated the story he had told so many times, but in the light of prosecution testimony it lost its force. On cross-examination Price found himself subjected to endless questions about his former marriage, his past conviction of crime, and his personal life. The prosecution did not consider his answers intrinsically important, but wanted to give the jury an impression of an immoral man trying to hide something. The following exchange is representative:

Q. How long were you married to Mary Fridley before you committed adultery?

Objection. Sustained.

Q. You never went with a woman very long, did you, Price, unless you had sexual relations with them?

Objection. Sustained.

Q. Would you mind naming the name of the lady who went with you when you went on your trip through the east?

Objection. Sustained.

Q. Did you love your wife, Mary Fridley?

A. I certainly did.

Q. You were heart broken when she died, and said 'May, May, [*sic*] speak to me,' and pretty near threw yourself over the cliff in your anxiety to get down to her?

Mr. [Michael C.] Brady [*Price's attorney*]: We object to this on the ground that it is absolutely unfair, incompetent, prejudicial—

The Court: It is a matter of discretion as to just how this should be conducted. I will not interfere as long as he keeps within reasonable bounds. Go ahead. Objection overruled.

A. It was a great shock to me, yes, sir.[25]

The jury undoubtedly drew the unfavorable inferences which the prosecution meant to be drawn. It almost looked as if Price's counsel forgot the legal rule that if the defendant willingly takes the stand—and he cannot be made to do so—he must submit to full and exhaustive cross-examination about his character and credibility. Price's character, as his attorney knew, could not stand that kind of examination.

The defendant's own testimony was the major defense effort, and shortly after Price left the witness stand both sides rested. Price's poor showing on cross-examination probably justified the assistant county attorney's melodramatic words in his summation to the jury: "It was because she (Mary Fridley) had money, gentlemen of the jury, that her blood was spilled on the rocks at the foot of that chasm. . . . Little Mary Fridley, simple little

Mary Fridley, not attractive, undersized, less than a hundred pounds in weight, not attractive, not voluptuous, not good looking, simply pure and sweet and good. . . . The only reason that he married her was because her father, old Dave, stingy old Dave, had some money and property. . . . I believe he (Fred Price) is absolutely without moral character. . . . What Fred Price wants is right, and what he wants he will do, and if he wants it bad enough he will commit any crime to get it."[26]

In spite of an equally impassioned defense argument, the jury on January 15, 1916, found Price guilty of first degree murder. Three days later the court sentenced him to life imprisonment. His attorney moved for a new trial and, when this was denied, appealed to the Minnesota Supreme Court. At the very end of the year, on December 26, 1916, the supreme court affirmed Price's conviction, stating that his twenty-seven assignments of error were not well taken. Frederick T. Price would henceforth lie in the state penitentiary forever separated from Carrie Olson for whom he had committed murder. The county attorney quietly dismissed the charges against Etchison, who had also been indicted for first degree murder, and he was never prosecuted.[27]

Without question Frederick T. Price was justly accused, tried, and convicted. Like Mary, he only followed where nature led, but like many another he could not withstand the tempting prospect of money and a pretty young thing. To secure both he had only to rid himself of a woman who bored him. Had he been less impetuous he might have had his cake and eaten it too. Nothing indicates that up to the moment of her death Mary had any inkling of Fred's inamorata, and even avaricious mistresses have been known to accept less than their demands. Fred was impatient; he was also incautious. He murders best who murders alone should be an axiom for practitioners of the art, and Price was neither the first nor the last to have his plans shattered by an ill-chosen accomplice.

15

Murder by Professionals

ALTHOUGH DECEMBER AND MAY MARRIAGES are not necessarily fatal, history shows them to be unwise. Cicero was wretched with his Publilia, King Mark of Cornwall had little pleasance in his Isolde, and Stanislaus Bilansky learned too late about his Ann. Frank and Alice Dunn moved in immortal company.

On August 4, 1914, Frank J. Dunn, a widower of forty, married Alice M. McQuillan, twenty-four, at St. Luke's Church in St. Paul. Dunn was a prosperous horse trader and teamster who for years had held a government contract for carrying mail from the trains to the post office. Alice was the daughter of James F. McQuillan, a plumbing contractor, whose firm still survives in present-day St. Paul. The young girl fell in love with the older man, as these things happen. Her mother said that "she was plumb crazy about" Frank.[1]

The newlyweds took a two-day honeymoon trip to Duluth which was apparently a disaster. They did not get along. Although Alice was probably too reticent to admit it, she may have had some difficulty in psychological or physical adjustment. Frank said, "She was very nervous and kind of sick to her stomach."[2] The two had not reached a stage of compatibility when they returned to St. Paul, where they began their married life at 210 Smith Avenue in a house owned by Dunn.

In early October—only two months after the marriage—Alice's mother visited her and found her crying. Frank, who was there, was rude and savage. When his mother-in-law tried to speak to him outside the house—he refused to go in—he snarled, "God damn you, get in there or I won't say what will happen to you."[3]

On October 14, 1914, Alice could stand the situation no longer and returned to her parents' house at 793 Selby Avenue. They felt, however, that she ought to rejoin her husband, and on October 19 she went back to Frank's home. This time he bolted. He left the house and flatly refused to return.

When Frank ran, he did not run far, since he also owned the dwelling next door at 202 Smith Avenue. He took his belongings to 202, leaving Alice in possession of 210, and for a time they lived side by side, married but apart.

On June 25, 1915, Alice moved to end the deadlock by beginning an action for judicial separation. She prevailed, and the court required Frank to pay her seventy dollars a month, secured "by affixing liens on his property."[4] The judgment aroused unending fury in Frank. It became his obsession, a monument of indignity, the symbol of a bloodsucking woman, he said, encouraged by a bloodsucking family.

Alice herself does not seem to have wanted the separation. During the entire time that she and Frank were apart, she wrote him letters regularly offering to come back whenever he would take her, but Frank stayed in offended isolation, remarking frequently and angrily that Alice was bleeding him. Friends tried to reconcile the two, but Frank would have none of it. He said that Alice's friends and family had too much influence over her and directed that influence against him. Feeling that matters were hopeless for the time being, Alice finally left the house on Smith Avenue and went to live with her parents.

The years passed. Frank traveled to Montana in 1915. Alice went to the Far West in 1916 and 1917, working as a stenographer in various places including Montana. She returned to St. Paul on Good Friday, April 6, 1917, the day America entered World War I, and on reaching the city she got in touch with Frank at once.

The man Alice saw in April, 1917, was far different from the bitter husband of 1915. On Easter Sunday, April 15, they met and had a long talk at a drugstore, for Frank was not yet willing to call at the McQuillan house. Alice's mother remembered that when Alice "came home she was all broke up. She said 'Mamma' she said, 'Frank cried all the time all the way up the street,' and he said, 'What a mistake our life has been,' and he tried to make up and I told him, she said, 'that it was him.'" Four nights later they met again at the drugstore. A witness saw them and heard Frank say, "My, that is a pretty coat you are wearing. . . . Take it off, won't you. Let me see whether you appear better without it on." Alice look puzzled, but complied.[5]

When Frank and Alice were leaving the drugstore, they met an acquaintance to whom Alice said eagerly, "We are going back to keep house together." Frank had agreed, but upon one condition, saying, "now remember, Alice, when we start up again I am not going to start in St. Paul. . . . If we don't go any farther we'll go to Minneapolis." Alice, anxious to help during the time when Frank would be disposing of his business in St. Paul, went to Minneapolis to apply for a job.[6]

On April 25 they were still apart but their plans to come together were nearly complete. On that same day a brief newspaper article commented on the mysterious disappearance of George Connery, a Minneapolis police officer who had simply vanished from his post of duty. Since he was a quiet, married man with a good departmental record, he seemed to have no reason for an abrupt departure. Frank Dunn spent the evening of April 25 at the Knights of Columbus Hall. Alice stayed home and went to bed early.[7]

On Thursday, April 26, 1917, St. Paul was shocked to learn that burglars had broken into the McQuillan home and murdered Alice with three shots from a .44 caliber Colt revolver. She and Frank would never be reunited in this world. The *Pioneer Press* of April 26, 1917, stated that prowlers entered a rear window of the house at about 1:45 A.M. After cutting the telephone wires, they went to the second-floor bedroom which Alice shared with her nineteen-year-old sister, Katherine. Both were awake and talking about hearing a noise in the house. Flashing a light on the two girls, the murderer swiftly beat Alice over the head with a pistol and then fired three shots into her head and body. Katherine was unharmed. It was a puzzling burglary; the thieves did not take Alice's two large diamond rings, and the only items missing from the house seemed to be Mr. McQuillan's checkbook and his pocketbook, which contained a check for $10.45.

The family summoned the police at once, and the officers lost no time in calling upon Frank Dunn. He was awakened at 3:30 A.M. and taken to the Central Police Station. After being questioned, he was released when it was obvious that he could not have been near the McQuillan residence that night.

Under the direction of John J. O'Connor, St. Paul chief of police, detectives worked swiftly and, as events proved, brilliantly. They took measurements and impressions; they classified fingerprints; and they questioned, questioned, questioned. They also took Frank Dunn back into custody, in spite of being told about his planned reconciliation with Alice. It is an axiom of police work that when one spouse dies the other is not always completely prostrated with grief.

On April 28 two schoolboys found Mr. McQuillan's checkbook and pocketbook not far from the house. All the burglars' loot, such as it was, had been recovered. On that same day the unhappy and unfortunate Alice Dunn was buried in Calvary Cemetery. Frank remained in jail. He did not even ask permission to attend the funeral.

By Sunday, April 29, three days after the murder, the police had uncovered several critical facts; a coast-to-coast manhunt had begun; and in St. Paul detectives worked patiently to unravel the details of an involved assassination plan. Chief O'Connor released —and the *Pioneer Press* published—a summary of the important facts already known: Frank Dunn had mysterious dealings with some Montana men in 1915 at the time of Alice's separation suit, in 1916 someone tried to arrange her murder, and fingerprints on the McQuillan window sill corresponded to those of a notorious trigger man.

In hasty response to an invitation from the St. Paul police, Albert F. Brown and Sylvester C. Ferdig of Montana arrived in the city on May 1, 1917, to describe a series of meetings with Frank Dunn in Billings and St. Paul during the summer of 1915. They told their stories in the presence of Frank—now sullen, silent, and far different from the man who could produce copious tears as he walked with his estranged wife.

The Montana men said they met Dunn in Billings on July 4, 1915, a little over a week after Alice began her separation suit. Frank clearly had more on his mind than smoothing his ruffled feathers in injured isolation. "I married one of the McQuillan girls and then my trouble started," Dunn told Brown. "Do you know of anybody that wants to make $10,000? . . . I want to get rid of my wife. . . . I don't give a damn how they do it so long as they get rid of her." Brown suggested that a Reno divorce would be far simpler, but Frank's conscience as a Catholic would not let him accept this solution because, as he said, "under the rules of my church I can never get married again." When Brown pointed out that murder always involved unpleasant brushes with the law, Dunn answered, "We can't get in any trouble at all, because I have got legal advice . . . from my attorney; he gave me all the advice I wanted." [8]

Ferdig said Dunn "told me that he wanted to get rid of her for the reason that she was bleeding him and that he couldn't get married any more. . . . He said he had attempted to do it himself and crawled into the basement and broke the gas line and tried to smother her, but she woke up. And he asked me if I would do it. And I told him I would. And he wanted to know for how much. I told him $10,000." [9]

On July 23, 1915, the two Montana men went to St. Paul, where Frank gave Ferdig a thousand dollars, pointed Alice out to him, and took him to see the McQuillan home. "Best place," Dunn told Ferdig, "would be to get her coming down those stairs. . . . Just knock her in the head, or . . . she quite often goes out to the lake, and if the old man is with her, kill him, too. . . . I've got it in for him just as well as I have for her." Ferdig wanted to know when he would be paid. Frank replied that "he could pay the money over as soon as she was in the morgue, but he didn't want to pay it before. And he said that I should take her diamonds and everything she had on so to make it appear as a robbery. He said she had a diamond that she wore that cost $500; he said I could just keep that. . . . He said he wanted me to let him know about the night I was going to do it so he could be at lodge or some public place." [10]

Four days later the measure of his supposed allies and the risks he had taken were brought home to Frank Dunn. Brown and Ferdig threatened to disclose all their conversations with Frank to the police and demanded payment for their silence. They apparently planned the entire scheme to blackmail Frank. He did the only thing he could, paying them four thousand dollars to keep their mouths shut and leave town.

In October, 1915, his Montana friends went back to St. Paul to see Frank again, as blackmailers do, but this time they were content with six hundred dollars. Even as he paid, Frank said, "I'll tell you, Ferdig, while you are a man that don't do a job of that kind, but . . . you might know somebody. . . . I still want the job done . . . I'll pay $10,000 for it. . . . if you can get any one for half that, why . . . you can just as well make that much." [11] Neither Brown nor Ferdig, however, wanted any further involvement. Their blackmail scheme had worked and they were satisfied.

They returned to Montana and did not see Dunn again until summoned to St. Paul by the police in 1917. Their disclosures forced concentration upon Frank as a principal suspect, although he had been able to explain his whereabouts during the entire night of April 25–26. In order to connect him with the murder the investigators must find some link, as yet unknown, or else conclude that Dunn was innocent and free him.

By May 4, 1917, the police knew who murdered Alice Dunn, and knew further that the same man killed Police Officer Connery in Minneapolis. Fingerprints identified the murderer as one Joseph P. Redenbaugh, a teen-age Kansas City gunman. The police also had reason to believe that Frank McCool, another Kansas City underworld character, had acted with Redenbaugh.

The disappearance of Connery on April 25 was one of those coincidences which often wreck mighty plans. On that day McCool and Redenbaugh were driving from St. Paul to Minneapolis when the capital city police arrested them for speeding. They paid a fine which took nearly all their ready cash. When they crossed the line into Minneapolis, they were again stopped for speeding. Connery made the arrest and entered the automobile to guide them to police headquarters. Having no money with which to pay the Minneapolis fine and having an important murder to commit in St. Paul, McCool and Redenbaugh were not going to let themselves be jailed for a traffic offense. One of them drew a pistol and held Connery prisoner while the other drove the automobile into the woods north of Minneapolis where Connery was shot — accidentally, the two men said, but his condition when he was found indicated otherwise.

It was not until May 6, eleven days after he was killed, that the police came upon Connery's body. An anonymous telephone call, which proved accurate, directed them to look in the woods one and a half miles north of Fridley. Tire track comparisons showed that an automobile abandoned in St. Paul, presumably by the killers, had taken Connery to the lonely spot. Since both Alice Dunn and George Connery were killed by .44 caliber bullets, there was little question that the Dunn and Connery murders were connected.

Police success comes from hard work, luck, and tips. In the Dunn case three tips provided the information needed to unravel a complicated murder scheme. Two of these were telephone calls, one of which led to the finding of Connery's body. The other call was made by an anonymous informant, known only as "Madame D," who told headquarters that Redenbaugh and McCool had been in the Twin Cities on April 25 and 26. By coincidence the discarded fourth wife of Brown, the Montana blackmailer, was visiting in St. Paul when Alice was murdered, and she speedily told the police about her husband's conversations with Frank Dunn in 1915.[12]

Who hired Redenbaugh to kill Alice Dunn remained a question. It was unlikely that criminals operating in Nebraska and Missouri were acquainted with Alice or had motives for killing her. Gradually the police investigation uncovered an answer. Underworld information hinted that Frank Dunn had invited Redenbaugh to St. Paul about a week before the murder and had seen him at a saloon known as Chickett's Buffet. Another bit of information hinted that Michael J. Moore, a bartender at Chickett's, had something to do with making the arrangements.

The case became a matter of cops and robbers on a national scale. On May 8, 1917, McCool was found in North Platte, Nebraska. He admitted being in Minneapolis when Connery disappeared but protested that he had nothing to do with the officer's death. He was nevertheless indicted for murder. The grand jury may have found it difficult to believe him completely innocent when told that at the time of his arrest he had Connery's revolver in his possession.

Joe Redenbaugh and his wife, Pearl, were apprehended in San Francisco on May 11, fifteen days after the murder. Redenbaugh admitted having robbed a bank at University Place, Nebraska, and said that he was in the Twin Cities on April 25 and 26. Although he strenuously denied having anything to do with the Connery and Dunn murders, he and his wife were returned to Minnesota.

Upon reaching the Twin Cities, Redenbaugh was coldly advised that the authorities planned to indict his wife as a principal in the murder, along with McCool and himself. Threatening his eighteen-year-old wife seems to have been the one way to reach him. In order to save Pearl from standing trial, he broke down, admitted killing both Connery and Alice Dunn, and revealed to the St. Paul police who had hired him. It was Frank Dunn, he said.

Redenbaugh was nineteen. Neat and well dressed, five feet six inches tall, and of fair complexion, he looked more like a high school student spruced up for a prom than a criminal. Nevertheless he had committed his first crime when he was nine years old, had spent much time in reform schools and prisons, had progressed steadily in criminal expertness, and in 1917 was known as the "toughest kid in America." [13]

Redenbaugh admitted visiting St. Paul in October, 1916. He said that Mike Moore, the bartender at Chickett's, offered him two thousand dollars to kill Alice Dunn. "But I did not feel like it at the time," Redenbaugh said, "so I went down to University Place and did the bank job." With the $1,981 he took from the bank, he felt rich enough to marry and did so in Kansas City the next day. His money did not last long, however, and in 1917 he reopened negotiations with St. Paul.[14]

Pearl Redenbaugh told the world that she had married Joe to reform him, although in the next sentence, with feminine lack of logic, she insisted that she could not believe him a criminal. Joe, however, would not have his underworld standing demeaned and said, "Sure, it's all true, kid. I did it for you." He explained, "I was broke and up against it . . . and had to think of my little girlie. The Connery job was an accident. Then we needed money to make a get-away. Although I've got to pay the penalty, I sure am sorry for the little wife, but you are as game as I am, ain't you, kid?" he asked, hugging her. "Sure I am, Joe," the little girlie answered. "Guess this is the last trip we'll make together for a while. I'll be waiting for you when you come out, and won't be very gray haired, either." [15]

Redenbaugh's confession led to the immediate arrest of Mike Moore, whose wife did not take his confinement as philosophically as Pearl Redenbaugh. "It's an outrage," she fumed, "locking a fellow up without any cause, and letting his wife meet the bills all alone, that's what it is." [16] Further police work revealed that another gunman known as John Doyle, whose real name was Orrin Shea, had also taken part in the Dunn murder, and on May 25 the grand jury indicted the complete roster of Doyle, Dunn, McCool, Moore, and Redenbaugh.

On the same day Redenbaugh pleaded guilty to the murder of George Connery, was sentenced to life imprisonment, and was immediately transported to the state prison. McCool pleaded not guilty, stood his trial, was convicted of third degree murder, and was sentenced to thirty years imprisonment at hard labor. Neither was ever brought to trial for the Dunn murder, although Redenbaugh was to appear in court again many years later in connection with it.[17]

Mike Moore and Frank Dunn, defendants in the Alice Dunn murder case, chose to be tried separately. On June 6, 1917, the trial of Mike Moore opened before Judge Hugo O. Hanft, a jurist of legendary strictness and a terror to the Ramsey County bar. Redenbaugh was brought from prison to testify. When Alice's mother saw how young he was, she could not keep from going up to him and saying, "Oh, you poor boy; you poor, poor boy. You can't realize what you have done." Four days later, on June 10, the jury found Moore guilty of murder in the first degree. He was sentenced to life imprisonment. Yelling "To hell with you, you dirty rat" at Judge Hanft, he was led off to the penitentiary.[18]

The Moore trial was a curtain raiser for the prosecution's main attempt, which would be to convict Frank Dunn of having hired professional assassins to murder his unwanted wife. It has been said that Anglo-American law does not care as much about the truth or falsity of matters at issue as it does about whether the party asserting a claim can prove it within the rules of evidence. County Attorney O'Brien had Redenbaugh's confession, but he still had to connect Redenbaugh with Dunn. So far as anyone knew, Dunn and Redenbaugh had never met. Such careful avoidance looks suspiciously as if Dunn had been right when he said in 1915 that he had secured legal advice. Redenbaugh dealt only with intermediaries. Under what the law calls the hearsay rule, Redenbaugh could not testify that an intermediary named Dunn as his principal unless this conversation took place in Dunn's presence. In addition, under the rule of relevancy all testimony must relate to the particular crime for which the defendant is being tried, and not some other one. This rule might exclude what Brown and Ferdig, the Montana blackmailers, had to say about their experiences with Dunn in 1915.

The prosecution had only one lawful way to introduce the evidence needed to convict Dunn. If a criminal conspiracy is proved, the prosecutor may show all acts and words in its furtherance. Even here, County Attorney O'Brien would be hampered by having to work backward: he would have to introduce acts and words carrying the conspiracy into execution in order to prove that it existed. The conspiracy was, of course, the mutual effort of Frank Dunn and his hirelings to murder Mrs. Dunn. Defense counsel knew the prosecution must cross these hurdles, and both knew they would inevitably clash over this point somewhere in the trial.

Dunn's trial for murder in the first degree opened on Thursday, June 14, 1917, and continued until June 29. The trial was a local sensation. It began with the deputy coroner's testimony describing Alice's death wounds. He was followed by her parents, James and Mary McQuillan, and by James Warren McQuillan, Alice's brother, all of whom described the family's experiences on that horrible night of April 26, 1917.

All three heard people moving around and all three tried to cross the hall. Each found someone stopping him. Warren was told, "Don't move, or . . . I will blow your brains out." In a moment "Katherine was screaming, and in the front room" Warren "heard a voice tell her to 'Be calm, he was just going to do a little shooting.'" A second later, three shots were fired. Mrs. McQuillan ran into the front room screaming, "Alice! Alice!" only to hear Katherine say, "Mamma, Alice is killed!" and to see both of her daughters covered with blood.[19]

Katherine McQuillan was sleeping in the same bed with Alice. Hearing a noise on the stairs, Katherine sat up and asked who was there. At this, Alice awakened and said, "Kathy dear, you are dreaming again; lie down," (her last words) and put her hand over Katherine's mouth. Katherine was, however, wide awake, and in a moment she saw a man enter Alice's old bedroom across the hall.[20]

"I says, 'Who is it?'" Katherine testified, "and I didn't get any answer, and then I heard Warren's bedroom door open, and I heard some noise in the hall, and I said, 'Alice, Alice, there is somebody in this house,' and as soon as I said Alice this man jumped right in our room, and I wanted to know who he was and what his business was, and he said, none of my business, 'To be calm, be calm; he was only going to do a little shooting.' And I had Alice in my arms tight, and he came over to the bed and he hit Alice. First he shot the light in our face, a flashlight, and I had Alice tight."[21]

Just before the man entered the girls' room, Katherine said, "Alice, let me take your diamonds," and put Alice's rings on her own hand, not to conceal them but to distract attention from Alice. The intruder, who was a short man wearing a dark suit, a white mask, and a cap pulled down over his face, paid no attention to the rings. Katherine continued, "And then he flashed the light, and as he did he hit Alice on this side of the head, and I was so tight that it hit me on this side, our two heads bumped . . . and then he fired three shots one right after another, just as quick as a flash . . . he pushed me aside before he did any shooting. . . . there was a big hole; the whole side of her head was gone." Such was the death of Alice Dunn.[22]

Joseph Perley Redenbaugh, whose life outside prison walls had ended for a long time to come, took the witness stand. He, too, was in a sense a tragic character, as the following colloquy shows:

Q. How old are you, Redenbaugh?
A. 20 years old.
Q. When were you 20?
A. Today.

The date was June 21, 1917.[23]

At this point in the trial, when Redenbaugh was asked to describe his negotiations with Moore about killing Alice Dunn, the defense raised its inevitable challenge to testimony concerning conversations with persons other than Frank Dunn. County Attorney O'Brien argued that he could show acts and words in furtherance of conspiracy; defense counsel objected that no one had shown a conspiracy; and Judge Hanft had before him the issue which both sides knew must be resolved. He ruled in favor of the prosecution. Those who followed the trial saw this ruling correctly as the one which led to Dunn's conviction. The county attorney was now free to show all deeds and speeches from which the jury could deduce a conspiracy.

Redenbaugh then said that he went to St. Paul in October and stayed until November 6, 1916. One Robert Emmett Hickey had told him that a St. Paul man wanted someone in Montana killed and would pay three thousand dollars for the job. At that time Alice was working in a Montana law office. The offer interested the nineteen-year-old gunslinger enough for him to meet Mike Moore and discuss the problem with him at Chickett's Buffet. Frank McCool was also present during the conversation. After talking the assignment over, Redenbaugh felt that the job did not interest him sufficiently at the time, and he left St. Paul with Hickey. Joe said that he went first to Omaha and then to University Place, Nebraska, where he robbed a bank.

Moore kept in touch with Redenbaugh by mail. On February 27, 1917, Moore wrote Redenbaugh that the offer was still open — "Hickey mentioned it to you — the Montana deal." Redenbaugh wired Moore that he would go to St. Paul to discuss it. On April 13 or 14, 1917, Redenbaugh, McCool, and Doyle left Kansas City for St. Paul. Redenbaugh went immediately to see Moore at Chickett's Buffet. The bartender then told him that the victim would be a woman and that his principal would pay three thousand dollars, of which Moore was to keep one thousand. Redenbaugh wanted to know why the woman was to be killed, and, as he testified, "I believe he told me at that time that this woman was obtaining money from this fellow, something similar to blackmail, I disremember, that was the way he meant me to take it." They reached no agreement because Redenbaugh did not feel that he was being offered enough money.[24]

The three Kansas City gunmen stayed in the Twin Cities for the next two weeks, negotiating with Moore and moving constantly from place to place. On April 19 Mike Moore took Redenbaugh to a drugstore in St. Paul where he pointed out Frank and Alice Dunn. Redenbaugh had not yet learned the woman's name or for whom Moore was acting. At the drugstore Redenbaugh watched Frank persuade Alice to take off her coat—so that the watching gunman could identify her at another place and time. The murderer said he saw Dunn on one other occasion and never conversed with him.

On April 24, Moore told Redenbaugh that Dunn had agreed to pay four thousand dollars for the job, which would give Doyle, McCool, Moore, and Redenbaugh a thousand dollars each. Redenbaugh accepted. That day, frolicking as criminals will, Doyle, McCool, and Redenbaugh stole an automobile at Stoddard, Wisconsin, and drove it through the Twin Cities. This frolic resulted in the two arrests for speeding and George Connery's murder. The car was abandoned behind the Rex Theater in St. Paul, where it was found that night.

Connery's disappearance would inevitably lead to police activity making it unhealthy for Redenbaugh and his pals to linger in the Twin Cities. Moore had told them that Mrs. Dunn planned to move to Minneapolis in a few days and asked them not to kill her in St. Paul. The Connery matter, however, changed everything. Redenbaugh reasoned that if Mrs. Dunn's murder "was to be done at all it would have to be done right away."[25] Final plans had to go into effect at once, and Alice must die in the McQuillan residence.

Moore told the group who would be in the McQuillan house that night. He also relayed a message from Frank Dunn "That it would be considered a good idea if it came off as if it happened during a robbery. . . . we was told that she had some diamonds. We was also told that she had a younger sister and not to mistake her." On the afternoon of April 25 McCool and Redenbaugh went to see the house, in order to note possible entrances and ways of escape. Returning to their rooming house, they waited until midnight and then started for the McQuillan residence with Doyle, who had joined them during the evening. They approached it from the rear. After finding several windows locked, they at last found one open. Redenbaugh crawled through it and unlocked the kitchen door. The killers cut the telephone wires, and all three then went upstairs. Redenbaugh looked through Mr. McQuillan's clothes before entering the girls' room. "I had on a gray suit," he said, "and a gray cap and a white handkerchief over my face." [26]

As he went into Alice's room, he heard someone talking. The following matter-of-fact statement is the murderer's description of what transpired:

> Q. What did you hear said?
>
> A. I heard Mrs.—well, I don't know who it was—but one of them said there was somebody in the house. I believe she called Alice. . . .
>
> Q. Alice?
>
> A. Alice; and she answered and told her 'No, you must be dreaming,' and she said, 'No, I am not dreaming,' and they were talking there, I didn't pay much attention to what was said.
>
> Q. Did you hear them call any one?
>
> A. When I started—yes, just before I went in the room I heard them say, 'I wonder if that is Jack [*a McQuillan brother not living at home*],' and after I got into the room they asked me if I was Jack. I don't remember what I said then, but I—said something—about Jack, I don't know what it was, I disremember, and then they started screaming, I then shot Mrs. Dunn and left the room.
>
> Q. How many times did you shoot her?
>
> A. Three times.
>
> Q. And where did you shoot her?
>
> A. I shot her once in the side and twice in the head, if I remember right.[27]

The three men then fled in haste, Redenbaugh testified, and returned to their rooming house, having thrown away the pocketbook and checkbook taken from Mr. McQuillan's clothes. They made no further effort to create the appearance of robbery. Murder apparently did not keep them awake, and they slept until about ten o'clock the next morning. After they read the newspaper account of their work, they called Mike Moore at Chickett's. Moore visited the killers at noon.

"He told us," Redenbaugh continued, "that he didn't think it looked very much like a burglary, and he said that he had seen Mr. Dunn and that the statement had come from him." Moore brought only a small amount of money and told the three gunmen that he had an appointment with Dunn to get the rest of it at two o'clock that afternoon. When Moore left, Redenbaugh said, "I told him to intimate to Mr. Dunn that he had better come across with the money and not take any unnecessary time about it; that if he didn't something might happen to him." McCool remembered Redenbaugh's warning as even more pointed. He told him, McCool said, that he thought "Dunn was stalling; said that he had better have it there at 2 o'clock or he would get the same medicine that his wife got." Moore returned speedily with the money. Redenbaugh, McCool, and Doyle took their shares and fled St. Paul. A custodian testified that Dunn had visited his safe-deposit box at 12:50 P.M. on April 26 and had withdrawn something from it.[28]

The testimony of Redenbaugh and McCool gave a vivid picture of the murder plan and its execution but offered little connecting Dunn with the crime. The prosecution did not call Mike Moore. Brown and Ferdig, describing their Montana conversations with Frank, proved helpful in showing Dunn's determination to get rid of Alice at all costs and the similarity between the murder plan recommended by Dunn in 1915 and the one carried out in 1917.

Another valuable witness was Carmen W. Chickett, Mike Moore's employer. He testified that Frank Dunn often came to the saloon looking for teamsters to hire, but in July, 1916, Dunn had developed a considerable interest in Mike Moore, wanting to know what kind of man he was. "He asked me if Mike done a lot of time," Chickett said, "he said he thought he was a pretty tough character, something like that."[29] The saloonkeeper testified that he did not know what came of Frank's inquiry.

A witness who did know was Robert Emmett Hickey, forty-nine, a small-time conman who hung around bars looking for handouts, tips, or jobs. After being sworn as a witness, he tried to insist that he was a waiter, at which the following exchange took place:

> Q. When did you work last as a waiter? . . .
>
> A. Well, to shut all that off, I'll tell you: I am just as they say I have been—that I have stole for a living.

Q. Yes, you are a thief?

A. Yes, exactly.

When he was allowed to come to the point, however, Hickey's testimony was highly important. In October, 1916, he said that he was undergoing an inconvenient one hundred and eighty days' detention in the workhouse when Mike Moore came to see him and asked him to call at Chickett's after he was released. Hickey got out of jail on October 22 and went to see Moore at once. The bartender had a proposal. "Why, he told me," Hickey testified, "that there was a party in town that a woman was bleeding and that this party wanted her bumped off and he asked me if I would take ahold of the matter. He says, 'There is 3,000 in it for you.' And I says, 'I don't want nothing to do with it, I wouldn't touch a woman under no circumstances.'"[30]

While Hickey's chivalry, he said, kept him from accepting the assignment, he nevertheless took up residence over Chickett's Buffet, and was living there with Redenbaugh on November 6, 1916. On that date Hickey needed money and asked Mike Moore to advance him some. Hickey was in the saloon when Frank Dunn entered and had some conversation with Moore. During the course of their talk, both men kept looking over at Hickey. Then, Hickey testified, "Mike Moore says, 'I'll introduce you to Hickey.' And his [*Dunn's*] exact words is, 'That is not necessary, it is better we should not know each other.'"[31]

Moore and Dunn went on with their conversation. Dunn handed Moore a fifty-dollar bill and, as Hickey began to leave the bar, "Mike took and handed me this bill and told me—he says, 'That is the party I was referring to,' and he said, 'If you decide to change your mind, your expenses will be paid to Montana and you can take whoever you wish with you.'" When asked whether Moore had revealed the purpose of this trip, Hickey replied, "Why, to murder Miss [*sic*] Dunn." The prosecution rested.[32]

Defense efforts were primarily confined to showing Frank Dunn's reputation for good character. After numerous witnesses testified, Dunn himself took the stand. He shrugged off Brown and Ferdig's stories as complete fabrications for blackmail purposes, admitting only that he had met the men in Montana. He said that he had been introduced to Mike Moore in July, 1916, but denied ever making any arrangements with him. Since the prosecution had only the testimony of rather slippery individuals to show that Dunn knew Moore at all, this admission helped the state's case. Frank also denied arranging drugstore meetings with Alice at Moore's request. Alice set the time and place for all these, he insisted. In fact, she abruptly changed the place of their April 19 meeting, which Redenbaugh alleged that Moore set up for the murderers to identify their intended victim. Dunn maintained that there was nothing unusual in his visit to his safe-deposit box on April 26, the day following his wife's murder. He went there nearly every day, he said, in the ordinary course of business. On April 26 he merely deposited some receipts.

On June 29, 1917, the case went to the jury, which promptly found Dunn guilty of first degree murder. He was sentenced to life imprisonment at hard labor. His counsel appealed to the Minnesota Supreme Court, which affirmed Frank's conviction.[33] The high court found the evidence, while circumstantial, more than sufficient to justify the conviction, and upheld Judge Hanft's critical ruling allowing testimony on the acts and words of conspirators.

In July, 1920, John Doyle, the third man in the McQuillan house when Alice was murdered, was arrested in Tacoma, Washington, and taken to St. Paul for trial. The McQuillan family had to recount again in court what had happened on that dreadful night in 1917. This time Pearl Redenbaugh also appeared as a witness, identifying Doyle as the man who left the rooming house with McCool and her husband. Doyle was convicted of first degree murder and sentenced to life imprisonment. Like Dunn, he appealed to the Minnesota Supreme Court, where his conviction was affirmed. Thus all five men—Dunn, Redenbaugh, McCool, Moore, and Doyle—who took part in the murder of Alice Dunn were finally convicted and imprisoned. On August 30, 1938, Joe Redenbaugh was again taken before the district court of Ramsey County, where he pleaded guilty to murder in the third degree and received a sentence of from seven to thirty years' imprisonment for shooting Alice Dunn.[34]

There seems no question of Frank Dunn's guilt, although it took the testimony of an unsavory gallery of criminal characters to convict him. In the history of crime, this case is unusual in having an older man exert mighty efforts to rid himself of a young wife. The age-old pattern is the young wife conspiring with her young lover to dispose of an elderly husband. The Dunn case is also unusual in having an elaborately prepared murder scheme which really fits the old legal phrase, *deliberately premeditated malice aforethought*. Most murders are committed much more offhandedly. Because of the problems of legal proof involved in showing that Dunn was, in fact, Redenbaugh's principal, the case is of continuing interest to lawyers.

Frank Dunn died in prison on February 26, 1958. Joe Redenbaugh, the boy killer, served forty-five years. During that time, attitudes toward criminals changed, and the emphasis shifted from punishment to rehabilitation. On May 9, 1962, the graying, sixty-four-year-old Joe Redenbaugh was released. Although the *Pioneer Press* of May 9 reported that Joe was still married, it noted that he had not seen or heard from Pearl for twenty-five years.

Over the years from 1858, when Minnesota became a state and Charles Rinehart was lynched, to 1962, when a man guilty of two murders walked quietly from prison to re-enter society, social revolutions erased not only the frontier but also much of the vindictive spirit that characterized early America's criminal code. In 1858 Redenbaugh might well have been lynched; in 1898 he would almost certainly have been hanged; in 1962 he was salvageable human material. If Sibley, Minnesota's first governor, could have lived to see Redenbaugh's release, he would probably have thought that the world had turned upside down. Elmer L. Andersen, the twenty-eighth man to serve as the state's chief executive, and his colleagues on the board of pardons would probably agree — that in 104 years the 1858 world had been turned upside down to some purpose.

APPENDIX
Those Who Were Hanged

1860, March 23 — *Ann Bilansky* — St. Paul

On March 3, 1859, Stanislaus Bilansky, the third member of a classic triangle consisting of himself, his wife, Ann, and his wife's lover, John Walker, came down with an indisposition which all the medicines carefully administered by his wife did not cure. He died on March 12 of arsenic poisoning. Convicted of murder, Ann fought a yearlong battle with the executive, legislative, and judicial powers of Minnesota, but ultimately lost and faced the gallows. Mrs. Bilansky was the first and only woman hanged in Minnesota. See Chapter 3.

1861, March 1 — *Henry Kriegler* — Albert Lea

Kriegler (also spelled Kriegerlee and Craggler) was unkind to his wife, who found refuge with the family of Nelson Boughton. On a summer's day Kriegler confided to a neighbor that he was going to stab Boughton. A week later, on September 6, 1859, Kriegler did so. In view of the circumstances, Kriegler's assertion that Boughton provoked him by stabbing at him three times with a pitchfork was not believed. Kriegler went to the gallows "on the Commons in the Village of Albert Lea" in the presence of a large number of witnesses.[1]

1868, March 6 — *Andreas Roesch* — St. Peter

On September 6, 1867, Roesch, a Swiss immigrant of sinister reputation, came across sixteen-year-old Joseph Saurer, who was hunting and carried a gun. Seizing the weapon, Roesch struck the boy repeatedly with it, killed him, and carried his body to a near-by lake. Andreas

Roesch, Jr., was the only eyewitness and gave the damning testimony which sent his father to the gallows. Repeating, "Ach, Gott in Himmel!" the elder Roesch mounted the platform, insisting in German that he was innocent and that he left himself in the hands of God. When his body was cut down, his wife refused to accept it, and the sheriff had to arrange for burial.[2]

1885, August 28 *John Waisenen* Duluth

On November 20, 1884, after drinking a quart of whisky, this Finnish immigrant and an accomplice seized clubs, bashed in Joseph Farley's head, stole his belongings, and dragged his body to a near-by shanty which they set afire. Waisenen got thirty dollars; his accomplice vanished and the Finn faced the last march alone. A huge crowd saw him walk fifty yards from the jail to the gallows, and the police had great difficulty keeping the mob out of the enclosure. Those who did watch, it was reported, found their appetite for the spectacle somewhat reduced after they saw "the hands turn purple."[3]

1888, April 13 *Nels Olson Holong* Fergus Falls

This Norwegian immigrant farm hand was apparently in love with Lilly Field, his employer's fifteen-year-old daughter. He fancied himself slighted by her, and on May 26, 1887, committed one of the most revolting murders in Minnesota history by cutting the girl's throat, slitting her corpse open as a butcher would an animal carcass, and throwing the body to the hogs. It may be more than coincidence that he was a contemporary of Jack the Ripper. Saved from lynching, he was hanged by legal process. Using the same rope that hanged John Waisenen in 1885 and saying, "Be a man, Nels," the sheriff swung Holong off so quickly that he had no chance to utter any memorable last words.[4]

1889, February 15 *John Lee* Alexandria

When at 11:00 P.M. on July 19, 1888, Lee and his friend Martin Moe emerged from the saloons of Brandon, where they had spent the evening, they saw approaching them on the moonlit street Charles Cheline, Lee's rival in the affections of young Sophia Mathieson. At Moe's prompting Lee shot Cheline through the head. Both Lee and Moe were sentenced to hang, and they had already begun their walk to the scaffold when news arrived that Governor William R. Merriam had commuted Moe's sentence. Lee continued his slow walk, alone. Just before the drop fell, Lee said, "I know my sins are forgiven and in 10 minutes I shall be in a better place."[5]

1889, March 22 — *Peter Barrett and Timothy Barrett* — Minneapolis

On July 27, 1887, these delinquents, whose family ran an illicit saloon called the "Hub of Hell," held up a horsecar and shot its conductor, Thomas Tollefson. The robbery netted them twenty dollars. Their brother, Henry, who had also taken part in the crime, confessed and furnished the testimony which sent them to the rope. They were hanged on a double gallows in the midst of their prayers. On the same day the pretty widow of their victim went quietly to Osceola, Wisconsin, where she remarried.[6]

1889, July 19 — *Albert Bulow* — Little Falls

On November 24, 1888, this ne'er-do-well stood idly by a bridge until he got a lift from Franklin Eich, who drove up with his fine, matched team. When they reached the woods near Royalton, Bulow shot Eich behind the left ear and made off with the team. He was swiftly captured, made no defense, refused the proffered legal services of Charles A. Lindbergh, Sr., pleaded guilty, and was hanged. He left behind a plaintive memento in the form of an "Execution Song," which he composed four days before his hanging. Bulow was not his legal name; he had acquired it in the course of a long criminal career, and his real name has not been found.[7]

1889, September 20 — *Thomas Brown* — Moorhead

Brown appears to have had a strong dislike for policemen. On October 18, 1888, he went to Moorhead to avoid arrest elsewhere and sauntered into a dance hall, where he was displeased to see two police officers on duty to keep order. Drawing a revolver, saying nothing, and using gestures, he forced the two lawmen down the stairs and into the street. At this moment a third officer, Peter Poull, walked up the street and noticed that his associates were in trouble. He rushed to help. Brown shot Poull without saying a word. True to the bad man's pose he had adopted, Brown was hanged without making any farewells.[8]

1890, June 27 — *William Brooker* — Pine City

After a domestic uproar, Brooker's wife took refuge in the home of Mrs. William P. Coombs, her sister. On November 2, 1889, Brooker strode up to the house carrying a double-barreled rifle and demanded his wife's return. Mrs. Coombs chose to argue and was shot; when Coombs ran up to help his wife he, too, was shot. Brooker coolly walked to the nearest neighbor and told him what he had done. Although he insisted that he acted to defend himself and his family, the court was not persuaded that this was the case. At 3:00 A.M. on the day of his execution, after taking a "strong drink of liquor" and smoking a cigar, he walked to the gallows, said a short prayer with an attending clergyman, and was hanged.[9]

1891, October 17 — *William Rose* — Redwood Falls

Enraged by disputes with a neighbor named Moses Lufkin, Rose mounted his horse on the evening of August 22, 1888, galloped through the moonlight to Lufkin's home, and fired into the parlor window, thereby committing the second great moonlit murder of 1888, the first being John Lee's shooting of Charles Cheline. The victim's last words reveal a talent for homely metaphor which makes one wish he could have used it in less melancholy circumstances: "Help, quick! I am shot through the body deader than hay!" After the jury disagreed twice, Rose was convicted of murder on a third trial. He asserted his innocence to the end, ate a hearty breakfast of eggs and oysters, mounted the scaffold imperturbably, said "Goodbye, all," and hurtled through the drop. To the scandal of Minnesota, the rope broke. But Rose was hanged on the same double gallows which served the Barrett brothers in 1889, and another noose dangled at the ready. Rose, unconscious, was rapidly resuspended by the other rope, which did the job.[10]

1891, October 23 — *Adelbert Goheen* — Fergus Falls

Finding his paramour, Rosetta Bray, an encumbrance, this young man of twenty-one freed himself by shooting her on March 22, 1891. Caught and convicted, he whiled away his time by writing bad poetry, cursing his family, and playing the accordion. He nevertheless went to the gallows with courage, leaving this world by saying to the sheriff, "Let her go, Jack; good bye." It is likely that the sheriff was the more nervous of the two; he had learned all he knew of the hangman's art at William Rose's bungled execution the week before.[11]

1894, October 19 — *Charles Ermisch and Otto Wonigkeit* — St. Paul

On May 2, 1894, these nineteen-year-old youths, who had already spent two years in the St. Cloud Reformatory, committed a needless murder by killing William Lindhoff as they tried to rob his saloon. They left the world together on a double gallows "attired in the neat dark gray suits which the sheriff had purchased for them." The lawman was said to prefer gray suits to black ones "which he thought had altogether too somber an appearance." Each man wore a rose in the lapel of his coat. The intended effect of simultaneity was somewhat marred when the trap beneath Ermisch stuck and had to be released by hand. Wonigkeit was already swinging. "A few convulsive twitches, the shoulders drawn up as though for breath, and both bodies hung motionless."[12]

1895, December 11 — *Harry T. Hayward* — Minneapolis

Hayward was a gambler strapped for funds. He persuaded his dear friend Kitty Ging to insure her life for ten thousand dollars and deposit the policies with him. On December 3, 1894, she was coaxed into taking a nocturnal buggy ride with Hayward's accomplice, Claus Blixt, who shot her on a lonely road near Lake Calhoun. Hayward's scheme was discovered when his brother, Adry, decided to tell all. To the end Hayward kept the pose of a casual gambling man who had made a bet and lost. He ascended the gallows in formal evening dress. His last words were: "Pull her tight; I'll stand pat." He was not, however, permitted to leave this world abruptly. The fall did not break his neck, and he slowly strangled to death. See Chapter 11.

1896, July 23 — *John E. Pryde* — Brainerd

In midwinter Pryde, a cookee in a lumber camp, was enticed into a gambling game where he lost all his wages. In order to recoup, he persuaded Andrew Peterson, a logger, to meet him at a secret rendezvous on February 24, 1896. There Pryde shot Peterson and took forty-one dollars from him. "Nothing but gambling has brought me to this," Pryde said on the eve of his execution. "I hope every gambling hell in the city may be closed by law and kept closed." After a snack of fried chicken, fruitcake, apple pie, peaches, and a bowl of cream, he ascended the scaffold, repeated after the pastor, "God forgive me for my sins, and save my soul for my Savior's sake, amen," and was hanged.[13]

1898, March 18 — *John Moshik* — Minneapolis

This St. Paul incorrigible and onetime leader of the "Rice Street Gang" committed his most serious crime in Minneapolis. On October 22, 1897, after he had been released from a long term in the state prison, he met John Lemke, a perfect stranger, at the Union Station in Minneapolis, enticed him to a remote part of the city, and there shot him twice in the back, beat him over the head with a pistol, and took fourteen dollars from him. Amazingly, Lemke lived long enough to describe the crime and identify his murderer. Moshik was hanged wearing the same black cap that Harry Hayward wore on a similar occasion in 1895. Just before leaving this world he seemed primarily concerned about the preparations for his journey. First he complained, "You haven't got the rope tight enough about my neck," and then, in his last words, "My legs, my feet," urged that his limbs be bound more tightly. Perhaps his suggestions sped him on the way; he was dead in three minutes.[14]

1898, October 20 — *Joseph Ott* — Granite Falls

Ott was a German Jew who turned to farming in western Minnesota. A thoroughly brutal character, he found his chief recreation in beating his wife. She had twice begun divorce proceedings but each time had been persuaded to rejoin her husband. On May 18, 1898, he again beat the unhappy woman with his fists but this did not satisfy him. Seizing a leather bludgeon loaded with shot, he beat her to death as she pleaded for mercy. After saying farewell to his six children, he mounted the gallows saying coldly, "I bid you all good evening," and danced on air in the presence of some four hundred spectators.[15]

1901, March 29 — *Franz Theodore Wallert* — Gaylord

Wallert had domestic troubles and finally separated from his wife. After three months of living apart, he returned surreptitiously on August 20, 1900, set the barn afire, then killed his wife and four of his five stepchildren with a butcher knife. A posse of neighbors caught him. As he was swung off on the same scaffold from which Ott had dangled in 1898, "Not a word did he utter." In view of his record there was not much he could have said.[16]

1902, February 18 — *Andrew Tapper* — Chaska

On June 3, 1901, Tapper, age thirty-five, infatuated, wretched, and enraged, stabbed Rosa Mixa, an eighteen-year-old waitress in the same hotel at which he worked as bartender and hostler, and cut her throat with his pocketknife. In passing sentence on Tapper, Judge Francis Cadwell said, "I am opposed to capital punishment," a sentiment with which the condemned man no doubt heartily agreed, "but the law is as it is, and I had to obey it." Tapper was hanged on the same gallows from which both Ott and Wallert had dangled previously. A hundred and fifty observers, sworn in as deputy sheriffs, attended the event.[17]

1903, March 6 *Charles E. L. Henderson* Duluth

Henderson was a Negro barber and a veteran of the Spanish-American War. When on June 21, 1902, he suspected that Ida McCormack, his mistress, was wavering in her affections, he hid in a closet until he overheard her tell a woman friend of her new interest in life. Springing from his hiding place, Henderson stabbed his faithless inamorata while her friend, understandably disturbed, jumped out the window. On the day of his execution he ate two meals of chicken and champagne, spoke with orotund eloquence for thirty minutes as he stood on the scaffold, and died bravely. Henderson was the only Negro ever legally executed in Minnesota. (Three Negro members of a traveling circus, however, were lynched at Duluth on June 15, 1920, for alleged assault on a white girl.)[18]

1903, March 20 *Ole G. Olsson* Aitkin

Enraged because his eighteen-year-old daughter, Josephine, was marrying someone other than the man to whom she was betrothed in the old country and, it was hinted, because he was exceptionally fond of her himself, this Swedish farmer stabbed and killed his daughter with a butcher knife on March 21, 1902. He repented at once but was nevertheless hanged, muttering, "Jesus Christ, receive my soul."[19]

1904, August 30 *William Chounard* Walker

Chounard's career paralleled a popular joke; he played the piano in a whore house. As he prospered, the whore house became his own. When his consort, Dora, gave him cause to suspect her faithfulness to him, he killed her on January 26, 1904. This curious insistence on chastity in one who ornamented his place of business led Chounard to the hangman. His death appears to have been edifying. He fell through the drop while repeating the Lord's Prayer, and a newspaper reported with satisfaction, "The execution was successful in every way, not the least hitch occurring during the entire proceeding."[20]

1905, December 5 *Claud D. Crawford* Elk River

On November 30, 1904, this veteran of the Philippine insurrection was riding in a railway baggage car with one George R. Palmer and others. Crawford and Palmer, confederates in crime, proceeded to hold up the others, and in the melee Heino Lundeen was killed. The two men were captured promptly. Palmer confessed and saved his skin but Crawford was condemned. As he went to the gallows, Crawford said, "I wish you all good luck. These are the last words I have to say on earth. Goodbye." The man's name was not Crawford, but he refused to give his family name and his secret died with him.[21]

1906, February 13 *William Williams* St. Paul

When on April 12, 1905, Mrs. John Keller tried to break up the passionate attachment of Williams and her sixteen-year-old son, Johnny, the Cornish immigrant shot both the boy and his mother. Williams' hanging was bungled; the rope was six inches too long, and he choked to death. Williams was the last person executed in Minnesota. See Chapter 12.

A Note on Criminal Procedure

THE FOLLOWING OUTLINE sketches the general steps in a murder case. Most of these procedures were in effect during the entire period covered by this book. The defendant is entitled to counsel at every step. If he cannot afford to pay, an attorney will be furnished at public expense.

1. INQUEST. When a person is found dead apparently as a result of violence, the county coroner holds an inquest and hears witnesses. If the county coroner concludes a murder was committed by a definite person, the coroner may issue a warrant for his arrest.

2. INVESTIGATION. If the coroner does not accuse any definite person, the proper law enforcement agency — which is the police department of an organized municipality or the sheriff in a rural area — conducts an investigation. If the results indicate that a definite person is probably guilty, a warrant is obtained from a magistrate and he is arrested.

3. PRELIMINARY EXAMINATION. The arresting officer takes his prisoner before a magistrate for a preliminary examination. The magistrate hears witnesses and decides whether the evidence indicates that the defendant may be guilty. If so, he is held in jail. At this point the defendant may secure his release on bail.

4. GRAND JURY. The county attorney convenes a grand jury of from sixteen to twenty-three people, usually twenty-three, who hear witnesses and again decide whether the evidence indicates that the defendant may be guilty. If twelve jurors concur, the grand jury brings in an indictment formally charging the defendant with murder.

5. TRIAL. The defendant will have his trial in the district court before a judge and a petty (petit) jury of twelve persons. The county attorney or the state's attorney general will conduct the prosecution; the defendant's counsel will conduct the defense. Witnesses for both sides testify and are cross-examined by opposing counsel. At the close of testimony counsel for the prosecution and defense argue to the jury, the judge charges the jury on the law, and the jury reaches a verdict. If the verdict is not guilty, the defendant is discharged at once; if guilty, the judge will pass sentence. Since 1980, sentences are determined according to sentencing guidelines. First degree murder is excluded from guidelines because it carries a mandatory life sentence.

6. APPEAL. A convicted person may appeal to the Minnesota Court of Appeals for review of issues of law, sufficiency of evidence, and constitutional issues. If the conviction is for first degree murder, the appeal is made directly to the Minnesota Supreme Court. If some error has occurred, the reviewing court may reverse the conviction, order a new trial, or modify the sentence. The Minnesota Supreme Court also considers appeals from decisions of the Minnesota Court of Appeals. An appeal from the highest state appellate court to hear a case may be brought to the United States Supreme Court. In criminal cases, review by the United States Supreme Court usually centers on constitutional issues.

7. EXECUTION. The sherriff of the county in which the defendant is tried and convicted carries the sentence of the law into execution. At present he takes the defendant from the courtroom, delivers him to the commissioner of the Department of Corrections, gets a receipt for the defendant, and files the receipt with the district court. Before 1911 a transcript of all proceedings resulting in a death sentence went to the governor. If he was satisfied with the result, he issued his warrant (the "death warrant") directing the sheriff to hang the defendant. The sheriff did so, endorsed on the warrant that he had completed the task, and returned it to the governor. With this the law had had its say. The defendant's body, after an autopsy, was turned over to his family for burial, in contradistinction to English law which required burial within the confines of the prison where executed. Capital punishment is no longer used in Minnesota.

Footnotes

Chapter 1 – *Death Travels by River Boat*

[1] Since this case never came to trial, no court records exist. Contemporary accounts, printed in the newspapers of the day, agree upon the main facts but differ on details. Several spellings are available for the names of the two principals. The author has chosen to follow the version of Bodell's name used by the *Minnesota Free Press* (St. Peter), which made an effort to determine the correct spelling. Rinehart is the spelling which occurs most frequently in the various accounts consulted. In addition to the sources cited below, information here presented was drawn from the *Henderson Democrat*, October 29, November 12, 26, December 3, 1858; *Minnesota Statesman* (St. Peter), December 3, 1858; *St. Paul Pioneer and Democrat*, October 31, November 2, 6, 9, 13, December 1, 9, 1858; William G. Gresham, *History of Nicollet and Le Sueur Counties, Minnesota*, 1:542–544 (Indianapolis, 1916); and "Lexington Lynching in 1858," in *Southern Minnesotan*, vol. 2, no. 4, p. 5, 16–18 (October, 1932).

[2] *Democrat*, December 10, 1858.

[3] *Democrat*, December 10, 1858.

[4] *Free Press*, November 10, 1858.

[5] *Free Press*, November 3, 1858.

[6] T. M. Newson, *Pen Pictures of St. Paul*, 412–414 (St. Paul, 1886).

[7] *Free Press*, November 10, 1858.

[8] *Pioneer and Democrat*, November 5, 1858.

[9] See *Free Press*, November 17, 1858.

[10] *Pioneer and Democrat*, December 31, 1858.

Chapter 2 – *War in Wright County*

[1] Background information on the area and a general account of the affair, incorrect in some details, is in Franklyn Curtiss-Wedge, *History of Wright County, Minnesota*, 1:194–205 (Chicago, 1915). In addition to the sources cited below, other facts here presented were drawn from the *Monticello Times*, October 2, 23, 1858; *St. Paul Pioneer and Democrat*, October 8, 1858; April 10, 12–16, 25, 28, 29, May 11, July 27, August 4–7, 13, 16, 1859. Only Jackson's indictment is on file in the Wright County Courthouse, Buffalo.

[3] Journal A, 77, Governors' Collection, Minnesota State Archives, St. Paul.

[3] Journal A, 95.

[4] The letters quoted here and below as well as "Report of the Attorney General on Proceedings in Wright County," August 12, 1859, p. 1, 10–13, are in file no. 67, Governors' Collection.

[5] Sibley to Lawrence and Bertram, August 10, 1859, in file no. 67, Governors' Collection. On the troops, see Minnesota, *House Journal*, 1859, p. 28; 1860, p. 287, 296, 789.

[6] *Pioneer and Democrat*, April 28, 1859.

Chapter 3 – *Not to Foster, But to Slay*

[1] For information on the events discussed here and in the paragraph below, see William W. Folwell, *A History of Minnesota*, 2:37–62 (St. Paul, 1961).

[2] The inquest described here and below is reported in the *Pioneer and Democrat*, March 15, 16, 1859. Stanislaus' death notice appears on March 12. Many variations in the spellings of the names occur. The author has chosen to follow those used in the *Pioneer and Democrat's* report of Mrs. Bilansky's trial, May 23–June 6, 1859. A brief, somewhat inaccurate account of the case appears in J. Fletcher Williams, *A History of St. Paul and the County of Ramsey, Minnesota*, 121, 388 (*Minnesota Historical Collections*, vol. 4, St. Paul, 1876).

[3] *Pioneer and Democrat*, March 16, 1859.

[4] *Pioneer and Democrat*, March 15, 1859.

[5] *Pioneer and Democrat*, March 16, 1859.

[6] *Pioneer and Democrat*, May 25, 1859.

[7] *Pioneer and Democrat*, March 15, 19, 1859.

[8] *Pioneer and Democrat*, March 16, 1859.

[9] The second inquest is covered in issues of the *Pioneer and Democrat* for March 16–18, 1859. Quoted material below is from the issues of March 16 and 17.

[10] *Pioneer and Democrat*, May 25, 1859.

[11] On the preliminary examination, see the *Pioneer and Democrat*, March 18, 19, 1859.

[12] The trial is fully reported in the *Pioneer and Democrat*, May 23–June 6, 1859. Mrs. Kilpatrick's testimony appears in issues of May 23–25; Rosa's (below) on May 25; Dr. Morton's on May 27, 28; and Walker's on June 1.

[13] *Pioneer and Democrat*, June 4, 1859.

[14] Ramsey County Probate Court file no. 233 shows that on March 11, 1859, the day of Stanislaus' death, creditors filed a petition for general administration, and that the estate then consisted of real property appraised at $2,212 and personal property appraised at $190.26, but sold at auction for $55.40. The estate was not closed until August 24, 1875, when in file no. 1400 the probate court assigned 52.3 acres of land appraised at $600 to Mary E. Truette, formerly Mary Bilansky, and her children, Benjamin, John, and Catherine Bilansky. The second proceeding is curious in that it ignored Ann and assumed Mary to have been Stanislaus' widow.

[15] On this phase of the case, see State of Minnesota *v.* Ann Bilansky, 3 *Minnesota* 246 (Gil. 169); *Pioneer and Democrat*, July 9, 1859; Criminal Register A, 83, 150, in the office of the clerk of district court, Ramsey County Courthouse, St. Paul.

[16] *Pioneer and Democrat*, July 26, 27, August 6, 1859. The sheriff's descrip-

tion is quoted from the issue of July 27. Manly Wade Wellman in his book entitled *Dead and Gone: Classic Crimes of North Carolina*, 24 (Chapel Hill, 1954), ventures the guess that Ann Carver Simpson, who poisoned two husbands with arsenic, and Ann Bilansky were one and the same person. He describes Mrs. Simpson as being of small stature with black eyes and a small nose. In view of the Ramsey County sheriff's description of Mrs. Bilansky, it seems unlikely that she was Mrs. Simpson.

[17] *Pioneer and Democrat*, August 2, 3, September 14, 1859.

[18] *Pioneer and Democrat*, December 3, 1859.

[19] The sentence is given here as it appeared in the *Pioneer and Democrat*, December 3, 1859. A slightly different version appears in file no. 77, Governors' Collection.

[20] See file no. 77, Governors' Collection, for numerous letters and petitions, including the Flandrau letter quoted here.

[21] *House Journal*, 1859, p. 50, 154.

[22] On Rosa's death, see the *Pioneer and Democrat*, January 10, 1860.

[23] *Pioneer and Democrat*, March 24, 1860.

[24] For a copy of Ramsey's order, see file no. 77, Governors' Collection.

[25] *House Journal*, 1860, p. 368, 407; Minnesota, *Senate Journal*, 1860, p. 402, 423.

[26] *House Journal*, 1860, p. 695–699. See also Journal A, 174, Governors' Collection, for a version with minor differences in wording.

[27] *Pioneer and Democrat*, January 26, 1860.

[28] *Pioneer and Democrat*, March 24, 1860. For the remarkable "Statement of Mrs. Bilansky," March 17, 1860, setting forth her last views of her trial and sentence, see file no. 77, Governors' Collection.

[29] The account of the execution covers a full page in the *Pioneer and Democrat* of March 24, 1860. Quoted passages here and below are from this source. On the following day, the paper noted that the priest attending Mrs. Bilansky stated that she did not speak the words "which was committed by another."

Chapter 4 *The Christmas Murders*

[1] For a good, brief account of the Sioux Outbreak, see Kenneth Carley, *The Sioux Uprising of 1862* (St. Paul, 1961).

[2] On the Jewett murders and John Campbell's capture discussed below, see Folwell, *Minnesota*, 2:347; Thomas Hughes, *History of Blue Earth County*, 147–158 (Chicago, [1909?]).

[3] The trial and the hanging described below are reported in the *St. Peter Tribune*, May 10, 1865; *Mankato Weekly Union*, May 5, 1865; *St. Paul Pioneer*, May 5, 1865.

[4] Hughes, *Blue Earth County*, 157; Adjutant General, *Reports*, 1863, p. 132, 135, 138; State of Minnesota *v.* John Gut, in 13 *Minnesota* 357 (Gil. 330).

[5] *Pioneer*, January 3, 1867; *Weekly Union*, January 11, 1867; 13 *Minnesota* 355 (Gil. 329). Various spellings of the names of these two men occur in the sources. Campbell is sometimes referred to as Charles rather than Alexander. The author has chosen to follow the names as they appear in the legal records.

[6] *Weekly Union*, January 4, 1867.

[7] Accounts of events in the saloon and at the jail discussed here and below may be found in 13 *Minnesota* 355 (Gil. 328); *Tribune*, January 9, 1867; *Weekly Union*, January 4, February 8, 1867.

[8] 13 *Minnesota* 355 (Gil. 328).

[9] 13 *Minnesota* 355 (Gil. 329).

[10] *Tribune*, December 26, 1866; *Weekly Union*, January 11, 1867.

[11] *Weekly Union*, January 4, 1867; *Tribune*, January 2, 1867. The funeral of the two men (below) is described in the *Union* of January 11, 1867. For New Ulm's side of the story, see letters of Daniel G. Shillock in the *St. Paul Daily Press*, December 30, 1866, January 12, 1867.

[12] *Weekly Union*, January 4, 18, 1867; Hughes, *Blue Earth County*, 162. See also a manuscript transcript of the inquest in the files of the Brown County Historical Society, New Ulm.

[13] *Weekly Union*, February 8, 1867.

[14] *Weekly Union*, February 8, 1867; Minnesota, *General Statutes*, 1866, ch. 64.33, 93.1; *General Laws*, 1867, p. 156.

[15] The names of the twelve men are listed in the *Weekly Union* of October 4, 1867.

[16] The trial is reported in the *Weekly Union*, February 7, 1868. See also *Appellant's Brief* in State of Minnesota *v.* John Gut, Minnesota Supreme Court files, July term, 1868, calendar no. 16, in the Minnesota Law Library, State Capitol, St. Paul; "Court Record," 380, 382, 393–402, a manuscript record of the trial in the office of the clerk of district court, Nicollet County Courthouse, St. Peter, Minnesota.

[17] Minnesota Constitution, Article I, section 6; United States Constitution, Amendment VI.

[18] *Appellant's Brief*, 29. The *Respondent's Points* may also be found in the supreme court files, July term, 1868, calendar no. 16.

[19] 13 *Minnesota* 357 (Gil. 331).

[20] John Gut *v.* State of Minnesota, 9 Wall. (76 U.S.) 37 (1869).

[21] *General Laws*, 1868, p. 129; Journal E, 164, Governors' Collection.

Chapter 5 – *Rally, Philadelphians!*

[1] Biographical data on the Northup family was drawn from A. B. Easton, *History of the Saint Croix Valley*, 1:324–326 (Chicago, 1909); *Minnesota in the Civil and Indian Wars, 1861–1865*, 1:3, 57 (St. Paul, 1890); *Duluth Minnesotian*, September 11, 1869.

[2] See *St. Paul Daily Dispatch*, August 28, 1869. For information on Duluth in 1869 and a summary of the Northup murder, see Walter Van Brunt, *Duluth and St. Louis County*, 1:185–190 (Chicago, 1921).

[3] Records in the case of the State of Minnesota *v.* Thomas Stokley *et al* are preserved in file no. 261, Governors' Collection, and in Minnesota Supreme Court files, January term, 1871, calendar no. 43. See also 16 *Minnesota* 282 (Gil. 249). The quotation here is from page 31 of the manuscript "Record of Testimony" in the Governors' Collection, which will be cited hereafter as "Record." Other material here presented and not cited elsewhere is from issues of the *Minnesotian* for August 14, 28, October 23, 30, 1869; August 20, September 3, October 8, 1870.

[4] "Record," 34.

[5] "Record," 32.

[6] According to the *Minnesotian*, August 21, 1869, the other suspects imprisoned were: William Hopkins, Thomas J. Courtney, Henry Russell, Joseph J. Lyons, E. J. Paulin, Benjamin F. Zaracher, and James Ott. See "Record," 7, for an account of their confinement in which the material here quoted appears. Van Brunt, *Duluth*, 1:190, states that an anti-Philadelphia vigilante

group existed in Duluth before George Northup's death. But the dates are confused in his account, which was written some forty years after the events transpired, and the contemporary transcript of the trial indicates that the murder provided the occasion for an attempt to organize such a group. Van Brunt also indicates that Anson Northup had earlier led a party which gave one of the Philadelphia Roughs a well-deserved hiding. If this occurred before George's murder, however, it seems odd that the county attorney did not mention it at the trial, since such an occurrence would have provided a possible motive for the unexplained attack on the Northups. See also Anson Northup's affidavit in supreme court files, January term, 1871, calendar no. 43, p. 16–18.

[7] "Record," 8.

[8] "Record," 3.

[9] *Minnesotian*, August 13, 1870.

[10] "Record," 15.

[11] *Minnesotian*, August 21, 1869.

[12] "Record," 34, 44, 48.

[13] Petitions and letters mentioned here and below, as well as a copy of Stokley's pardon dated December 20, 1871, and pertinent correspondence between Jackman and Austin regarding Stokley's release, are preserved in files number 242 and 261, Governors' Collection.

Chapter 6 – *Bobolink's Last War Whoop*

[1] For a summary of the case discussed below and background on the area, see Alvin Wilcox, *A Pioneer History of Becker County*, 250, 379, 386–408, 438, 555 (St. Paul, 1907). On the Oak Lake station, see *Detroit* (Lakes) *Weekly Record*, June 1, 1872.

[2] The account presented in this chapter is based upon a thirty-page manuscript "Record of Testimony, State vs. Kahkahbesha" preserved in file no. 252, Governors' Collection, and cited hereafter as "Record." The author has chosen to follow the spelling of the names as they appear in this source.

[3] Mrs. Small's testimony appears in "Record," 2.

[4] Sheriff L. L. S. Burgar to Austin, April 27, 1872, and the Oak Lake settlers' petition of May 1, 1872, are preserved in file no. 252, Governors' Collection.

[5] On the proclamation, see *St. Paul Daily Pioneer*, May 14, 1872. For quoted material, see Day to Austin, June 6, 1872, p. 11, 13, in file no. 252, Governors' Collection.

[6] Brackett's report to Austin, undated, is in file no. 252, Governors' Collection. The St. Paul detective concluded that the "outrage was committed by a small party of Chippewa Indians from Leech Lake called the 'Pillager Indians.' "

[7] William W. Warren, *History of the Ojibway Nation*, 256–260 (*Minnesota Historical Collections*, vol. 5, St. Paul, 1885); Austin to Walters, January 13, 1872, in file no. 252, Governors' Collection.

[8] The following story of Bobolink's capture is based on Whitehead's testimony, "Record," 18–23. Quoted material below appears on page 19. See also *Brainerd Tribune*, May 25, 1872.

[9] "Record," 20.

[10] See *Weekly Record*, May 25, June 29, July 7, 1872; *Daily Pioneer*, June 14, 1872.

[11] This confession is fully reported in the *Weekly Record*, June 29, 1872. Quoted material below is from this source.

[12] Undated "Interview of Jno. Batiste [*sic*] Bottineau with Kah-kah-bin-ese," in file no. 252, Governors' Collection. See also *Weekly Record*, June 22, 1872. In Bottineau's notes the three are named as Bahgonegeshig, Keg-wadab, and Benesewigwan; in the newspaper as Kaguaguaydule, Pahguara-gushiek, and Penessewegun. Bahgonegeshig may be Bugonaygeshig who took part in the Leech Lake Uprising of 1898. See Louis H. Roddis, "The Last Indian Uprising in the United States," in *Minnesota History*, 3:273–290 (February, 1920).

[13] This confession is in Whitehead's testimony, "Record," 18–23.

[14] *Weekly Record*, November 30, 1872.

[15] See chapter 7 below for the story of Helen McArthur. On the danger that Bobolink might be lynched, see John Gurrell to Austin, January, 1873, file no. 252, Governors' Collection; and the *Tribune*, January 18, 1873.

[16] Peter Roy to Austin, June 5, 1872, in file no. 252, Governors' Collection.

[17] Flat Mouth and other Pillager chiefs to Austin, June 6, 1872, in file no. 252, Governors' Collection. See also *Tribune*, June 8, 1872; *Weekly Record*, June 15, 1872.

[18] *Weekly Record*, June 15, 22, 1872.

[19] The following account of the trial is based on the "Record." Pyle's testimony appears on pages 7–11, 25; Dr. Calkins' on page 13; the two Indians' on page 24; and that of the doctors for the defense on page 26.

[20] *Weekly Record*, February 8, 15, 1873.

[21] *Tribune*, February 22, 1873; *Weekly Record*, February 15, 1873; Whitehead to Austin, February 20, 1873, in file no. 252, Governors' Collection. On the troops, see also file no. 294, Governors' Collection.

[22] *Daily Pioneer*, May 20, 1873.

[23] *Daily Pioneer*, July 25, 1872.

Chapter 7 – *The Lady Vanishes*

[1] *St. Paul Daily Pioneer*, July 20, 24, 1872. The spelling of the Indian names in this chapter follows that of the *Detroit* (Lakes) *Weekly Record*, which printed accounts of the matter on July 20, 27, August 3, 11, 1872. See also the *St. Paul Dispatch*, July 25, 26, 1872; and Folwell, *Minnesota*, 3:79 (St. Paul, 1926) for a concise review of the events here discussed.

[2] *Brainerd Tribune*, May 18, 1872.

[3] For a different version of the arrest, see the *Tribune*, July 13, 1872.

[4] The confessions described here and below were reported in the *Daily Pioneer* of July 27, 1872.

[5] *Weekly Record*, July 27, 1872.

[6] *Daily Pioneer*, July 27, 1872.

[7] *Weekly Record*, July 27, 1872; *Daily Pioneer*, July 26, 1872.

[8] Journal E, 62, Governors' Collection.

[9] Journal E, 67.

[10] Journal E, 61.

[11] On the troops, see Adjutant General, *Reports*, 1872, p. 21, 23–25; *Daily Pioneer*, July 25, 1872; Journal E, 63–66, 69; Folwell, *Minnesota*, 3:80.

[12] John G. Morrison, Bemidji, to the author, August 24, 1960. Mr. Morrison is Helen's nephew by marriage.

[13] *Minneapolis Star*, June 24, 1959.

Chapter 8 — *Highwaymen Came Riding*

[1] This chapter is based largely on contemporary reports in the *St. Paul and Minneapolis Pioneer Press and Tribune*, September 8–October 21, November 15–23, 1876, and in the *Faribault Republican*, September 13–October 4, 1876. See also George Huntington, *Robber and Hero; the Story of the Raid of the First National Bank of Northfield, Minnesota, by the James-Younger Band of Robbers, in 1876* (Northfield, 1895), which contains biographical sketches of Heywood and other Minnesotans involved; Thomas C. Younger, *The Story of Cole Younger*, 79–93 (Chicago, 1903); John Jay Lemon, *The Northfield Tragedy; a History of the Northfield Bank Raid and Murders* (St. Paul, 1876).

[2] These and other facts on the careers of the James-Younger boys were drawn from Robertus Love, *The Rise and Fall of Jesse James* (New York, 1926); Homer Croy, *Last of the Great Outlaws: The Story of Cole Younger* (New York, 1956); H. H. Crittenden, comp., *The Crittenden Memoirs*, 131–374 (New York, 1936).

[3] *Pioneer Press and Tribune*, September 27, 1876.

[4] *Pioneer Press and Tribune*, September 20, 1876

[5] *Pioneer Press and Tribune*, September 9, 1876.

[6] *Pioneer Press and Tribune*, September 9, 1876.

[7] *Pioneer Press and Tribune*, September 8, 9, 1876.

[8] *Pioneer Press and Tribune*, September 9, 1876.

[9] *Pioneer Press and Tribune*, September 8, 9, 1876.

[10] Bunker recovered within three weeks. See *Pioneer Press and Tribune*, September 9, 27, 1876.

[11] *Pioneer Press and Tribune*, September 8, 1876.

[12] *Pioneer Press and Tribune*, September 9, 1876.

[13] *Pioneer Press and Tribune*, September 8, 9, 1876.

[14] See *Pioneer Press and Tribune*, October 4, 1876; Croy, *Last of the Great Outlaws*, 105.

[15] *Pioneer Press and Tribune*, September 10, 20, 1876.

[16] *Pioneer Press and Tribune*, September 9, 10, October 14, 1876. Copies of the photographs are in the Minnesota Historical Society's picture collection.

[17] *Pioneer Press and Tribune*, September 9, 13, 1876; *Republican*, September 13, 1876.

[18] *Pioneer Press and Tribune*, September 15, 1876.

[19] Huntington, *Robber and Hero*, 101–119; *Pioneer Press and Tribune*, October 21, November 20, 21, 1876.

[20] *Pioneer Press and Tribune*, September 20, 1876.

[21] In order to protect Sorlen from possible reprisals, his name was publicly announced as Oscar Suborn. Members of the posse were: William W. Murphy, Sheriff James F. Glispin, Thomas L. Vought, B. M. Rice, George A. Bradford, C. A. Pomeroy, S. J. Severson. See *The Northfield Raid*, 20 (Northfield, 1933); Huntington, *Robber and Hero*, 61–71.

[22] *Pioneer Press and Tribune*, September 23, 1876.

[23] *Pioneer Press and Tribune*, September 24, 1876. See also Younger, *Story of Cole Younger*, 76, for Cole's later explanation of the Minnesota raid.

[24] *Pioneer Press and Tribune*, September 23, 27, 1876.

[25] *Pioneer Press and Tribune*, September 24, 1876.

[26] *Pioneer Press and Tribune*, September 26, 1876. On the activities of Hoyt's militia, see Albert Castel, *A Frontier State at War: Kansas, 1861–1865*, 43 (Ithaca, N.Y., 1958).

[27] *Republican*, September 27, 1876; *Pioneer Press and Tribune*, September 26, 1876.

[28] *Pioneer Press and Tribune*, September 26, 1876. For various explanations of the disposition of the bodies, see Francis F. McKinney, "The Northfield Raid, and its Ann Arbor Sequel," in *Michigan Alumnus*, 61:38–45 (December 4, 1954); *St. Paul Daily News*, November 20, 1921; Croy, *Last of the Great Outlaws*, 115–119.

[29] *Pioneer Press and Tribune*, September 27, 1876.

[30] *Pioneer Press and Tribune*, October 5, 1876.

[31] *Pioneer Press and Tribune*, September 28, 1876. On the James brothers' movements, see James D. Horan, *Desperate Men: Revelations from the Sealed Pinkerton Files*, 130 (New York, 1949).

[32] *Pioneer Press and Tribune*, September 22, 26, 1876.

[33] *Pioneer Press and Tribune*, November 18, 1876.

[34] *Pioneer Press and Tribune*, November 21, 1876.

[35] *Pioneer Press and Tribune*, November 21, 1876; *House Journal*, 1877, p. 41, 388; *General Laws*, 1877, p. 178, 262, 271.

[36] Minnesota, *Executive Documents*, 1876, p. 34.

[37] Journal G, 26, Governors' Collection. Supporting letters to Pillsbury from Missourians may be found in file no. 428 of the same collection. In this file, too, is an interesting seven-page pamphlet entitled *A Brief History of the Younger Brothers and the Reasons Why They Should Be Pardoned* (n.p., [1881?]), which calls them "the last victims of a Civil War which has now been over for sixteen years."

[38] For the story of Bronaugh's efforts, see his volume entitled *The Youngers' Fight for Freedom* (Columbia, Mo., 1906).

[39] Bronaugh, *Youngers' Fight*, 179, 207; Bronaugh-Younger Papers in Minnesota Historical Society manuscripts collection, a series of photostats made from originals at the University of Missouri, Columbia; *General Laws*, 1895, p. 6; 1897, p. 18–20. The creation of a pardon board was suggested by Pillsbury as early as 1878. See his *Annual Message to the Legislature of Minnesota*, 30 (Minneapolis, 1878).

[40] *House Journal*, 1901, p. 182, 408, 409; *Senate Journal*, 1901, p. 712.

[41] *St. Paul Daily Pioneer Press*, July 7, 9, 10, 11, 1901. Quoted material is from the issue of July 11. See also file no. 644, Governors' Collection, for letters for and against pardoning the Youngers.

[42] *Pioneer Press*, October 21, 1902, April 9, 1904.

[43] File no. 644, Governors' Collection.

[44] *St. Paul Dispatch*, October 20, 21, 23, 1902; *Pioneer Press*, October 20–22, 1902.

[45] On Cole's pardon, see the *Dispatch*, February 4, 1903. At least one author claims that Cole, near death, at last confirmed the popular rumor that Jesse and Frank James were in Northfield. See Carl W. Breihan, *Younger Brothers*, 186–191 (San Antonio, 1961).

Chapter 9 – *A Night with French Lou*

[1] *Winona City Directory*, 1879, p. 199–201 (Winona, 1879). The facts on the cases here presented were drawn from the *Record*, *Appellant's Brief*, and *Respondent's Brief* in State of Minnesota *v.* Edward Lawlor, Minnesota Supreme Court files, April term, 1881, calendar no. 106; *Winona Republican*, July 28–August 1, October 15–30, November 5, 6, 1879.

[2] *Record*, 57.
[3] *Record*, 27, 178; *Republican*, July 28, 1879.
[4] *Record*, 96, 103.
[5] *Record*, 85.
[6] *Record*, 28.
[7] *Record*, 180.
[8] *Record*, 86.
[9] *Record*, 182.
[10] *Record*, 88, 98.
[11] *Record*, 89.
[12] *Record*, 183.
[13] *Republican*, July 29, 30, 1879.
[14] *Record*, 169, 219–221. See also *Republican*, October 29, 1879.
[15] *Record*, 189.
[16] *Republican*, October 30, November 5, 6, 1879.
[17] Mitchell to Pillsbury, August 27, 1880; Bentley to Pillsbury, September 1, 1880, in file no. 428, Governors' Collection.
[18] *Record*, 195.
[19] *Record*, 123.
[20] *Record*, 27.
[21] *Record*, 29, 31.
[22] *Record*, 57.
[23] *Record*, 117.
[24] *Record*, 41.
[25] *Record*, 66.
[26] *Record*, 63.
[27] *Record*, 118, 120.
[28] *Record*, 140.
[29] State of Minnesota *v*. Edward Lawlor, in 28 *Minnesota* 216, 226; 6 *Northwestern Reporter* 698.
[30] See *Record*, 143–150, for the gunsmith's testimony. Quoted material is from 28 *Minnesota* 225.

Chapter 10 – *Two Affronted Ladies*

[1] *St. Paul and Minneapolis Daily Pioneer Press*, April 8, 1887. Available records on the State of Minnesota *v*. Bertha Hegener are in the *Pioneer Press* of April 7–12, 1887, March 1–3, 1888, and file no. 1739 in the office of the clerk of district court, Ramsey County Courthouse.
[2] This letter and that discussed below appear in the *Pioneer Press* of April 8, 1887.
[3] *St. Paul Dispatch*, April 8, 1887.
[4] *Pioneer Press*, April 8, 1887.
[5] *Pioneer Press*, April 7, 1887.
[6] Arthur Conan Doyle, *The Adventures of Sherlock Holmes*, 127 (New York, 1930).
[7] *Pioneer Press*, April 8, 9, 1887.
[8] *Pioneer Press*, April 8, 12, 1887.
[9] *Pioneer Press*, February 29, 1888.
[10] *Pioneer Press*, March 1, 1888.
[11] *Pioneer Press*, March 3, 1888.
[12] On the case discussed below, see *Minneapolis Evening Journal*, August

15–20, September 3, 4, 20, November 15–17, 1888, and file no. 2736 in the office of the clerk of district court, Hennepin County Courthouse, Minneapolis.

[13] *Evening Journal*, August 16, 1888.

[14] *Evening Journal*, August 15, 1888.

[15] *Evening Journal*, August 17, 1888.

[16] *Evening Journal*, August 17, 1888.

[17] *Evening Journal*, August 16, November 17, 1888.

[18] *Evening Journal*, November 15, 1888.

[19] *Evening Journal*, November 16, 1888.

[20] *Evening Journal*, November 17, 1888.

[21] *Evening Journal*, November 17, 1888.

Chapter 11 – *High Stakes and Green Goods*

[1] *Minneapolis Journal*, December 7, 1894. Although the murder of Katherine Ging was widely reported in the local press, the author has elected to rely primarily on the *Minneapolis Journal*, December 4–10, 1894, December 7–11, 1895, and the trial *Record*, *Appellant's Brief*, and *Respondent's Brief* found in State of Minnesota *v.* Harry T. Hayward, Minnesota Supreme Court files, October term, 1895, calendar no. 99, in the office of the clerk of the supreme court, State Capitol, St. Paul. The spelling of Miss Ging's first name, given in various sources as Catherine or Katherine, is taken from the *Record*. For additional information on the case, which is one of the better-known Minnesota murders, see Criminal Register, 4389, State of Minnesota *v.* Claus Alfred Blixt, in the office of the clerk of district court, Hennepin County Courthouse, Minneapolis; *The Ging Murder and the Great Hayward Trial: The Official Stenographic Report* ([Minneapolis?], 1895); *Minneapolis Times*, January 22–March 9, 1895; *The Ging Murder: Being a Complete Version of the Most Horrible Event in the Criminal History of the World* ([Minneapolis?], 1894), compiled from contemporary accounts published in the *Minneapolis Tribune*; Stewart H. Holbrook, *Murder Out Yonder*, 69–93 (New York, 1941).

[2] *Journal*, December 5, 1894.

[3] *Record*, 71, 72, 75.

[4] *Record*, 15.

[5] *Record*, 12.

[6] *Record*, 69, 70.

[7] *Journal*, December 6, 1894.

[8] *Journal*, December 6, 1894.

[9] *Record*, 230.

[10] *Record*, 85. Harry seems to have anticipated the device – drowning – used in New York much later, which gave birth to Theodore Dreiser's *An American Tragedy*.

[11] *Record*, 32.

[12] *Record*, 32. Administrators of Miss Ging's estate handled a total of $4,860.20 – all of it from the New York Life Insurance Company policy. The net estate, after expenses, came to $2,601.95. The Travelers Insurance Company denied liability on its policy, which did not cover intentional injuries, and it was sustained in Julia A. Ging *v.* Travelers Insurance Company, 74 *Minnesota* 505; 77 *Northwestern Reporter* 291. The final account in the estate was allowed on August 6, 1900. See "The Estate of Catherine Ging," in Henepin County Probate Court file no. 4781.

[13] *Record*, 35.
[14] *Record*, 36.
[15] *Journal*, December 10, 1894.
[16] *Journal*, December 10, 1894; *Record*, 39.
[17] *Record*, 43.
[18] *Record*, 41.
[19] *Record*, 41.
[20] *Record*, 58, 59.
[21] *Record*, 99.
[22] See *ante*, chapter 10.
[23] *Record*, 82, 83.
[24] *Record*, 138.
[25] *Record*, 301, 374.
[26] *Record*, 318.
[27] Criminal Register, 4391, State of Minnesota *v.* Harry T. Hayward in the office of the clerk of district court, Hennepin County Courthouse.
[28] State of Minnesota *v.* Harry T. Hayward, 62 *Minnesota* 114, 474–476; 64 *Northwestern Reporter* 90; 65 *Northwestern Reporter* 63. According to the *Journal* for December 2, 1895, the governor was besieged by letters from Illinois, Hayward's birthplace, and surrounding states, asking for clemency. These letters have not been preserved in the Governors' Collection, which does, however, contain in file no. 642 two letters from Minnesotans who made their opposite views known to Clough. Evert Nymanover, on November 18, 1895, wrote: "In a society where temptation is supreme, capital punishment is an awful injustice!" Axel Jorgensen, writing on November 30, 1895, said, just as seriously if not as grammatically, "If H. Hayward are not deelt out justis to the full extent of the Law as his act deserves then non[e] ever ought to be punished. If he deserves succor or sympathy then throw law, Court and jurror system to the Dog and let us have direct anarcky and let the rich and mighty hawk over the week and poor." Some affidavits of Illinois residents, containing information on Hayward's ancestry, may be found in the *Record*.
[29] *Journal*, December 7, 9, 11, 1895. Two letters, dated April 24 and June 21, 1895, written by Hayward while he languished in prison, are in the James Gray Papers in the collections of the Minnesota Historical Society. Both voice his views on newspaper stories about him.
[30] The full interview is published under the title *Hayward's Confession* (Minneapolis, 1895).
[31] The quotations in this and the following two paragraphs are from the *Journal*, December 11, 1895.
[32] *Journal*, January 19, 1930; a review of the entire case also appears in this issue. See also *Minneapolis Tribune*, December 11, 1960.
[33] This version of the ballad, which was published by the *Journal* in 1924, is preserved in volume 6 of the collection of old songs in the Music Room of the Minneapolis Public Library.

Chapter 12 – *The End of the Rope*

[1] *St. Paul Dispatch*, May 17, 1905.
[2] *St. Paul Daily Pioneer Press*, April 14, 21, 1905; *Dispatch*, May 18, 1905.
[3] *Daily Pioneer Press*, April 13, 1905.
[4] *Dispatch*, May 12, 18, 1905.

[5] State *v.* William Williams, 96 *Minnesota* 354, 368; 105 *Northwestern Reporter* 265.

[6] 96 *Minnesota* 354–357, 367; 105 *Northwestern Reporter* 265.

[7] *Daily Pioneer Press*, May 16–20, 1905. A typed transcript of the trial record plus the appellant's and respondent's briefs are in file no. 14459 in the office of the clerk of the Minnesota Supreme Court, State Capitol.

[8] 96 *Minnesota* 370; 105 *Northwestern Reporter* 265; *Dispatch*, May 20, 1905.

[9] 96 *Minnesota* 364–378; 105 *Northwestern Reporter* 265.

[10] *Dispatch*, February 13, 1906.

[11] The hanging is fully reported in the *Dispatch*, February 13, 1906; *St. Paul Daily News*, February 13, 1906.

[12] *General Laws*, 1889, p. 66. The law resembles the English law of 1868 which ended public executions and required hangings to take place within jails. See *Statutes of the United Kingdom*, 31 and 32 Victoria, ch. 24 (London, 1868). The John Day Smith law was challenged in 1889 and upheld by both the Minnesota Supreme Court and the United States Supreme Court. See State *v.* Clifton Holden, 42 *Minnesota* 350; 44 *Northwestern Reporter* 123; 137 *United States Reports* 483; 11 *Supreme Court Reporter* 143; 34 *U.S. Supreme Court Reporter* (Lawyers' Edition) 734.

[13] *Little Falls Transcript*, July 19, 1889; *Fergus Falls Daily Journal*, October 17, 1891; *Sherburne County Star News* (Elk River), December 7, 1905. See also "Those Who Were Hanged," below, pages 219–226.

[14] State *v.* Pioneer Press Company, 100 *Minnesota* 173; 110 *Northwestern Reporter* 867.

[15] 100 *Minnesota* 173–178; 110 *Northwestern Reporter* 867.

[16] For a Minnesota example, see John E. Hartmann, "The Minnesota Gag Law and the Fourteenth Amendment," in *Minnesota History*, 37:161–173 (December, 1960).

[17] 100 *Minnesota* 173; 110 *Northwestern Reporter* 867; the Dean of St. Asaph's case is in 21 *State Trials* 1040 (1783).

[18] 100 *Minnesota* 177; 110 *Northwestern Reporter* 867.

[19] Criminal Register I, 4695, in office of the clerk of district court, Ramsey County Courthouse.

[20] *General Laws*, 1883, p. 164; 1911, p. 572. Among the difficult cases are those reported in State *v.* John Ryan, 13 *Minnesota* 370 (Gil. 343); State *v.* George Lautenschlager, 22 *Minnesota* 514; *ante*, chapter 8.

[21] Carrie Cropley, "The Case of John McCaffary," in *Wisconsin Magazine of History*, 35:281–288 (Summer, 1952); *General Laws*, 1911, p. 572.

Chapter 13 – *Six Women Who Kept a Secret*

[1] The account presented in this chapter is based upon contemporary newspaper sources cited below and on information about the case contained in file no. 5156 in the office of the clerk of district court, Ramsey County Courthouse.

[2] *St. Paul Pioneer Press*, May 14, 1909.

[3] *Pioneer Press*, May 15, 1909.

[4] *Pioneer Press*, May 20, 25, 1909; *St. Paul Daily News*, May 21, 1909.

[5] *Pioneer Press*, May 14, 1909.

[6] Quoted material here and in succeeding paragraphs is from the *Pioneer Press*, May 14, 15, 1909.

[7] *Minneapolis Journal*, May 16, 1909. See also *Pioneer Press*, May 18, 1909.
[8] *Pioneer Press*, May 19, 1909; *Daily News*, May 22, 1909.
[9] *Minneapolis Tribune*, May 18, 1909.
[10] *Daily News*, May 17, 1909.
[11] *Journal*, May 17, 1909; *Pioneer Press*, May 21, 1909.
[12] *Pioneer Press*, May 21, 1909.
[13] *Daily News*, May 21, 1909.
[14] *Pioneer Press*, July 15, 1909.
[15] *Daily News*, May 13, 1909.
[16] *Pioneer Press*, June 10, 1909. The most scandalous of theoretical motives for the crime is suggested by the *Minneapolis Tribune* of June 3, 1909, which referred to "a story of unlawful relations between father and daughter, pretty Louise Arbogast, followed by the inevitable discovery by Mrs. Arbogast." This tale, for which no substantiation was found, persists in St. Paul folklore; the author heard it several times in 1962.
[17] The trial is fully reported in issues of the *Pioneer Press* for October 18–November 5, 1909. Quoted material here and below is from this newspaper. The preliminary testimony of Ida, Minnie, and Flora is covered in issues of October 21, 22; that of Spangenberg, Abrahamson, and Flora again on October 23; and that of Mrs. Garvey and her daughter on October 26, 27.
[18] *Pioneer Press*, November 2, 1909.
[19] "Estate of Louis Arbogast, Decedent," in Ramsey County Probate Court file no. 16961, shows personal property valued at $12,586.45 and real property valued at $3,225.00 on hand for final distribution.

Chapter 14 — *The Case of the Convenient Cliff*

[1] For information on the Fridley family, see Albert M. Goodrich, *History of Anoka County*, 218 (Minneapolis, 1905). Full accounts of the case may be found in the *Minneapolis Journal*, November 29, 1914, December 1–28, 1915, January 2–16, 1916; legal proceedings are recorded in State *v.* Fred T. Price, 135 *Minnesota* 159; 160 *Northwestern Reporter* 677; Criminal Register, 13543, in the office of the clerk of district court, Hennepin County Courthouse.
[2] *Journal*, January 11, 12, 1916.
[3] *Journal*, January 10, 1916.
[4] *Respondent's Brief*, 8, in State *v.* Price (Cases and Briefs) 135 *Minnesota* 159 in the Minnesota Law Library; 160 *Northwestern Reporter* 677.
[5] *Respondent's Brief*, 11.
[6] *Respondent's Brief*, 3.
[7] *Journal*, January 8, 1916.
[8] *Respondent's Brief*, 4.
[9] "Estate of Mary Fridley Price," Hennepin County Probate Court file no. 16920.
[10] *Journal*, October 19, 24, November 1, 1915; *Appellant's Brief*, 70, in State v. Price, (Cases and Briefs) 135 *Minnesota* 159; 160 *Northwestern Reporter* 677.
[11] *Journal*, December 6, 1915, January 12, 1916.
[12] *Journal*, December 1, 1915.
[13] "Estate of Mary Fridley Price," Hennepin County Probate Court file no. 16920, remained open until January 31, 1921. Price got the better of the bargain; he had squandered the assets so completely that David Fridley, as

administrator, was able to recover only the land, valued at $7,150, and $4,000 from the sureties on Price's administrator's bond (on which Fridley had to pay $2,000 in attorneys' fees).

[14] *Journal*, December 7, 1915.
[15] *Journal*, December 7, 8, 1915.
[16] *Journal*, December 11, 1915.
[17] *Journal*, December 12, 1915.
[18] *Journal*, December 13, 1915.
[19] *Journal*, January 4, 1916.
[20] *Journal*, January 6, 1916.
[21] *Respondent's Brief*, 13.
[22] *Journal*, December 13, 1915; *Respondent's Brief*, 14.
[23] *Journal*, December 13, 1915; January 11, 1916; *Respondent's Brief*, 14.
[24] *Appellant's Brief*, 48.
[25] *Appellant's Brief*, 60.
[26] *Appellant's Brief*, 13.
[27] *Journal*, January 15, 1916; 135 *Minnesota* 159; 160 *Northwestern Reporter* 677.

Chapter 15 – *Murder by Professionals*

[1] *Record*, 358, in State of Minnesota *v.* Frank J. Dunn, (Cases and Briefs) 140 *Minnesota* 308, Minnesota Law Library. See also State *v.* Frank J. Dunn, in 140 *Minnesota* 308; 168 *Northwestern Reporter* 2; Criminal Register, 7603, in the office of the clerk of district court, Ramsey County Courthouse.
[2] *Record*, 951.
[3] *Record*, 44.
[4] 140 *Minnesota* 312.
[5] *Record*, 353; *St. Paul Pioneer Press*, May 16, 1917.
[6] *Record*, 356, 667.
[7] *Pioneer Press*, April 25, 1917.
[8] *Record*, 440, 441.
[9] *Record*, 499.
[10] *Record*, 504, 505.
[11] *Record*, 521.
[12] *Pioneer Press*, April 29, May 4, 6, 7, 1917.
[13] *Pioneer Press*, May 15, 1917.
[14] *Pioneer Press*, May 15, 1917.
[15] *Pioneer Press*, May 16, 21, 1917.
[16] *Pioneer Press*, May 16, 1917.
[17] *Pioneer Press*, May 26, June 19, 1917.
[18] *Pioneer Press*, June 8, 10, 1917.
[19] *Record*, 49, 59, 60.
[20] *Record*, 75.
[21] *Record*, 76.
[22] *Record*, 77, 91.
[23] *Record*, 225.
[24] *Record*, 154, 163.
[25] *Record*, 168.
[26] *Record*, 137, 170.
[27] *Record*, 135.
[28] *Record*, 173, 174, 397.

[29] *Record*, 320. In 1900 Moore was in the penitentiary on a charge of grand larceny. He was released in 1903, after being transferred to a hospital for the insane.

[30] *Record*, 267.

[31] *Record*, 267.

[32] *Record*, 269, 270.

[33] 140 *Minnesota* 310; 168 *Northwestern Reporter* 2.

[34] State *v.* Orrin Shea, Alias John Doyle, 148 *Minnesota* 368; 182 *Northwestern Reporter* 445.

Appendix – *Those Who Were Hanged*

[1] File no. 107, Governors' Collection; *St. Paul Pioneer and Democrat*, March 8, 1861.

[2] File no. 192, Governors' Collection; *St. Paul Daily Pioneer*, March 7, 1868; *St. Peter Tribune*, March 11, 1868.

[3] *Duluth News Tribune*, August 29, 1885; *St. Paul Daily Pioneer Press*, August 29, 1885.

[4] State *v.* Holong, 38 *Minnesota* 368; 37 *Northwestern Reporter* 587.

[5] *Alexandria Post*, February 15, 1889; *Minneapolis Journal*, February 15, 1889.

[6] State *v.* Peter Barrett, 40 *Minnesota* 77; 41 *Northwestern Reporter* 463; State *v.* Timothy Barrett, 40 *Minnesota* 65; 41 *Northwestern Reporter* 459.

[7] *Little Falls Transcript*, July 19, 1889.

[8] State *v.* Brown, 41 *Minnesota* 319; 43 *Northwestern Reporter* 69.

[9] *St. Paul Daily News*, June 27, 1890.

[10] State *v.* Rose, 47 *Minnesota* 47; 49 *Northwestern Reporter* 404.

[11] Trenerry, "The Bray-Goheen Murder Case," in *Minnesota History*, 38:11–20 (March, 1962).

[12] *St. Paul Pioneer Press*, October 19, 1894.

[13] *Brainerd Dispatch*, July 24, 1896.

[14] *Minneapolis Journal*, March 18, 1898.

[15] *Granite Falls Journal*, October 22, 1898.

[16] *Gaylord Hub*, March 29, 1901.

[17] *Weekly Valley Herald* (Chaska), February 20, 1902.

[18] *News Tribune*, March 6, 1903; Earl Spangler, *The Negro in Minnesota*, 100 (Minneapolis, 1961).

[19] *Aitkin Age*, March 24, 1903.

[20] State *v.* Chounard, 93 *Minnesota* 176; 100 *Northwestern Reporter* 1125.

[21] State *v.* Crawford, 96 *Minnesota* 95; 104 *Northwestern Reporter* 768, 822.

Index